COMMUNICATION SKILLS
FOR
DEPARTMENT CHAIRS

COMMUNICATION SKILLS
FOR
DEPARTMENT CHAIRS

Mary Lou Higgerson

Foreword by William E. Cashin
Introduction by Walter H. Gmelch

ANKER PUBLISHING COMPANY, INC.
Bolton, MA

Communication Skills for Department Chairs

ISBN 1-882982-13-4

Composition by Deerfoot Studios
Cover design by Deerfoot Studios

Anker Publishing Company, Inc.
176 Ballville Road
P.O. Box 249
Bolton, MA 01740-0249

To my family for their love,
patience, and unfailing support

ABOUT THE AUTHOR

Mary Lou Higgerson brings to this text 20 years of experience that spans every administrative level of a multicampus university system. Higgerson holds a PhD from the University of Kansas where she studied and conducted research in organizational communication. Combining her knowledge of communication literature and skills with her administrative experience, Higgerson has focused her writing, consulting, and training activities on the application of communication and management theory utilizing video vignettes and case studies. Since 1990, Higgerson has taught on a variety of topics for the American Council on Education in seminars offered through the Department Leadership Program. Currently a professor of speech communication at Southern Illinois University at Carbondale, Higgerson teaches courses in organizational communication and the university as an organizational culture. Higgerson has coproduced training videos on communication strategies relevant for higher education administrators and has written articles that have appeared in such publications as *The Chronicle of Higher Education, Journal of College and University Personnel Association, Continuing Higher Education Review,* and *The Department Chair.* She coauthored a book titled *Complexities of Higher Education Administration: Case Studies and Issues,* which is designed for formal classroom use, workshops and seminars, and self-directed professional development.

CONTENTS

About the Author   *vi*

Foreword   *ix*

Introduction   *xi*

Preface   *xiii*

Author's Introduction   *xv*

Index of Cases by Higher Education Issues and Administrative Tasks   *xix*

Part One: Cultivating the Department Culture   1

  1. Structuring the Department Mission   2

  2. Enhancing the Department Climate   36

  3. Defining the Department Ethics   69

Part Two: Working with Faculty   105

  4. Conducting Performance Counseling   106

  5. Managing Conflict   139

  6. Implementing Change   169

Part Three: Interfacing with External Publics   201

  7. Working with the Dean   202

  8. Building Alliances   228

  9. Promoting the Department   253

References   280

Index   282

FOREWORD

There is a saying that higher education is staffed mainly with amateurs. The typical Ph.D. program provides a wealth of knowledge and beginning research skills but rarely provides systematic education or training in how to teach—the primary activity of most faculty. Likewise, most academic department chairs receive no systematic training in administration—the primary activity of chairs. Fortunately, academic amateurs are good learners, as long as we have good teachers. This book is a good teacher of important administrative skills.

This is a teaching book. It has a great deal of information, and it has evocative case studies: 36 if you are counting. Higgerson takes the reader through the learning experience systematically, discussing "relevant communication concepts and strategies," then presenting cases that require the application of those concepts and strategies. After each case is a commentary—not giving an answer but highlighting the issues. Then it is the reader's turn to respond to specific questions about the case; to describe how the reader would act were he or she the chairperson in the case.

This is a working book. It is rich with content, information, principles—and with practices that adroitly develop administrative skills. Reading the cases is interesting, but the reader must do the homework by completing the practices in order to develop substantive skills. The reader should complete the practices. For some cases, Higgerson suggests that we decide on the actual wording we would use—a very good suggestion from both the communication and learning points of view.

This book is realistic, sometimes painfully so when a case comes close to one's own experiences. The realism is a reflection of the breadth and depth of the author's experience: as a teacher and researcher, as a department chair, as an associate dean, as an associate provost, as a consultant and trainer. The cases describe real problems with enough detail that the reader enters into the situation; at times I found myself getting angry at some of the behavior described.

This book is about more than communication skills in the narrow sense. Higgerson has taught and done research in the area of organizational communication. As the reader will discover, this includes organizational behavior and organizational change as well as administrative and managerial skills. Yes, to be effective, chairs need to be administrators and managers as well as teachers, researchers, and academics. And like teaching and research, administrative and managerial skills are learnable. Some academics disdain anything to do with business and industry. That is truly unfortunate because business and industry have learned a great deal about what works in complex organizations—and colleges and universities are definitely complex organizations.

This book is valuable for people in other roles, as well as for academic department chairs. True, the case studies are set in the context of the academic department, and readers put themselves in the role of the chair. But the concepts and strategies apply to all academic administrators. Little imagination is needed to make the context a college or an entire institution, or for that matter, a program within a department.

This book is well worth your time and effort if you seek to be an effective administrator. Like a good teacher this book makes you think and work. In the process, you learn!

William E. Cashin
Center for Faculty Evaluation and Development
Kansas State University

INTRODUCTION

Department chairs face the difficult task of representing both department needs and institutional priorities. This "in the middle" position requires chairs to communicate effectively within and outside the department. Virtually every task assigned to department chairs requires effective communication skill. Whether a department chair is counseling individual faculty on teaching effectiveness or convincing the dean that the department needs more space, communication determines the chair's success. The need for strong communication skills is especially crucial when chairs must handle uncomfortable tasks such as managing conflict or leading change. In *Communication Skills for Department Chairs,* Mary Lou Higgerson offers specific insights and strategies for enhancing chair communication for managing administrative tasks.

With a background in organizational communication, Higgerson has held administrative positions at every level of a multi-campus university system, and in each of these positions she has applied, tested, and honed communication strategies. This breadth of experience allows her to understand the chair's roles and responsibilities from a number of different vantage points. She has also conducted extensive training workshops in communication, and in this book synthesizes her experiences into fascinating, complex, and realistic case studies. These case studies present typical situations faced by department chairs, and then analyze the communication principles and options within the situation. The case studies examine situations from various perspectives and ask the readers to participate in articulating possible solutions to the problems presented. The case studies also present communications dilemmas involving the full range of chair interactions, including working with faculty; representing both the department and the administration; and interfacing with outside constituencies and stakeholders. The book presents lucid explanations of necessary communication principles and can be used equally well in workshops and seminars or for self-directed, individual professional development.

Mary Lou Higgerson is uniquely qualified to author a communications resource for department chairs; in fact, it is difficult for me to cite anyone in higher education today who can better address the critical subject of communication and the department chair. She has for many years worked with the American Council on Education in training department chairs, is a regular presenter at the Kansas State University conference for department chairs, and is a frequent invited consultant/trainer for department chairs at colleges and universities across the country. Dr. Higgerson is able to apply her rigorous research in the field to situations that will resonate with all department chairs and will enable them to understand the nature and importance of communication strategies.

Communication Skills for Department Chairs helps chairs to: 1) sharpen their analytical skills by reviewing relevant communication concepts; 2) heighten their ability to think and reason rigorously by applying theory; and 3) develop a focal point around which they can use their own expertise and experience. This book renews the sense of fun, excitement, and creativity that can accompany the job of chairing an academic department. Readers of this book will be come away charged with the certainty that effective communication is a great challenge—intellectually, politically, socially, and intuitively. And they will come away, also, equipped with new tools and strategies for meeting their myriad challenges.

I recommend this splendid book for those who wish to make a difference by leading the most important and central unit in the academy: the academic department.

Walter H. Gmelch
Center for the Study of the Department Chair
Washington State University

PREFACE

I first recognized the need for this book while serving as a department chair in the early 1980s. I witnessed the advantage of training in communication as I sat with my chair colleagues in meetings with the dean. Subsequently, observations made while serving in administrative positions at the dean and provost levels further convinced me of the value of communication skills training for department chairs. Department chairs who possess some understanding of organizational communication and exhibit strong communication skills have a noticeable advantage in carrying out the multitude of roles and responsibilities assigned to them.

Although the need for this text was readily apparent more than a decade ago, it took two specific experiences for me to determine how to write the book. The first relevant experience came from teaching the effective use of communication in managing several of the specific duties and responsibilities typically assigned to department chairs. Some of this work involved teaching for the National Seminar on Chairing the Academic Department that the American Council on Education (ACE) offers through its Center for Leadership Development. The seminar typically enrolls 80 to 100 department chairs and deans from roughly 60 to 80 institutions. In addition, I conducted seminars for department chairs at various institutions of higher education. These leadership development programs were custom designed to meet the specific needs of chairs, deans, and provost's staff on a particular campus. The experience enabled me to develop and refine a methodology for presenting theoretical content on organizational communication in a format that is relevant to specific administrative tasks handled by department chairs. Over time, the work for ACE and numerous institutions allowed me to develop a method for translating relevant communication theory into prescriptive guidelines that are immediately useful to department chairs. The teaching method employed uses original case studies and other activities designed to help department chairs sharpen their communication skills for managing the department.

The second experience that helped to shape this book was the completion of an earlier text titled *Complexities of Higher Education Administration: Case*

Studies and Issues. This book, coauthored with Susan Rehwaldt, illustrates the value of the case study method outside a formal classroom or workshop setting. Comments from those using the book illustrate its usefulness as a course text and as a tool for individual professional development. That reaction was critical to the writing of this volume because skill development is essential to improving the department chair's effectiveness. The success of the *Complexities* text is evidence that practicing administrators can improve their professional communication skills by placing themselves as first-person participants in a case study and by taking seriously the structured questions and other exercises designed to practice the seemingly commonsense communication guidelines and principles.

This book presents information about communication as it affects some specific responsibilities and duties assigned to the department chair. The text offers prescriptive guidelines for immediate use. In addition, practicing chairs can expand their repertoire of communication skills and become more proficient communicators by adopting a first-person participant's role when reading this book. Those willing to place themselves in the scenarios described and answer the questions asked will find that they don't have to "live it to learn it." The ultimate goal is to make the more salient lessons of my discipline relevant and useful to the department chair practitioner.

To be certain that the communication strategies are clear and useful to chair practitioners and that the cases are realistic, I piloted portions of this text with colleagues and practicing administrators. Special thanks are due to all of these reviewers who read early versions of the manuscript:

John B. Bennett, Quinnipiac College
Sarah Blackstone, Southern Illinois University at Carbondale
Walter H. Gmelch, Washington State University
Irene W. D. Hecht, American Council on Education
Allan Karnes, Southern Illinois University at Carbondale
Lee I. McCann, University of Wisconsin at Oshkosh
Barry McCauliff, Clarion University

AUTHOR'S INTRODUCTION

Too often, successful teachers and researchers with little or no administrative training find themselves promoted into department chair positions. Unfortunately, many of the skills needed to be an effective department chair are not those that one cultivates while teaching and conducting research. Successful administration at any level of the university requires effective communication.

The need for strong communication skills is particularly acute for department chairs because they face some special challenges. First, the chairs must work closely on a daily basis with the faculty over whom they have administrative responsibility. Unlike the dean or provost, the chair has an office near the faculty. The chairs live among the faculty about whom they must make decisions. This closeness heightens the need for effective communication skills. Second, department chairs are both faculty and administrators. The central administration is likely to view the department chair as having more faculty allegiance whereas faculty may perceive the chair as having more loyalty to the administration. That dual role makes it imperative that the chair establish and maintain credibility with both the faculty and the central administration.

This text is a resource for practicing department chairs. Each chapter describes communication strategies that are useful in handling an important administrative task. The theoretical information is then applied to specific situations so the reader observes the impact of communication in carrying out the chair's duties and responsibilities. The text organization walks the reader through real-life situations that allow the reader to develop critical thinking skills and practice a repertoire of communication skills for more effectively managing similar situations. The book can be used for self-directed professional development or in a seminar and workshop setting. The objective is to equip practicing department chairs with information and to coach them through structured applications in order to make the chair's role more comfortable and manageable.

The text is organized around three major communication contexts for department chair activity. Within each context, individual chapters focus on the more dominant administrative tasks that require strong communication skills. Consequently, the text blends the teaching of communication skills with those administrative duties typically assigned to department chairs.

The focus of Part One, Cultivating the Department Culture, is on the preconditions to effective department communication. A healthy department culture sets the stage for effective administration. Even difficult tasks such as managing conflict are easier in a healthy department than in a department where there is little or no trust and respect among colleagues. Part One includes chapters on structuring the department mission, enhancing the department climate, and defining department ethics.

The focus in Part Two of the text is on the interpersonal communication skills needed to work effectively with faculty. Part Two includes chapters on three of the more difficult, but essential, tasks performed by department chairs: conducting performance counseling sessions; managing conflict; and implementing change.

The focus for Part Three is the communication strategies essential to interfacing with external publics. The chair needs to position the department favorably with relevant external publics, including the central administration, alumni, legislators, governing boards, accrediting agencies, prospective students, granting agencies, and industry. Part Three contains chapters on working with the dean, building alliances on and off campus, and marketing the department.

Special Features

Relevant communication concepts and strategies

For each administrative task, relevant communication theory is presented in the form of practical guidelines for department chairs. Special care is taken to interpret communication theory and research findings in a way that is meaningful to practicing department chairs who may lack formal training in communication. The objective is to equip department chairs with information that can be immediately useful in carrying out their administrative duties.

Putting theory into practice

Short case studies follow the sections on relevant communication concepts and strategies. The case study method allows theory to be translated into practice. It also allows the reader to observe how communication functions in the context of real-life situations and, in particular, to witness how effective communication affects specific administrative duties. By using case studies, department chairs can think through strategies for the implementation of the pragmatic communication guidelines.

The case study method provides readers with an opportunity to learn from the experience of others in a risk-free environment. The use of case studies accelerates the type of learning that typically accompanies professional work experience. For this benefit to be fully realized, the reader must remain an active participant and not slip into the more comfortable role of third-person observer. Department chairs will benefit most from placing themselves in the case situations, analyzing the available alternatives, and developing strategies for managing the administrative challenge presented in the case study.

Let's analyze the case

This text does not supply "the answers" because no simple answer transcends all institution and personality types. Successful department chairs seldom start with all the information necessary to solve a given problem, but they must be able to recognize and articulate the important questions that need to be answered. The text helps the reader identify and analyze the key issues, variables, and options. A brief analysis that delineates the major components of the case study and describes the challenges that face the department chair follows. By structuring the problem set forth in the case, the reader is better able to devise a plan for managing the dilemma described in the case.

It's your turn

Each case is followed with a series of questions. These queries invite the reader to participate in the case scenario. They offer the reader an opportunity to consider alternatives and make decisions from the role of the department chair in the case. The questions are carefully structured to help the reader systematically analyze the relevant variables and determine a reasonable course of action. Occasionally, the questions direct the reader to practice the communication strategies by scripting comments or drafting a response. The final stage of self-directed professional development occurs when readers, who have participated fully in the case study analysis, evaluate their own handling of the case situation.

Critical thinking skills are a combination of knowing the questions to ask, using the information assembled, applying the appropriate communication and management skills, and making decisions with clarity and vision. Analyzing cases in this directed format will improve a person's ability to think critically. The text is designed to provide practicing department chairs with an opportunity for skill development. This learning, whether done independently or as part of a professional seminar or workshop, will serve to sharpen one's communication skills for more effectively managing the academic department.

Please consider

Sometimes new case information and other considerations are presented that alter how the reader would approach the case. Each case addendum is intended to keep the reader from truncating the analysis of the problem before gaining a complete understanding of all variables. These sections help the reader comprehend the true complexity of each case by illustrating how the case issues influence, and are influenced by, other variables. Solutions are only workable if they accurately allow for the dynamic interrelationship of all relevant components of the problematic situation.

Let's recap

This section completes the loop, moving the reader from the specific case back to the theoretical guidelines that were described earlier in the chapter. It presents readers with a checklist for assessing the merit of their derived strategy for managing the case situation. It also serves to reinforce the broader theoretical concepts that can be generalized to situations beyond the text case studies.

Index of cases

Realistic case studies usually encompass several issues. The reader may wish to analyze additional cases that relate to a particular administrative task. All the cases included in this text are organized by higher education issue and administrative task to help the reader find other cases on similar issues.

The Index of Cases by Higher Education Issue and Administrative Task also enables the reader to locate relevant communication strategies for a particular administrative task or issue without reading the text from beginning to end. A reader seeking insight on managing a new assessment initiative, for example, can check the index to identify those cases that deal with assessment. The communication strategies presented with these case studies will be maximally relevant to the administrative task at hand.

INDEX OF CASES
BY HIGHER EDUCATION ISSUE
AND ADMINISTRATIVE TASK

Academic Dishonesty
    Case 3.3, Reward or Punishment   92
    Case 5.1, The Accusation   149
    Case 5.2, Letter of Recommendation   155

Affirmative Action
    Case 2.1, The Inner Circle   43
    Case 2.3, This Is Important   57
    Case 2.4, Equality?   63
    Case 7.3, Please Say No   219

Alumni Relations
    Case 2.3, This Is Important   57
    Case 8.3, Marketable Collaborations   243
    Case 9.1, Operating in the Dark   260
    Case 9.2, Mobilizing the Fans   266
    Case 9.3, Mounting an Offensive   270

Assessment of Student Learning
    Case 1.4, Tough Times: Foreign Languages' Response   31
    Case 6.1, Another Mandate!   179
    Case 6.2, Spare the Messenger   183
    Case 8.2, Meeting Accreditation Standards   238
    Case 8.3, Marketable Collaborations   243

Budget (see Fiscal Management)

Campus Climate
    Case 1.1, Changing Times and Sinking Ships   14
    Case 1.3, Tough Times: Theater's Response   25
    Case 1.4, Tough Times: Foreign Languages' Response   31

Case 6.1, Another Mandate! 179
Case 6.3, A New Playing Field 191
Case 6.4, Checkmate 196
Case 9.3, Mounting an Offensive 270

Campus Constituencies
Case 1.3, Tough Times: Theater's Response 25
Case 1.4, Tough Times: Foreign Languages' Response 31
Case 2.3, This Is Important 57
Case 8.3, Marketable Collaborations 243
Case 8.4, Campus Networks 247
Case 9.3, Mounting an Offensive 270
Case 9.4, Marketing the Department Mission 274

Collegiality
Case 2.1, The Inner Circle 43
Case 2.2, Making No-Win Decisions 51
Case 2.3, This Is Important 57
Case 2.4, Equality? 63
Case 3.1, Mixed Messages 75
Case 3.2, The Written Record 87
Case 3.3, Reward or Punishment 92
Case 4.3, The Self-Centered Team Member 126
Case 5.1, The Accusation 149
Case 5.3, Self-Interest 157
Case 5.4, The Chair's Bias 163

Crisis Management
Case 1.3, Tough Times: Theater's Response 25
Case 1.4, Tough Times: Foreign Languages' Response 31
Case 5.1, The Accusation 149
Case 9.1, Operating in the Dark 260
Case 9.2, Mobilizing the Fans 266
Case 9.3, Mounting an Offensive 270

Delegation of Duties
Case 1.4, Tough Times: Foreign Languages' Response 31
Case 2.4, Equality? 63
Case 3.3, Reward or Punishment 92
Case 3.4, The Reaction 98
Case 6.1, Another Mandate! 179
Case 6.2, Spare the Messenger 183

Case 7.2, Passing the Buck   216
Case 7.3, Please Say No   219

Department Climate
Case 1.1, Changing Times and Sinking Ships   14
Case 1.2, The Assigned Mission   18
Case 1.3, Tough Times: Theater's Response   25
Case 1.4, Tough Times: Foreign Languages' Response   31
Case 2.1, The Inner Circle   43
Case 2.2, Making No-Win Decisions   51
Case 2.3, This Is Important   57
Case 2.4, Equality?   63
Case 3.1, Mixed Messages   75
Case 3.2, The Written Record   87
Case 3.4, The Reaction   98
Case 4.3, The Self-Centered Team Member   126
Case 5.1, The Accusation   149
Case 5.3, Self-Interest   157
Case 5.4, The Chair's Bias   163
Case 6.1, Another Mandate!   179
Case 6.2, Spare the Messenger   183
Case 9.1, Operating in the Dark   260

Department Image and Reputation
Case 1.1, Changing Times and Sinking Ships   14
Case 1.2, The Assigned Mission   18
Case 2.1, The Inner Circle   43
Case 2.3, This Is Important   57
Case 6.2, Spare the Messenger   183
Case 6.3, A New Playing Field   191
Case 6.4, Checkmate   196
Case 8.1, Join the Winner's Circle   233
Case 8.2, Meeting Accreditation Standards   238
Case 8.3, Marketable Collaborations   243
Case 9.1, Operating in the Dark   260
Case 9.2, Mobilizing the Fans   266
Case 9.3, Mounting an Offensive   270
Case 9.4, Marketing the Department Mission   274

Development/Fundraising

    Case 8.1, Join the Winner's Circle   233

    Case 9.1, Operating in the Dark   260

    Case 9.2, Mobilizing the Fans   266

    Case 9.3, Mounting an Offensive   270

Discrimination

    Case 2.2, Making No-Win Decisions   51

    Case 2.3, This Is Important   57

    Case 2.4, Equality?   63

    Case 3.2, The Written Record   87

    Case 3.3, Reward or Punishment   92

    Case 3.4, The Reaction   98

    Case 5.3, Self-Interest   157

    Case 5.4, The Chair's Bias   163

    Case 7.3, Please Say No   219

Due Process and Individual Rights

    Case 3.3, Reward or Punishment   92

    Case 3.4, The Reaction   98

    Case 5.1, The Accusation   149

    Case 5.2, Letter of Recommendation   155

    Case 7.3, Please Say No   219

Enrollment Management

    Case 1.2, The Assigned Mission   18

    Case 1.3, Tough Times: Theater's Response   25

    Case 1.4, Tough Times: Foreign Languages' Response   31

    Case 2.3, This Is Important   57

    Case 4.3, The Self-Centered Team Member   126

    Case 6.3, A New Playing Field   191

    Case 6.4, Checkmate   196

    Case 8.3, Marketable Collaborations   243

Evaluation (see Performance Counseling)

Faculty Development

    Case 2.2, Making No-Win Decisions   51

    Case 2.4, Equality?   63

    Case 3.1, Mixed Messages   75

    Case 3.2, The Written Record   87

    Case 4.1, Superstar or Naive   115

    Case 4.2, The Encounter   119

Case 4.3, The Self-Centered Team Member 126
Case 4.4, The Follow-up 134
Case 7.3, Please Say No 219

Faculty Complaints and Grievances
Case 2.1, The Inner Circle 43
Case 2.2, Making No-Win Decisions 51
Case 2.4, Equality? 63
Case 3.1, Mixed Messages 75
Case 3.3, Reward or Punishment 92
Case 3.4, The Reaction 98
Case 4.3, The Self-Centered Team Member 126
Case 5.1, The Accusation 149
Case 5.3, Self-Interest 157
Case 5.4, The Chair's Bias 163

Fiscal Management
Case 1.1, Changing Times and Sinking Ships 14
Case 1.2, The Assigned Mission 18
Case 1.3, Tough Times: Theater's Response 25
Case 1.4, Tough Times: Foreign Languages' Response 31
Case 2.2, Making No-Win Decisions 51
Case 5.3, Self-Interest 157
Case 7.2, Passing the Buck 216
Case 7.4, Listen Carefully 223
Case 8.1, Join the Winner's Circle 233
Case 8.2, Meeting Accreditation Standards 238
Case 9.1, Operating in the Dark 260
Case 9.2, Mobilizing the Fans 266
Case 9.3, Mounting an Offensive 270

Governance Issues
Case 2.1, The Inner Circle 43
Case 2.2, Making No-Win Decisions 51
Case 2.4, Equality? 63
Case 3.3, Reward or Punishment 92
Case 3.4, The Reaction 98
Case 5.1, The Accusation 149
Case 7.2, Passing the Buck 216
Case 7.3, Please Say No 219
Case 8.2, Meeting Accreditation Standards 238

Implementation of a New Initiative
    Case 1.4, Tough Times: Foreign Languages' Response   31
    Case 6.1, Another Mandate!   179
    Case 6.2, Spare the Messenger   183
    Case 6.3, A New Playing Field   191
    Case 6.4, Checkmate   196
    Case 7.4, Listen Carefully   223
    Case 8.1, Join the Winner's Circle   233
    Case 8.3, Marketable Collaborations   243
    Case 9.4, Marketing the Department Mission   274

Instructional Quality
    Case 1.2, The Assigned Mission   18
    Case 1.3, Tough Times: Theater's Response   25
    Case 1.4, Tough Times: Foreign Languages' Response   31
    Case 2.3, This Is Important   57
    Case 4.1, Superstar or Naive   115
    Case 4.2, The Encounter   119
    Case 4.3, The Self-Centered Team Member   126
    Case 4.4, The Follow-up   134
    Case 6.1, Another Mandate!   179
    Case 6.2, Spare the Messenger   183
    Case 8.2, Meeting Accreditation Standards   238
    Case 8.3, Marketable Collaborations   243

Job Search
    Case 1.1, Changing Times and Sinking Ships   14
    Case 2.1, The Inner Circle   43
    Case 2.4, Equality?   63
    Case 5.2, Letter of Recommendation   155
    Case 8.4, Campus Networks   247

Legal Liability
    Case 3.1, Mixed Messages   75
    Case 3.2, The Written Record   87
    Case 3.3, Reward or Punishment   92
    Case 3.4, The Reaction   98
    Case 4.1, Superstar or Naive   115
    Case 4.2, The Encounter   119
    Case 4.4, The Follow-up   134
    Case 5.1, The Accusation   149

Case 5.2, Letter of Recommendation 155
Case 7.1, Sharing the Liability 211
Case 7.3, Please Say No 219

Management of Conflicting Interests
 Case 1.1, Changing Times and Sinking Ships 14
 Case 1.2, The Assigned Mission 18
 Case 1.3, Tough Times: Theater's Response 25
 Case 2.1, The Inner Circle 43
 Case 2.2, Making No-Win Decisions 51
 Case 2.3, This Is Important 57
 Case 3.1, Mixed Messages 75
 Case 4.1, Superstar or Naive 115
 Case 4.2, The Encounter 119
 Case 4.3, The Self-Centered Team Member 126
 Case 5.1, The Accusation 149
 Case 5.2, Letter of Recommendation 155
 Case 5.3, Self-Interest 157
 Case 5.4, The Chair's Bias 163
 Case 6.1, Another Mandate! 179
 Case 6.2, Spare the Messenger 183
 Case 6.3, A New Playing Field 191
 Case 6.4, Checkmate 196
 Case 7.2, Passing the Buck 216
 Case 7.3, Please Say No 219
 Case 7.4, Listen Carefully 223
 Case 8.2, Meeting Accreditation Standards 238
 Case 9.3, Mounting an Offensive 270

Merit Pay
 Case 3.3, Reward or Punishment 92
 Case 3.4, The Reaction 98
 Case 5.3, Self-Interest 157
 Case 5.4, The Chair's Bias 163

Mission and Goals
 Case 1.1, Changing Times and Sinking Ships 14
 Case 1.2, The Assigned Mission 18
 Case 1.3, Tough Times: Theater's Response 25
 Case 1.4, Tough Times: Foreign Languages' Response 31
 Case 2.1, The Inner Circle 43

Case 4.1, Superstar or Naive   115
Case 6.3, A New Playing Field   191
Case 6.4, Checkmate   196
Case 7.2, Passing the Buck   216
Case 7.4, Listen Carefully   223
Case 8.2, Meeting Accreditation Standards   238
Case 8.3, Marketable Collaborations   243
Case 9.3, Mounting an Offensive   270
Case 9.4, Marketing the Department Mission   274

Performance Counseling
Case 3.1, Mixed Messages   75
Case 3.2, The Written Record   87
Case 3.3, Reward or Punishment   92
Case 3.4, The Reaction   98
Case 4.1, Superstar or Naive   115
Case 4.2, The Encounter   119
Case 4.3, The Self-Centered Team Member   126
Case 4.4, The Follow-up   134
Case 5.1, The Accusation   149
Case 5.2, Letter of Recommendation   155
Case 7.3, Please Say No   219

Policies and Procedures
Case 3.2, The Written Record   87
Case 3.3, Reward or Punishment   92
Case 4.1, Superstar or Naive   115
Case 5.1, The Accusation   149
Case 6.3, A New Playing Field   191
Case 6.4, Checkmate   196
Case 7.3, Please Say No   219
Case 8.4, Campus Networks   247

Policy Development
Case 2.2, Making No-Win Decisions   51
Case 4.3, The Self-Centered Team Member   126
Case 5.3, Self-Interest   157
Case 5.4, The Chair's Bias   163
Case 6.1, Another Mandate!   179
Case 6.2, Spare the Messenger   183
Case 7.2, Passing the Buck   216

Productivity: Department
Case 1.2, The Assigned Mission   18
Case 1.3, Tough Times: Theater's Response   25
Case 1.4, Tough Times: Foreign Languages' Response   31
Case 6.1, Another Mandate!   179
Case 6.2, Spare the Messenger   183
Case 6.3, A New Playing Field   191
Case 6.4, Checkmate   196
Case 7.4, Listen Carefully   223
Case 8.2, Meeting Accreditation Standards   238
Case 9.3, Mounting an Offensive   270
Case 9.4, Marketing the Department Mission   274

Productivity: Individual
Case 3.1, Mixed Messages   75
Case 3.2, The Written Record   87
Case 3.3, Reward or Punishment   92
Case 3.4, The Reaction   98
Case 4.1, Superstar or Naive   115
Case 4.2, The Encounter   119
Case 4.3, The Self-Centered Team Member   126
Case 4.4, The Follow-up   134
Case 8.4, Campus Networks   247

Program Evaluation
Case 1.1, Changing Times and Sinking Ships   14
Case 1.3, Tough Times: Theater's Response   25
Case 1.4, Tough Times: Foreign Languages' Response   31
Case 6.1, Another Mandate!   179
Case 6.2, Spare the Messenger   183
Case 8.3, Marketable Collaborations   243

Promotion and Tenure Decisions
Case 3.1, Mixed Messages   75
Case 3.2, The Written Record   87
Case 4.1, Superstar or Naive   115
Case 4.2, The Encounter   119
Case 4.4, The Follow-up   134
Case 7.3, Please Say No   219
Case 8.4, Campus Networks   247

Public Relations
    Case 1.2, The Assigned Mission 18
    Case 1.4, Tough Times: Foreign Languages' Response 31
    Case 2.3, This Is Important 57
    Case 4.3, The Self-Centered Team Member 126
    Case 5.1, The Accusation 149
    Case 6.3, A New Playing Field 191
    Case 8.1, Join the Winner's Circle 233
    Case 8.2, Meeting Accreditation Standards 238
    Case 8.3, Marketable Collaborations 243
    Case 9.1, Operating in the Dark 260
    Case 9.2, Mobilizing the Fans 266
    Case 9.3, Mounting an Offensive 270
    Case 9.4, Marketing the Department Mission 274

Roles and Responsibilities: Department Chair
    Case 1.3, Tough Times: Theater's Response 25
    Case 1.4, Tough Times: Foreign Languages' Response 31
    Case 2.2, Making No-Win Decisions 51
    Case 3.1, Mixed Messages 75
    Case 3.2, The Written Record 87
    Case 3.3, Reward or Punishment 92
    Case 3.4, The Reaction 98
    Case 4.1, Superstar or Naive 115
    Case 4.2, The Encounter 119
    Case 4.3, The Self-Centered Team Member 126
    Case 5.4, The Chair's Bias 163
    Case 6.1, Another Mandate! 179
    Case 6.2, Spare the Messenger 183
    Case 7.1, Sharing the Liability 211
    Case 7.2, Passing the Buck 216
    Case 7.3, Please Say No 219

Roles and Responsibilities: Dean and Central Administration
    Case 6.1, Another Mandate! 179
    Case 6.2, Spare the Messenger 183
    Case 7.1, Sharing the Liability 211
    Case 7.2, Passing the Buck 216
    Case 7.3, Please Say No 219

Roles and Responsibilities: Faculty
    Case 1.2, The Assigned Mission   18
    Case 1.3, Tough Times: Theater's Response   25
    Case 1.4, Tough Times: Foreign Languages' Response   31
    Case 2.1, The Inner Circle   43
    Case 2.2, Making No-Win Decisions   51
    Case 2.4, Equality?   63
    Case 3.1, Mixed Messages   75
    Case 3.2, The Written Record   87
    Case 3.3, Reward or Punishment   92
    Case 3.4, The Reaction   98
    Case 4.1, Superstar or Naive   115
    Case 4.2, The Encounter   119
    Case 4.3, The Self-Centered Team Member   126
    Case 5.1, The Accusation   149
    Case 6.1, Another Mandate!   179
    Case 6.2, Spare the Messenger   183
    Case 8.4, Campus Networks   247

Scientific Misconduct
    Case 5.1, The Accusation   149
    Case 5.2, Letter of Recommendation   155

Student Complaints and Grievances
    Case 2.3, This Is Important   57
    Case 4.1, Superstar or Naive   115
    Case 4.3, The Self-Centered Team Member   126

Student Recruitment and Retention
    Case 1.4, Tough Times: Foreign Languages' Response   31
    Case 2.3, This Is Important   57
    Case 4.1, Superstar or Naive   115
    Case 4.3, The Self-Centered Team Member   126
    Case 8.3, Marketable Collaborations   243
    Case 9.1, Operating in the Dark   260

Teaching Improvement
    Case 2.3, This Is Important   57
    Case 3.1, Mixed Messages   75
    Case 3.2, The Written Record   87
    Case 4.1, Superstar or Naive   115
    Case 4.2, The Encounter   119

Case 4.3, The Self-Centered Team Member 126
Case 4.4, The Follow-up 134
Case 7.3, Please Say No 219

Termination (possible) of Appointment
Case 4.1, Superstar or Naive 115
Case 4.2, The Encounter 119
Case 4.4, The Follow-up 134
Case 5.1, The Accusation 149
Case 5.2, Letter of Recommendation 155
Case 7.3, Please Say No 219
Case 8.4, Campus Networks 247

Workload Management: Department
Case 1.1, Changing Times and Sinking Ships 14
Case 1.2, The Assigned Mission 18
Case 1.3, Tough Times: Theater's Response 25
Case 1.4, Tough Times: Foreign Languages' Response 31
Case 5.3, Self-Interest 157
Case 6.1, Another Mandate! 179
Case 6.2, Spare the Messenger 183
Case 6.3, A New Playing Field 191
Case 6.4, Checkmate 196

Workload Management: Individual
Case 4.1, Superstar or Naive 115
Case 4.2, The Encounter 119
Case 4.3, The Self-Centered Team Member 126
Case 4.4, The Follow-up 134
Case 9.3, Mounting an Offensive 270

PART ONE

CULTIVATING THE DEPARTMENT CULTURE

This section of the text describes those characteristics of a healthy department culture that are preconditions to effective communication within the department. Emphasis is given to the department chair's role in influencing the department culture. Communication strategies for effective leadership in establishing and maintaining a healthy department culture are presented in relation to three of the more critical components of the department culture: the department mission, the department climate, and the department ethics.

Chapter 1: Structuring the Department Mission
describes how to build consensus for the department mission from shared values

Chapter 2: Enhancing the Department Climate
includes strategies for maintaining a climate that is conducive to high morale and productivity

Chapter 3: Defining the Department Ethics
examines the relationship between the chair's performance and department ethics

1

STRUCTURING THE
DEPARTMENT MISSION

In a healthy department there exists a common core of understanding, a basic agreement that defines the department and charts its general direction. This does not imply that all members of the department think alike or agree on everything. Indeed, perfect harmony negates the advantage of having diverse viewpoints. For the same reason that some conflict is important to reaching a better group decision, diverse views among faculty and staff are essential to the long-term growth of the department. Diversity is most advantageous (and less destructive) when a common core of shared basic values exists among department members.

Values underlie how individuals think and act. Values influence attitudes and guide behaviors. Shared values are the basic cornerstones for productive working relationships. With shared values come a common purpose, a basic agreement on what is important. Shared values yield a common language among members that allows them to collaborate. Shared values allow people to function independently and interdependently to achieve a mutually accepted purpose.

The accepted purpose is the department mission. Most department chairs recognize the importance of shared values to the overall sense of community within the department and to the general acceptance of the department mission. Less clear, perhaps, is the critical role of the department chair in building community through shared values. Effective department chairs create consensus around shared values. They pull individuals together and build a department community around a generally accepted mission.

The Objective

One goal of this chapter is to help department chairs understand their role in building consensus around shared values. Departments that are value-driven rather than event-driven typically have healthier climates and a greater tolerance for adversity. A second goal of this chapter is to equip chairs with some specific communication strategies for building consensus within the department around the department mission. Department chairs do not need to wait for a crisis to build consensus for a common purpose. The carefully structured department mission is a vehicle for involving individual department members in collective actions and shared successes. A third goal is to help department chairs realize the benefits of having a clearly articulated department mission. When a department tries to be all things to all people, internally and externally, it typically ends up being nothing to anyone. A clearly focused and accepted mission statement based on shared values accrues advantages both within and outside the department.

Defining the Task

Structuring the department mission involves building consensus about the future direction of the department. If the task begins as a writing assignment, department deliberations will focus on compromise language that is acceptable to everyone. Instead, the process should begin with the attitudes and beliefs currently held by the faculty and their expectations for the academic unit. The department members need to consider perceptions and expectations in relation to verifiable department strengths and potential strengths. Eventually, the department must measure this internal assessment against those external conditions that affect the department.

The department mission statement should describe the department's basic purpose and strategic direction. By doing so, the mission statement establishes an internal and external image of the department. Internally, the department mission clarifies the shared values that guide individual and collective department activities and provides a framework for resolving department conflict. An accepted mission statement equips faculty with a common language with which they can collaborate. Externally, the department mission statement educates the various external publics that interact with the department about the unit's strengths and resource needs.

An effective mission statement accomplishes the following objectives:

Provides a clear and compelling statement of future direction

An effective mission statement is not open to a range of interpretations. Rather, it offers a description of future department direction that is clear, concise, and feasible. A department mission statement should not be so general that any department could use it regardless of the discipline, size, institution, or geographic location. When departments draft mission statements without first building consensus, they typically use compromise language that is too general to be useful. Ideally, a department mission statement has a compelling or inspirational quality in that it serves to increase commitment to and build pride in the department purpose.

Specifies who the department serves and how

An effective mission statement gives a department an added dimension, a certain distinctiveness and character. That is particularly helpful in times of adversity. Whether adversity results from budget cuts, a change in campus leadership, or structural reorganization, departments with clear missions are in a stronger position to avoid the negative outcomes of these difficult times. The mission statement must indicate whom the department serves and how in order to demonstrate the significance of the department to the institution, region, and discipline. Clarifying this information moves the department from a defensive posture to a proactive position.

Identifies department priorities

An effective mission statement declares the values that are most important to the department. Consequently, it sets the tone for department activity and clarifies the unit's unique purpose. The mission statement helps faculty know what activities are important to the department and, therefore, most likely to earn reward. It clarifies for the central administration and other external publics what strengths the department is able to offer the institution, region, and discipline. The description should indicate the relative weight assigned to each of the shared values. The mission statement, for example, should make clear the value placed on undergraduate instruction relative to other department priorities such as research, public service, and graduate instruction.

Provides a description of how the department defines success

An effective mission statement links strategic direction to specific objectives that drive individual and collective actions. By doing so, the mission statement defines success. Consider, for example, the department mission that articulates the goal of educating and preparing needed speech pathologists for the state. This mission offers a profile of the department's special distinctiveness. It also sets up the measure for success in that the department's retention and graduation rates will be indicators of the department's effectiveness.

Demonstrates how the department mission
serves the institutional mission

It is suicidal to have a department mission that is not compatible with the mission of the institution. It is costly, for example, to ignore the institution's mission to undergraduate education and focus department effort exclusively on the graduate curriculum. That idea is easier to understand than to implement. Sometimes the institution's mission changes in response to externally imposed conditions before the institution formally revises the mission statement. Sometimes the central administration is slow or unwilling to acknowledge such imposed shifts in the institution's mission. That is likely to happen when external groups push the institution into a reactive mode. The state governing board of higher education may, for example, direct the institution to increase the attention given to undergraduate instruction. Responding to such pressure is likely to redirect resources away from other priorities and toward undergraduate education whether or not the administration formally acknowledges how this shift alters the institution's mission. Department chairs need to be alert to the operational mission of the institution. What activities does the institution value? What is the general direction of the institution? How do external pressures influence campus values? How might the department support the institutional mission? Are the department strengths and mission responsive to the external pressures that forced a shift in campus priorities? The answers to these and similar questions are important if chairs want the department mission to remain compatible with the institution's mission.

Relevant Communication Concepts and Strategies

Effective mission statements evolve from fully participative and serious deliberation. Whether department chairs are starting from scratch or working to revise an existing mission statement, it is imperative that all department members have a voice in the process. Consensus building, both about the need for a mission statement and the department priorities, should precede the drafting of a formal statement. The task of structuring the department mission is a process, not a single activity. It unfolds over time and not in any one meeting. The following communication strategies will help department chairs manage the process of structuring the department mission.

Determine key shared values

A department chair cannot proclaim department values. Developing shared values is a process that must begin with soliciting input from department members. The process is as important as the outcome. Individual perspectives will change as department members participate in the process. Consequently, the outcome represents an assimilation of ideas that all members can more easily accept. Participation in the process can help individual members accept ideas that they might otherwise reject because ideas are not presented as conclusions but grow out of department deliberation.

Reaching consensus is a win-win process that allows the members to express their values and aspirations for the department. Cultural, ethnic, and other kinds of diversity make the process more valuable and important because the final outcome is one that derives from full consideration of all diverse viewpoints. While diversity can be a source of strength, it can also make the process of building consensus more time-consuming and challenging. Department chairs who effectively lead faculty and staff through this deliberate and participative process can secure authentic consensus about core department values. Department values are more than individual observations, perceptions, or department procedures. Department values are those basic principles that department members deem to be most important to the department's welfare. Department values answer such questions as:

- Who are we?

- What is our purpose?

- What is most important to us?

- Where do we want to go in the future?

Department values may include statements like:

- Quality undergraduate instruction is the top department priority.

- The department's graduates must be able to obtain productive employment in discipline-related occupations.

It is important that all department members have an operational understanding of the department values. It is not enough, for example, for faculty to know that undergraduate instruction is a priority for the department. If undergraduate instruction is a priority for the department, then faculty need to know what that means in terms of the expectations for their individual behavior. Does it mean that faculty must help recruit and retain good students? Does it mean that faculty must work together to sequence the content covered in related courses? Does it mean that faculty must actively engage in research that supports undergraduate instruction? Until the faculty have an operational understanding of department values and priorities, the department will not realize the benefit of having a department mission. The process of consensus building allows individual department members to acquire an operational understanding of shared values.

Despite the benefits, consensus building can be a difficult process. The degree of difficulty depends on the department membership and profile. If, for example, you are a new chair in a department characterized by low morale and distrust, the task of building consensus will be especially difficult. The task of building consensus is difficult when department members hold widely different viewpoints and have no or little practice in communicating with one another. The task is also challenging if the department has even a few members who protect personal interests, fear confrontation, or fear examining facts and data. The remaining communication strategies are techniques for building consensus in order to structure the department mission.

Involve all faculty and staff

Effective mission statements represent a common core of understanding among the faculty as to the general direction to be pursued by the department. The department cannot reach consensus if the procedures used exclude some faculty from the process of discussing department goals and objectives. Some department chairs may believe that the task of structuring a department mission is only possible if a committee composed of faculty and staff who think alike complete the task. There is no doubt that the issue of department priorities is one on which individual members may disagree. One does not have to look far to find an example of the department in which the faculty seem to get along with one another only because they avoid any discussion of department priorities. Those departments typically lack functional mission statements. If the members of an academic department do not have a common understanding about the department's general direction and priorities, then external groups cannot possibly have a coherent perception of the department's worth. If the department is different things to different groups, it cannot succeed. Structuring the department mission requires consensus building. This means that faculty and staff with different views about department priorities must be able to discuss their views and reach some agreement about the department mission and goals. By doing so, all department members present similar impressions of the department and its unique niche on campus and within the discipline.

Faculty and staff will have a greater commitment to the department mission if they participate in deciding department priorities. It is harder for department members to reject priorities when they have participated in framing them. Furthermore, when members misinterpret the department mission or fail to have a clear sense of department priorities, they are less likely to engage in the activities that the department values. Individual and collective success requires that department members have a clear understanding of department priorities so they can perform valued tasks. Department morale improves when members know that their contributions are essential to the success and reputation of the department. Commitment to the department mission cannot be 100% if any subgroup of the faculty has not participated in the consensus-building process. Take, for example, the department that employs several part-time faculty. Typically, that department's mission will include some prescription about the population that the department serves primarily, if not exclusively, through the work of the part-time faculty. To establish department goals and priorities without input and participation from the part-time faculty leaves out those who are essential to achieving the mission. The part-time or adjunct faculty have firsthand experience that can help shape a more accurate statement of department priorities with regard to serving the population they teach.

Some departments are too large for the faculty to work as a committee of the whole in discussing department priorities. In those instances, the chair should structure a process to ensure that all department members participate in the process of determining department priorities and drafting the department mission statement. Consider again the department that uses a number of part-time faculty to teach service courses. Part-time faculty often hold more than one job. They do not spend all of their work week on a single campus and may not be able to attend department meetings. This does not diminish the importance of their perspective at least with regard to the student population they serve. The chair may schedule separate meetings for this group to organize their thoughts into a cohesive perspective. The chair of this subcommittee might then meet with the larger group that must consider the full range of perspectives. If that is not possible, a member of the larger group may sit in on the meetings of the part-time faculty to learn their perspective and report it to the larger group. The specific structure used will depend on the department size and profile. Regardless of the specific department characteristics, the department chair must establish a process that allows full participation or the process will not yield genuine department consensus.

Keep discussion focused on the department and not on individuals
Consensus is harder to reach when department members protect their own turf or advocate self-interest. The chair's objective is to keep the members from becoming defensive. The best way to reduce the potential for destructive conflict and individual defensiveness is to focus the discussion on the department as a whole. For example, it is one thing to discuss what the department needs to do to remain the state's major source of trained graduates in

the discipline and a very different matter to discuss how to update the content taught in a particular course, especially when that course is taught by the same person each term. The first issue frames the discussion from a department perspective in a constructive way. The second query focuses on an individual and frames the issue in a way that is likely to make at least one department member defensive. Department members will more likely reach consensus about department priorities if the department chair frames the issues so that no individual or group must defend current practice.

When the chair structures the consensus-building process so that department members are less defensive, the consensus-building process itself will promote cooperative behavior and a sense of community. It is important that members recognize how their specific roles are interconnected and important to department success. Competitive or independent action can be costly to the department. The consensus-building process calls for honest, professional, and persuasive communication, but has no room for name calling, accusations, or other personalized attacks. Ground rules established to preserve a constructive exchange of differing perspectives can spill over into department discussions on other issues. Chapter 5 of this text includes a list of specific ground rules that department chairs can use to minimize destructive conflict.

Identify department strengths and potential strengths

The department mission statement should describe the future direction of the department. It is important, therefore, that the discussion about mission explore potential strengths as well as existing strengths. This requires that department members be knowledgeable about the total offerings of the department. If the faculty only know about individual interests and discipline specialties, they cannot possibly assess the full range of department strengths. Member isolation is harmful in that it prevents productive collaboration among faculty and staff. Tunnel vision is typically an obstacle to consensus building.

The department also needs to recognize those existing strengths that may, for some reason, become a weakness in the future. For example, if one department strength derives from preparing students for technologically skilled employment, that strength could become a weakness unless the department remains current with technological advancements that are relevant to the degree program. The review of strengths and potential strengths must consider how external and internal factors influence these strengths. The department must consider such facts as changes in the state economy, discipline-related employment statistics, faculty retirements, campus priorities, and action taken by competing programs.

Know the institution's mission and environment

It is imperative that the department chair have a working knowledge of the institution's mission. It is not enough to read the approved mission statement for the institution. The department chair needs to know how the campus leadership carries out the institution's mission. What are the intentions of the central administration? What is the rank order of institutional priorities? The answers to those questions allow a chair to predict the preferences of the campus leadership. This is important information whenever promoting the department's mission. The department mission is more acceptable to central administration if it is compatible with the priorities of the institution.

The department chair also needs to watch for conditions that challenge or alter the institution's mission. For example, state budget cuts and increased external pressures for institutional accountability for undergraduate instruction may alter the institution's mission. Under such pressure, even strong research institutions may place a greater working emphasis on undergraduate instruction and decrease the emphasis given to graduate instruction and research. Departments need to stay ahead of such institutional changes. If there is increasing pressure for the institution to document undergraduate instructional quality, the department should not take action that gives the appearance of slighting undergraduate instruction. The department will be able to promote other department priorities only if it does not appear insensitive to the institution's increasing commitment to undergraduate instruction. The department will win more favor if it does not wait until the central administration requires it to give greater attention to undergraduate instruction.

Department chairs should discuss the institution's mission with the faculty. Faculty who are knowledgeable of the institution's mission and changing conditions are better able to represent the department in an appropriate manner. For example, a faculty member who complains about his or her course load relative to that typically assigned to colleagues in the same discipline at other institutions will irritate other faculty on campus who have heavier course loads. The ability to adapt to the campus audience requires a working knowledge of the institution's mission and operations. It is the chair's responsibility to help the faculty understand the context within which the department must work. Poor adaptation by the faculty or the department chair can be costly to the long-term mission and health of the department. Gary Larson made this point dramatically in one "Far Side" cartoon that featured Marie Antoinette's trip to the guillotine. The caption read, "Marie Antoinette's last ditch effort to save her head." The cartoon showed Marie Antoinette on her way to the guillotine exclaiming, "And ice cream. I said let them eat cake and ice cream." We know from history that such a last-ditch effort to adapt to the audience would only make matters worse for Marie Antoinette. Faculty who are familiar with the institution's mission and the campus culture are less likely to say and do things that will inadvertently harm the department.

Assess potential allies and markets

The department needs to identify the salient external publics and continuously review potential markets. External publics include, but are not limited to, the central administration, alumni, prospective students, granting agencies, accrediting boards, state boards of higher education, state legislatures, and area businesses. The department can identify the important external publics by asking a few key questions.

- Why is the department important to the college?
- Why is the department important to the institution?
- Why is the department important to the region?
- Whom does the department serve?

The answers to those questions will help develop an accurate list of relevant external publics that the department may serve or need. More specific information on how to communicate effectively with the external publics appears in Chapters 8 and 9.

The answers to the questions will also describe the perceived worth of the department to the various external publics. For example, the English department may be valuable to the institution because it teaches the composition courses required of all students. This does not mean that external publics dictate the department mission. Rather, the perceived worth of the department to external publics is a springboard for department advocacy. Consider again the English department that is valuable to the institution because it offers the required composition courses. That department could use this information to argue the merit of other department priorities. The English department may, for example, have a research priority that can benefit from the value placed on the composition course offering.

A mission statement must be dynamic. Just as conditions within the department change over time, relationships with external publics change. Department chairs need to continuously reassess potential allies and markets. The English department, for example, will gain another external public if accreditation guidelines in engineering require that students majoring in engineering take more courses in technical writing. In one sense, the engineering department becomes an external public to satisfy. On another plane, the engineering department becomes an ally because it is now important to engineering majors that the English department have sufficient faculty and resources to offer the technical writing courses required by their accrediting body. Those linkages are important in that they provide opportunities for the department to promote and achieve its mission.

It is also important to consider salient publics that are off campus. They surface in determining whom the department serves and why the department is important to the region, state, or discipline. It is important to determine the pulse of the external publics before initiating changes that will affect their relationship with the department. Take, for example, the music department that offers a series of musical performances for public enjoyment. In tight budget times, the music department may consider cutting back on the number of performances offered each year. Before making the decision, the department needs to ascertain the potential ramifications of this change for patrons that regularly purchase tickets to the events. The unit also needs to determine if the department would jeopardize other components of the program by cutting back on the performance schedule? For example, do the performances help to recruit students? Departments cannot make decisions in a vacuum without considering the potential impact on the department's relationship with salient external publics.

Write the mission statement, but don't file it

Effective mission statements are working documents. They are responsive to changing conditions and needs. If the department mission is to guide both collective and individual department activities, it must remain fresh and current in the minds of department members. It is not enough to write the mission down. Department members must understand and believe in it for the mission to drive individual and collective behavior.

It is the chair's responsibility to keep the department mission visible and present in everyday activity. This sometimes requires that chairs help faculty and staff translate the more general department values into specific activities. For example, consider the department that has a commitment to quality instruction and student success. The chair might lead an exercise in which all department members brainstorm the longer list of specific activities that support that value. The list might include the following actions:

• Faculty will monitor student progress through each course and keep students informed of their standing in the class.

- The department will limit class enrollment in skills courses to 20 students to ensure that students receive sufficient individualized instruction.

- Academic advisors will make certain that students have the appropriate prerequisites for each course.

Often the chair must serve as the constant reminder of the overriding purpose of the department. Some chairs convert the key components of the department mission into slogans or symbols that serve as a reminder. For example, one department focused on the need to remain creative as it lived through a time of severe adversity. That unit's symbol became the wings of a bird. The chair distributed lapel pins of a bird for faculty to wear. This helped everyone in the department to remember to be creative as they developed innovative solutions to the current dilemma. Regardless of the tactics used, it is the chair's responsibility to keep the department mission clear and visible in the daily activities of department members.

Putting Theory Into Practice

The strategies suggested for structuring the department mission will make intuitive good sense to those department chairs who recognize the value of an effective mission statement. On a philosophical level, the advantage of involving faculty and staff in building consensus about the department mission is clear. It is, however, quite another matter to engage in and manage a process with full faculty and staff participation. There are numerous reasons for truncating the process, including administrative deadlines, fiscal crises, heavy workloads, resistance to meetings, and conflict within the department. Department chairs typically do not find it easy to structure and carry out a planning process with full department participation.

In Case 1.1, Changing Times and Sinking Ships, a department must decide whether to maintain the current mission at significant cost or revise the department mission in response to external pressures at a considerable loss. The chair must lead the department faculty through this decision-making process while preserving the strong sense of department community. It is not easy because the faculty do not agree on what the department should do. Place yourself in the position of the department chair as you read the following case.

Case 1.1, Changing Times and Sinking Ships

Background Information

Since the early 1960s, the department of communication disorders at South Central University (SCU) has enjoyed healthy student enrollments. The only certified program in the southern part of a large midwestern state, the department currently enrolls roughly 200 baccalaureate, 65 full-time master's, and 30 doctoral students. In addition, there are another 75 students doing graduate work on a part-time basis. Since SCU is primarily an undergraduate teaching institution, the department's strong graduate enrollment gives it a high profile on campus.

The department boasts 14 full-time faculty who are known to the profession as excellent teachers and researchers. The strong research program conducted by the faculty earns much prestige off campus. On campus, the faculty frequently hold significant leadership posts on university committees, including the graduate council and the faculty senate.

The department owes much of its early success to a strong kinship with the administration. One of the institution's most respected presidents was a professor of speech pathology who held tenure in the department. That president served the institution and department well for 25 years before retiring five years ago. The president would frequently ask one of his department colleagues to chair a special campus-wide task force. As a result, the department faculty had significant influence in shaping campus policy.

The Present

The current decade has not gone as well for the department. Many of the old guard reached retirement age at the same time. In the last three years, seven of the 14 faculty retired. Unfortunately, the department did not fill all of the open faculty positions. The belief among the remaining faculty was that the department needed to be selective in hiring new people. The faculty feared that mediocre hires would damage the department's reputation in the discipline. The department managed to replace four of the seven, but elected to convert the remaining salary dollars to one-year term appointments in order to cover the curriculum while the department continued to search for stronger candidates.

This past year the state suffered a serious recession. The state drastically cut the institution's budget for the next fiscal year. The central administration absorbed all funds not committed to continuing personnel, and the department lost the three open positions. This leaves a faculty of 11 to cover the workload previously managed by a faculty of 14. Some faculty believe that the budget will be restored and the faculty lines returned to the department. These individuals suggest that everyone pitch in by teaching overloads, advising more students, and applying for more research grants until the budget picture turns around. They believe that this is the only course of action that will allow the department to preserve its reputation and program inventory. These faculty fear that any downsizing efforts might become permanent.

Other faculty believe that the department needs to take action to make the program manageable for the reduced department size. These faculty believe that it is time to sharpen the department focus. Some suggest eliminating the bachelor's component. Others want to drop audiology and return to the department's original focus in speech pathology. These faculty fear that any effort to retain the complete program that was staffed by 14 faculty will guarantee a visible decline in program quality that would have an even greater liability for the department in the future.

The department chair must lead the faculty through this decision.

Let's Analyze the Case

The department of communication disorders at South Central University is a strong department. The department mission exceeds university expectations in that SCU is primarily an undergraduate teaching institution and the department boasts a healthy graduate enrollment and strong research profile. The department lost three of 14 full-time faculty positions only because the positions were open at a time when the state suffered a serious recession. The central administration considered the positions open and available because the department had not filled them with tenure-track faculty. The department's effort to replace retiring faculty with only the highest quality applicants proved costly. Had the department been willing to appoint less experienced candidates, the positions would be filled and not lost abruptly to the institution's budget cut. The department seemed unaware of the risk it took by filling open tenure-track positions with one-year term appointments. For whatever reason, the department did not pay attention to the external economic pressures that were likely to affect the institution.

The central issue is whether or not the department should revise its mission in response to the recent loss of three faculty positions. Fundamental to making the best decision is the probability that the three open positions might be restored. Is the loss of three faculty positions temporary or permanent? How likely is it that the three positions will be returned to the department? The issue is easier to discuss because there exists a common understanding of the department mission. Before the budget cut, the department faculty agreed on the department's general direction and priorities. While the faculty disagree on the permanency of the recent budget cut, they continue to hold similar department values. The chair can use this strong sense of community as the department wrestles with how best to respond to the externally imposed reduction of the department's faculty.

It's Your Turn

Place yourself in the role of department chair and think through how you would structure faculty discussion of this issue.

1. How would you frame the issue? Give some thought to the language that you would use. Would you, for example, reference the decision to fill the open positions with term appointments as a "mistake" or the faculty disagreement as a "split" in the department? How would you engage the faculty in a candid airing of the issue without appearing to take sides?

2. What information would you gather in order to assess whether the loss of three faculty positions is likely to be temporary or permanent? Would you offer a personal assessment or limit your comments to concrete data such as the number of majors and credit hours generated?

3. How would you use your knowledge of the institution's mission? How much should the institution's focus on undergraduate education influence the planning done by the department? How might the department build continued support for a mission that exceeds university expectations?

Please Consider

The department must consider the fact that South Central University is primarily an undergraduate teaching institution. The obstacles to restoring the three positions in the department are more than budgetary. The department must assess whether the institution will invest in a strong graduate program and research initiative. If the state restores a portion of the institution's cut funding, would the communication disorders department be a high or low campus priority for receiving those funds? With the change in campus president, the department lost a significant link with the central administration. The department cannot assume that the new president has the same first-hand knowledge of the department and the discipline that the retired president had. The department needs to assess its current status on the campus to determine whether the lost faculty positions represent a top or bottom spending priority for the new central administration.

At the same time, the department needs to carefully assess the advantage accrued to the institution from the department's strong graduate program and research initiative. Part of the decision regarding the department mission hinges upon the department's ability to bolster its standing with the current campus leadership. This includes plans for regaining a central role on campus-wide policy-making groups. The department cannot assume that the current administration has the same favorable impression of the department's value that the former president held. The faculty cannot make a decision about whether to narrow the scope of the department's mission without a clear understanding of the larger institutional context. The following questions should help to focus this assessment.

1. What information could the department assemble and use to advocate the department's importance to the institution? Is there, for example, a need for trained and licensed speech pathologists and audiologists in the region? Is the market demand for graduates one that typically requires a graduate degree? If so, would the recruitment and retention of undergraduates decline if the department (and the institution) lost the graduate program?

2. Who makes decisions regarding the restoration of cut budgets? What sources will these decision-makers consult? What data will be perceived as credible and relevant? What action can the department take to become a higher priority for the institution? Are there, for example, other departments that rely on the communication disorders department? How does the institution benefit from the department's strong research profile?

3. What harm would accrue to the department and the institution if the department mission were narrowed? Would the department lose quality faculty? Would the department lose student enrollment? Is the central administration aware of the anticipated harmful outcomes?

Let's Recap

Take a moment and review your plan for handling the department meeting. If your approach does not incorporate the strategies for structuring the department mission, you may want to review the material presented earlier in this chapter on how to effectively structure the department mission. Does your approach

- identify and incorporate the key shared values?
- allow for full participation of department members?
- keep the discussion focused on the department and not on individuals?
- help faculty identify department strengths and potential strengths?
- introduce and describe the institution's mission and environmental conditions to the faculty?
- assess potential allies and markets?
- keep the department mission current and operational?

Putting Theory Into Practice

In Case 1.2, The Assigned Mission, the central administration does not know or accept the department's mission to build a strong creative writing program. Instead, the central administration defines the department's mission as service. From the administration's perspective, the department's objective is to provide the composition and technical writing courses needed to satisfy the degree requirements of other programs. The department pursues a mission that is broader than service. Place yourself in the role of the department chair as you read the following case.

Case 1.2, The Assigned Mission

The Department

The English department at Northern State University is small, overworked, but proud. The department is working hard to build a creative writing program. It is the goal of the department to become one of the best creative writing programs in the nation. Progress is slow but steady. The faculty redirect every available resource toward this objective. Recent progress is especially encouraging. Faculty work is being published, and a few faculty received prestigious awards for their creative writing products. One faculty member secured a modest grant from the National Endowment for the Humanities (NEH) to complete a volume of poetry. Another faculty member received a small stipend from the state arts council. The faculty remain very upbeat despite rather grim conditions on campus.

For the most part, the English department services other majors. The department teaches the English composition courses that are part of the institution's core requirement for all students. In addition, the department staffs a variety of upper-division technical writing and literature courses that other programs require. These service courses comprise about 75% of the department's total curricular offering.

Building the creative writing program is difficult because budget cuts translate into heavier teaching loads for all faculty. The English faculty typically teach 12 credit hours each semester, which exceeds the campus average of nine credit hours per faculty per semester. When the institution decided to increase the English composition component of the core curriculum from three to six credits, the English department had to staff twice as many sections of composition courses. The English faculty agreed to assume the heavier loads in order to avoid reducing the number of creative writing courses.

The Campus

Campus morale is generally low. The institution's current budget is 15% less than it was three years ago. The administration amortized the cuts across all departments with every program sharing the pain. To maintain faculty teaching loads at nine credit hours per semester, many departments reduced the size of their curricular offerings. With no relief in sight, many departments opted to downsize the program rather than to overload the faculty.

Last spring, the campus took a bold move and increased tuition 10%. If the increased tuition doesn't result in further decline in enrollment, the tuition increase will yield desperately needed revenue for the institution. Everyone is hopeful that the institution will maintain its enrollment level so conditions can improve. Even if the enrollment holds steady, the projected increase generated from increased tuition will not offset the three years of cumulative budget loss.

The Telephone Call

Maria Perez, the chair of the English department, is studying the fall schedule, trying to determine how she might give some course relief to those faculty who have funded grant projects. The grant awards are important to the department's goal to build one of the best creative writing programs in the country. Dr. Perez recognizes that the grants bring prestige to the department and believes that they should not result in larger workloads for the faculty who received them.

Dr. Perez is contemplating how she might reduce the teaching loads of the two grant recipients from 12 to nine credit hours when she receives a telephone call from the director of admissions, Joe McCray.

McCray: "Good news. The enrollment for fall semester is up despite the

10% increase in tuition. I don't have to tell you how pleased the provost was to get this news."

Dr. Perez couldn't decide why she was the recipient of this special "good news" bulletin but echoed the positive tone: "That's great. Perhaps the provost will work on restoring some of our budget."

McCray: "I don't know anything about that. The reason I'm calling is to let you know that we added five new sections of English composition to accommodate incoming freshmen."

Perez could not believe what she heard: "What? Who's going to teach them?"

McCray (chuckling): "Very funny, Maria. I'm sure your faculty don't believe that anyone else is qualified to teach English composition."

Perez: "My faculty cannot cover five more sections of English composition. What makes you think you can add sections without my approval?"

McCray: "I didn't. The provost authorized it. You can take it up with him, but I don't think you'll get anywhere. He's determined that we're not going to lose students to other institutions because they can't get freshman courses here."

Dr. Perez: "The provost knows that English faculty carry the heaviest teaching loads on campus. I can't believe he thinks we can cover this."

McCray: "I don't know what to tell you, Maria. All I know is that he told me to add the sections. I'm just calling to let you know about it so you can plan. I'm sorry if this upsets you. I'm glad you're not the type of person who kills the messenger. If there is any change, I'll let you know."

Perez (with a heavy sigh): "Thanks a lot, but I don't want any more news like this."

Maria Perez is numb as she hangs up the phone. How could the provost make a decision like that when he knows that the English department is understaffed? How could she possibly cover five more sections of English composition? The department would have to drop the entire creative writing sequence in order to cover the additional sections and bring the faculty course loads more in line with the campus average.

Let's Analyze the Case

In Case 1.2, the English faculty have a common understanding regarding the department's mission. Specifically, the English faculty strive to build a strong creative writing program. This goal drives faculty behavior and department decisions. Despite budget cuts, the department invests every possible resource toward enhancing the creative writing program. The faculty accept that they must teach English composition and technical writing courses as a service to the institution. They do not ignore the service component of the department mission. However, faculty achievements in relation to the creative writing program are the ones that carry pride for the department.

The campus has a different assessment of the department mission. The provost and the director of admissions function as though the English department's mission is exclusively service. The campus leadership does not acknowledge the English department's goal to build a creative writing program. Instead, the decisions made by the provost reinforce the service role of the English department. The provost expects the English faculty to teach the English composition courses required as part of the institution's core curriculum and the technical writing courses that service major requirements in other departments.

The department could reduce their large teaching loads by narrowing the department mission to that imposed by the campus. To maintain the goal of building a creative writing program, the department accepts a workload that goes above the average faculty workload and beyond campus expectations. If the department wishes to pursue its emphasis in creative writing, it must convince the central administration of the value of that goal. Until the administration understands and accepts the English faculty's view of their mission, external assessment of the department's productivity will not consider the effort expended toward the development of a creative writing program.

It's Your Turn

Place yourself in the role of Maria Perez, the chair of the English department at Northern State University, and decide how you would lead the faculty through this difficult situation.

1. Is it advisable for the department to maintain as part of its mission the goal to build one of the best creative writing programs in the nation? List the data you would use to make this determination. For example, to what extent would the provost's perception of the department mission sway you? Is the recognition received by faculty in the area of creative writing sufficient to maintain this goal?

2. What information would you present to the faculty to assist them in reaching a final decision? What steps might you take to get the administration to acknowledge and accept the department's mission to build a

creative writing program? What kudos do department achievements in creative writing bring to the institution?

Please Consider

The situations described in Cases 1.1 and 1.2 illustrate the value of a department mission. Both cases demonstrate the advantage of having an understanding among the department faculty. At the same time, both cases illustrate the liability that results when the department fails to promote the mission outside the department. In Case 1.1, the faculty did not respond to the change in campus leadership. They assumed that a new president would recognize their worth. In Case 1.2, the faculty elected to pursue a mission that was above and beyond the mission assigned by the campus leadership. That resulted in excessive faculty workloads and fueled the image that the English department faculty didn't support institutional goals. These cases demonstrate the value of a department mission statement that external publics accept. A clearly articulated mission statement benefits the department in numerous ways.

Clarifies performance expectations
and opportunities for external support

Mission statements demonstrate the importance of the department to the university, the region, the state, the accrediting association, and so on. A clearly stated department mission prepares students and faculty to project a more unified sense of department priorities and goals. Consequently, department mission statements must be promoted continuously.

An effective mission statement clarifies priorities for external audiences. When external publics know and understand the department mission, the department has more opportunities for forming productive alliances. A mission statement can promote the department's identity both on and off campus. In Case 1.2 the department did not successfully advocate a department mission that included a goal to build a creative writing program. Consequently, the central administration relates to the department exclusively on the basis of its view of the department's mission. Clear department priorities increase the opportunity for external support. For example, the department whose mission is to educate and train physician assistants who will work in the surrounding region can build effective and helpful alliances off campus. These alliances can be eventual sources of funding, equipment, support, student internships, and job placements for graduates.

Internally, the department mission establishes expectations for faculty and staff performance. Clearly communicated department priorities help faculty and staff know how to succeed. A working understanding of the department mission enables department members to engage in activities that will be rewarded. Furthermore, there is less anxiety about performance evaluation in a department when everyone knows and understands behavior expectations. The chair can begin performance appraisal by summarizing the progress made rather than by clarifying what should be done. This benefit is not realized if the reward system is inconsistent with the department mission and expectations for faculty performance. If the department mission statement claims a strong commitment to undergraduate instruction, then teaching excellence must be recognized and rewarded. If not, the chair cannot expect faculty to maintain a strong commitment to undergraduate instruction.

Offers a blueprint for decision-making
The department mission should guide decisions about curriculum, budget, and personnel. Without a clearly understood mission statement to guide decisions, the department chair is more subject to criticism for taking arbitrary and unilateral action. Consider the issue of spending finite equipment funds within the department. The chair of a chemistry department, for example, may need to decide whether to use the funds to purchase instructional supplies or to equip a research lab that will improve the department's potential for getting external grants. The department mission helps guide this decision by stipulating the relative priority of teaching to research. Without this blueprint, the chair's decision is subject to criticism regardless of the action taken. When a chair's decisions are obviously consistent with the department mission, the chair has an accepted and visible rationale for the action taken. This diffuses potential conflict because it lessens the likelihood that department members will perceive the chair as acting from personal bias.

Another example is the allocation of travel dollars within the department. Assume that a department chair has $2,000 for professional travel in a department with 10 faculty. All 10 faculty plan to attend at least one conference. Five of the faculty have paper presentations to make. One faculty member is planning to attend a conference in Europe. How should the chair divide the $2,000 among the faculty? Many chairs would look at that scenario and say it is a no-win situation because the small sum of money available for faculty travel makes it impossible to please anyone, let alone everyone. A clear mission statement, however, allows a department chair to make tough decisions while preserving personal credibility and advancing the department toward its goals. If, for example, the department has a commitment to increasing its visibility in the research arena, the chair should give preference to those faculty who will make presentations. If, however, the department goal is to support professional development that enhances instruction, the chair will need to consider the purpose of each trip.

Without a mission statement, decisions such as how to allocate equipment dollars or travel funds get made according to criteria that faculty may perceive as subjective. The allocation of travel funds without a clear basis for that decision will leave at least some faculty wondering why certain persons received more than others. When faculty must supply the logic or rationale for a chair's decision, the chair is subject to misinterpretation and criticism. This damages the chair's credibility. Further, decisions made may not safeguard the strengths of the department. For example, if the department chair divides equipment dollars across all special interests, it is likely that the allocation of resources will not serve any of the special interests completely. The result can be a decline in quality across all department areas and subspecialties.

Improves department climate and faculty morale
The climate among faculty within a department improves when the department chair eliminates the perception of a hidden agenda or favoritism. Faculty morale is hardest to maintain in departments when the rules are not known or applied consistently across faculty. By clarifying priorities and expectations, the department chair reduces the perception of a hidden agenda or favoritism. This does not mean that all faculty will like every decision but rather that faculty who disagree with the decision will still understand the basis for it and recognize it as fair or at least consistent with the department mission. Faculty and staff morale is always higher in departments when all members believe that everyone receives fair treatment in accordance with the department mission and goals.

Department chairs who build consensus around shared department values establish a healthy department community. These chairs help department members learn that everyone's interests will be best served when each contributes to a common purpose. By doing so, department chairs equip themselves with a clearly understood blueprint that guides decisions. Chairs also enhance their own credibility with faculty and staff. While department members tend to view autocratic chairs as arbitrary and ineffective spokespersons for the unit, they typically perceive consensus-building chairs as fair and effective advocates for the department.

Review the situations described in Cases 1.1 and 1.2 and consider whether the departments accrue the values mentioned above.

1. In both cases, the department mission statement clarifies priorities and expectations for faculty performance. How can the departments communicate their missions to the administration and other salient external publics?

2. In both cases, the department mission serves as a blueprint for making department decisions. Can the chairs in Cases 1.1 and 1.2 use their department missions to enhance the department's image with external publics?

3. Department morale in Cases 1.1 and 1.2 becomes vulnerable when the central administration's action undermines the department mission. Can faculty morale remain high if the department mission is not accepted on campus?

Putting Theory Into Practice

The situations described in Cases 1.3, Tough Times: Theater's Response, and 1.4, Tough Times: Foreign Languages' Response, take place on the same campus. A medium-sized public institution must down size its program inventory in response to repeated budget cuts. Case 1.3 examines the plight of the theater department. Imagine that you are the department chair as you confront the challenge presented in Case 1.3. Pay particular attention to the role of the department mission in this situation.

Case 1.3, Tough Times: Theater's Response

Background Information

Western State University (WSU) is a public institution with roughly 16,000 students. The campus is located in a rural part of the state so almost all of its students are residential. Although the institution was founded more than one hundred years ago, WSU grew rapidly from a small teachers college to its current size during the 1960s and 1970s. The state legislature invested in the institution in order to serve a large rural portion of the state. WSU is a comprehensive institution, offering undergraduate degrees in everything from fine arts to engineering. Although primarily an undergraduate institution, WSU boasts several research centers that link the institution with regional industry. The institution, for example, engages in research that helps area farmers improve harvest yields. The institution's mission includes a strong commitment to regional service, and the university enjoys a wonderful rapport with the community. The campus represents the nearest urban center for people living within a 300-mile radius of the campus.

University Mission Statement

WSU is a major public higher education institution dedicated to quality academic endeavors in teaching and research, to supportive programming for student needs and development, to effective social and economic initiatives in community, regional, and statewide contexts, and to affirmative action and equal opportunity.

Seeking to meet the educational, vocational, social, and personal needs of its diverse population of students and helping them fully realize their potential are central purposes of the university. Emphasis on accessibility and regional service that creates distinctive instructional, research, and public service programs gives WSU its special character among the nation's universities.

Committed to the concept that research and creative activity are inherently valuable, the university supports intellectual exploration in traditional disciplines and in numerous specialized research undertakings, some of which are related directly to the western region of the state. Research directions evolve from staff and faculty strengths, and mature in keeping with long-term preparation and planning.

The university continues a long tradition of service to its community and region. Its strength in the creative and performing arts provide wide-ranging educational, entertainment, and cultural opportunities for its students, faculty, staff, and the public at large. Its involvement in the civic and social development of the region are manifestations of a general commitment to enhance the quality of life through the exercise of academic training and the application of problem solving techniques. The university seeks to improve the well-being of those whose lives come into contact with it.

The Problem

WSU faces tough times. For the past six years, the institution received a budget appropriation that was less than the preceding year. Budget cuts, in addition to the customary increases in the consumer price index, force the leadership at WSU to reevaluate the institution's mission. The central administration is doubtful that the institution can continue to fulfill its broad mission.

To date, departments shared the pain resulting from reduced funding. Now, the administration believes that the institution cannot preserve program quality if it continues to amortize budget cuts across all departments. Instead, the institution will make some vertical cuts. The central administration prefers to cut a few weaker programs than to reduce the entire program complement to mediocrity. The campus leadership has taken great care to communicate this plan as one that will strengthen the university. The administration describes the process in terms of pruning the dead and dying branches from a healthy tree. The pruning will allow the remaining programs to flourish and grow stronger. The provost constituted a special campus-wide committee for the purpose of reviewing all programs. The committee will evaluate every program on campus and recommend every department for one of four possible fates: enhancement, maintenance, reduction, or elimination.

Department of Theater
The theater chair, Winston Porter, is pessimistic about the department's future. He knows that the department is vulnerable and likely to be targeted for reduction or elimination. He's not sure what to do about it.

The theater department has seven full-time faculty. Including Dr. Porter, there are three tenured full professors who teach playwriting, theater history, and theater education courses. The remaining four faculty are untenured assistant professors who teach production and performance courses. At the undergraduate level, the department offers the BA, BS in theater education, and BFA. At the graduate level, the department offers the MFA in performance studies, technical theater, and playwriting, and the MA in theater history. The department has about 60 undergraduate majors and eight students in the master's program. In addition, the department enrolls a sizable number of nonmajor undergraduate students who take theater courses in order to work on productions.

The department runs a very ambitious production schedule, presenting ten main stage productions each calendar year. Four of these productions run as a summer playhouse season, while the other six run during the academic year. Four of the ten productions are either musicals or light opera. The theater faculty work in collaboration with the music department to produce the shows. The productions attract season-ticket holders within a radius of 150 miles of campus. Seats sell out far in advance and, whenever possible, the cast runs an extra matinee to satisfy demand.

Winston Porter knows that the department has serious problems. The faculty are overworked. The department continues to offer a curriculum that was once staffed by 11 faculty. Because of budget cuts and other circumstances, the department lost a total of four positions over the last seven years. Each time, the faculty voted to take on more work rather than cut anything. The assistant professors do not want to cut any aspect of the performance program. These faculty believe that the BFA and MFA degrees are essential to recruiting undergraduate and graduate students that allow them to mount the ten main stage productions each year. The tenured full professors are unwilling to sacrifice the BA, BS, and MA degrees. They believe that the better known and respected theater programs offer the traditional BA and MA as well as the performance-oriented degrees. The BS in theater education provides an option for majors that prefer to teach drama in high school rather than pursue graduate study or work in professional theater. In general, all of the faculty oppose cutting degree programs. They worry that cutting degree programs will result in a reduction in the number of theater majors. They hope that the budget crunch is temporary and fear that program cuts would be permanent.

Dr. Porter believes that the department cannot survive unless it narrows its mission and reduces faculty workloads. It is difficult to know what to cut. The popular production series accrues a lot of visibility and prestige for the department. Box office revenues provide important relief to the financial strain of state budget cuts. Currently, the box office generates $.60 for every $1.00 of state funds spent on production. It is important that the department not lose its patron appeal. At the same time, Dr. Porter shares the view that the MA degree brings a respectability to the program. Furthermore, the tenured full professors contribute more to the MA than they would ever be able to contribute to the MFA.

It is even more difficult to know how to get the faculty to reach agreement about what might be cut. The faculty cannot agree. The tenured full professors contribute primarily to the BA, BS in theater education, and MA degrees. Students interested in theater history, theater education, and playwriting pursue those degrees. The untenured assistant professors teach the courses required for the BFA and MFA degrees. They also staff the production series by serving in roles such as director, technical director, and costume designer.

Let's Analyze the Case

The theater faculty do not have a common understanding regarding the department mission. Nor do the faculty order department priorities in the same way. The senior tenured faculty value tradition and seek to maintain a comprehensive inventory of theater programs, including degrees in theater history, theater education, and playwriting. The untenured faculty focus on performance. They prefer to invest in the BFA and MFA degrees that are indicative of a performance-oriented program. The sum of the two department missions is a workload that is too heavy for seven faculty. The chair points out that the current program inventory was once staffed by 11 full-time faculty.

The question is how to narrow the department focus. The information presented in the case suggests that the chair, Winston Porter, is the only person who recognizes the larger issue. Despite heavy workloads, faculty always vote to do more work than to drop any portion of the program. The expanded department mission is the product of a vote and not the outcome of consensus building. Without a common understanding, the faculty vote to defend turf and personal interest. The chair recognizes that the department must narrow the mission but doesn't know what to cut. Some portion of the faculty will perceive the chair as taking sides no matter what the chair recommends for elimination. If there were a common understanding among faculty, the department mission would guide such decisions. In Case 1.3, the chair believes that it is his responsibility to decide what to eliminate in order to reduce faculty workloads to a manageable level. The chair admits his uncertainty in knowing the best course of action.

It is not the responsibility of the department chair to unilaterally decide the department mission. Winston Porter is wrestling with the wrong issue. Instead of fretting over what to cut, he needs to focus on building consensus in the department. The chair needs to involve the faculty in the decision to redefine the department mission. This requires consensus on what is important to the long-term future of the department. A community of shared values and common purpose cannot develop unless faculty begin to discuss the strengths and potential strengths of the department in the context of the campus culture. Faculty must realize how their individual efforts are interconnected in order to begin isolating some common values that can become the core of a more tightly focused department mission.

It's Your Turn

Place yourself in Winston Porter's position as chair of the theater department and decide how you would initiate consensus building within the department.

1. What points of agreement exist among faculty? It seems, for example, that all faculty are willing to work overtime for the department's welfare. How could you use this to build consensus on other values and the department's mission?

2. How would you present the issue so that the faculty are less prone to defend personal interests? Would you make the faculty aware of the

administration's decision to preserve program quality by making vertical cuts and theater's vulnerability under this plan? Could these external conditions help shift the department discussion from "who gives up what" to "how can we survive and prosper in changing conditions"?

3. How might the department demonstrate that it is not one of the dead or dying branches that need pruning from the university tree? What data would you use to advocate the importance of the theater program to the institution?

Please Consider

The faculty repeatedly vote to take on more work rather than cut any component of the program. They fail to weigh the ramifications of their action in the context of the campus climate. The campus leadership believes that the institution must narrow its scope. The central administration is reevaluating the institution's mission with the hope of strengthening the university despite fiscal adversity. Remember that the administration described the painful process of downsizing in terms of "pruning the dead and dying branches from a healthy tree." In this context, the theater faculty's effort to retain all programs is not only futile but suicidal.

The faculty need to understand the larger context for department decisions if they are to move away from the practice of voting to protect turf and individual interest. Rather than framing the question for consideration as a department issue, the chair needs to outline department alternatives within the campus context. The reshaping of the issue redirects the concern from protecting individual interest to protecting the department from further cuts or possible elimination.

Let's Recap

If your approach to building consensus within the theater department does not incorporate the strategies for structuring the department mission, you may want to review the material presented earlier in this chapter on how to effectively structure the department mission. Does your approach

- identify and incorporate the key shared values?
- allow for full participation of department members?
- keep the discussion focused on the department and not on individuals?
- help the faculty identify department strengths and potential strengths?
- introduce and describe the institution's mission to the faculty?

- assess potential allies and markets?
- keep the department mission current and operational?

Putting Theory Into Practice

Case 1.4, Tough Times: Foreign Languages' Response, describes the response of the foreign languages department to the adversity experienced at Western State University. The foreign languages department is roughly the same size as the theater department. The faculty in foreign languages, however, sensed that the department was in trouble earlier when the number of majors hit a record low. Unlike the theater faculty, the foreign languages faculty took action to remedy the situation that threatened the department. Notice the different reaction to essentially the same set of circumstances as you read the following case.

Case 1.4, Tough Times: Foreign Languages' Response

Cases 1.3 and 1.4 take place on the same campus. Please refer to Case 1.3, Tough Times: Theater's Response, to review the characteristics and mission of Western State University (WSU) and the problem the institution faces.

Department of Foreign Languages

The department of foreign languages employs eight full-time faculty. There are three tenured full professors, three tenured associate professors, and two untenured assistant professors. In addition, the department hires between two and four part-time instructors to meet enrollment demands. The department offers course work in Spanish, French, German, Russian, and Japanese.

Seven years ago, the number of department majors dropped to an all-time low of 47. Course enrollment remained steady, however, because the college of liberal arts has a foreign language requirement for all students earning a BA degree in any of the 22 departments within the college.

The foreign languages faculty do not want to be exclusively a service unit. The faculty want to teach more than 100- and 200-level courses to non-majors who are satisfying a baccalaureate requirement. When the number of majors bottomed out at 47, the department took decisive action to build the major enrollment.

First, the department made the bachelor's degree more flexible. They converted separate BA degrees in Spanish, French, and German into one

BA degree with specializations in Spanish, French, German, Russian, and Japanese. Previously, students could only minor in Russian and Japanese. Now students can pursue any language or combination of languages to earn a bachelor's in foreign languages. The department also added a specialization in foreign languages and international business. The faculty designed this specialization in collaboration with faculty from the business college. The intent was to design a curriculum that would appeal to students who want to work in other cultures.

Second, the faculty, under the chair's leadership, assembled information attesting to the contemporary value of training in foreign languages. The faculty believe in the value of learning foreign languages, but they had never gathered objective evidence to substantiate their belief. The data collected included statements about the global economy and the need to educate government and business leaders who could cross cultural boundaries. They pulled employment statistics showing projected increases in the number of positions available for individuals who were proficient in at least two languages. Finally, they assembled a battery of quotes from current government and business leaders asserting the critical importance of training in foreign languages.

Third, the department developed an aggressive student recruitment plan. Faculty made speeches at regional high schools and community colleges. For three years, department faculty voted to spend all of the department's limited travel budget on student recruitment. On campus, the department chair approached every unit that might have students who would benefit from a second major in a foreign language. The chair even talked to the commanding officers of the campus ROTC army and air force programs. Internally, the department restructured its advisement system. Even though students are advised centrally at the college level, the department assigned a faculty mentor to every department major. The faculty mentors do not duplicate the curriculum advisement that is performed by the college advisement office. Instead, the faculty focus on helping students understand the full range of career options and on getting extracurricular experiences that will improve employment opportunities.

Current Situation
Enrollment in foreign languages is up to 75 majors and 20 minors. The specialization in foreign languages and international business enrolls 35 of the 75 majors. After about three years, the department was able to scale back its recruitment effort and target those sources with the highest return. For example, the faculty only make speeches at those high schools and commu-

nity colleges that are the department's best feeder schools. In place of the other travel, the department hosts a one-day festival on campus each winter. They invite all high school guidance counselors in the state along with community college advisors. It's an opportunity for the advisors to meet the faculty and learn more about the program offered.

Let's Analyze the Case

Unlike the theater department, the foreign languages department took early action to streamline the department's academic program. The department's action was motivated by a collective desire to have a mission that encompasses more than service courses required for all liberal arts majors. The decision to convert separate bachelor degrees in three different languages into one degree with five different language specializations had the effect of streamlining the degree program inventory while increasing the number of languages taught in the department.

The department initiated an aggressive recruitment program, including building linkages with other programs on campus. Those efforts helped to promote a more central perception of foreign languages instruction. Finally, the department collected information that demonstrates the value of foreign language instruction. Enrollment increased in foreign languages. Consequently, the foreign languages department is in a stronger position to face the campus-wide committee that will recommend it for enhancement, maintenance, reduction, or elimination than it was seven years earlier. The foreign languages chair has a different task than the theater chair.

It's Your Turn

Assume the role of the chair of the foreign languages department and determine how you would prepare for the review of the campus-wide committee.

1. Would you seek a recommendation of maintenance or enhancement from the campus-wide committee? If you elect to push for enhancement, how would you demonstrate that a department that was successful in growing on a reduced level of fiscal support needs an increase in support? Does the institution's mission help you formulate the argument?

2. Would you involve the faculty in preparing the information for campus committee review? How would you prepare the faculty for the committee review? Is there any formal or informal action that the faculty might take to strengthen the department's posture?

Please Consider

The foreign languages faculty worked on the problem of low enrollment over a period of several years. One senses a common understanding among the foreign languages faculty that does not exist in the theater department. The foreign languages faculty make department decisions within the larger context of campus issues. Note also that the faculty continuously revised their action as conditions changed. When enrollment increased, the department scaled back the aggressive recruitment effort and targeted only the sources that yielded the highest return. An effective department mission is dynamic in that it must remain responsive to changing external conditions that influence the operation and future of the academic department. Whereas the theater faculty in Case 1.3 continued to make department decisions in a vacuum, the foreign languages faculty incorporated changing external conditions into department decision-making. The chair of the theater department worried alone about the fate and future of the department. He believed that the task of deciding the department's future direction was his responsibility. Because it was difficult to "take sides" between the untenured assistant professors and the tenured professors, the theater chair put off making any decision. The chair of the foreign languages department involved the total faculty in developing and executing an action plan to remedy a dramatic drop in undergraduate enrollment.

Let's Recap

An effective mission statement provides a clear and compelling declaration of future direction. It specifies whom the department serves and how. An effective mission statement identifies department priorities and provides a description of how the department defines success. It also demonstrates how the department mission serves the institutional mission. Remember the story of the man who jumped from the top of the Empire State Building. As he descended past the 45th floor, he said, "So far, so good!" A functional mission statement spares the department such a "free-fall" experience. Instead, an effective mission statement provides guidance into the future.

The contrast between the foreign languages and theater departments on the same campus illustrates the tremendous strength and advantage that accompanies a clear sense of department mission. The faculty in the foreign languages department had consensus about the department mission. The theater faculty did not. The foreign languages department realized the benefits of having a clearly articulated and understood mission statement. Within the foreign languages department, there were clear expectations for faculty performance. When the department decided to initiate an aggressive student recruitment program, the faculty were expected to help. The mission also clarified opportunities for external support. The department began to think creatively about linkages with other units on campus that could improve the importance of the foreign languages department to the university. In contrast, the theater faculty worked to protect individual interests. They lacked an understanding of institutional expectations for faculty performance. Because the theater faculty made department decisions in a vacuum, they failed to identify opportunities for external support.

Effective mission statements yield a blueprint for decision-making. That was the case in the foreign languages department. The faculty wanted to be more than a unit that serviced other majors. To do that they needed to reverse the downward trend in major enrollment. The department goals dictated specific action plans that had the full commitment and participation of the faculty. The theater chair did not know what components of the program to eliminate because he had no rationale upon which to make that determination. Any decision would be an arbitrary choice because the faculty lacked a common understanding about the department mission.

Finally, effective mission statements result in improved faculty morale. Clearly, the foreign languages department could be more optimistic about the outcome of the campus-wide review of all programs than the theater department. When goals and performance expectations are clear, faculty are less defensive and more accepting of changing conditions. The theater department does not have consensus on shared values. There is no common community that can create a strong, unified presence on campus or off. With higher morale, the foreign languages faculty become more effective spokespersons for their department, both individually and collectively.

2

ENHANCING THE
DEPARTMENT CLIMATE

*C*limate refers to the personality of the department. The department climate is psychologically based and reflects how department members perceive and interpret daily experience. The department climate mirrors what is psychologically meaningful for department members. As the filter through which department members interpret information and events, the climate shapes the action and performance of department members.

It is important to distinguish climate from culture. Whereas culture derives from shared values, climate accrues from shared perceptions. Just as strongly held values change slowly over time, a group culture is resilient when facing sudden change. Climate, however, changes with variations in individual or group perceptions. Faculty may, for example, lose confidence in a department chair after just one or two incidents. This alteration in perception can quickly change the department climate. The department climate, then, is the barometer that measures faculty and staff satisfaction with the department.

The department climate does not automatically mirror the campus climate but develops from the perceptions of department members. While campus conditions may influence these perceptions, it is the internal department conditions that ultimately shape faculty and staff perceptions. That is why it is possible to have varying climates in different departments across a single campus. Regardless of the campus climate, department productivity is significantly stronger in departments with a positive climate. Effective department chairs work to establish and maintain a healthy department climate.

The Objective

One goal of this chapter is to describe the characteristics of a healthy department climate so chairs can recognize the benefits of a positive climate. A second goal is to help department chairs understand how their behavior enhances or detracts from the department climate. Department chairs have considerable influence over faculty and staff perceptions and, therefore, can help create a healthy department climate that, in turn, contributes to their success. A third goal is to equip department chairs with a working understanding of those factors that shape the department climate.

Defining the Task

The task of enhancing the department climate does not focus on keeping everyone happy or satisfied. Instead, enhancing the department climate requires the building of a productive work environment. Because climate reflects what is psychologically meaningful to department members, the task of enhancing the department climate translates into maintaining a work environment that individual members perceive as positive and constructive. The department climate sets the tone for how department members interact with one another and perform their assigned responsibilities. The department climate is a perceived condition that shapes individual and group performance. For a healthy department climate to exist, the department members must perceive the following characteristics.

High degree of mutual trust and respect

In a healthy department climate, faculty and staff may not be homogeneous or even similar in their professional interests and viewpoints. They must, however, have a high degree of mutual trust and respect for one another. This brings with it a freedom from second-guessing the decisions and actions of one another. Rather, it signifies a confidence in each other's professional performance in carrying out instructional, research, and service responsibilities. Individual paranoia does not exist in an environment characterized by a high degree of mutual trust and respect because the department members perceive one another as credible and competent to perform assigned duties.

Ability to openly air differences
constructively without fear of retaliation

A healthy department climate does not impose a single viewpoint. Instead, a healthy department climate encourages individuals to express personal viewpoints in a constructive manner. Important department decisions are made following an exhaustive review of all possible alternatives. Department members work together to analyze issues and reach well-reasoned conclusions. Without the fear of retaliation, department members can tackle the toughest issues in a candid and professional manner. The faculty in departments with healthy climates do not avoid issues. They are not afraid to discuss changing conditions that may affect the department's welfare. They are more likely to generate productive solutions to adverse conditions.

Norm of reciprocity

A healthy department climate is characterized by the presence of well-meaning cooperation among members. We tend to think of people as uncooperative if they fail to do what we want them to do. Cooperation, however, implies a joint effort, a productive working relationship. This norm of reciprocity extends beyond discipline focus. The faculty do not limit, for example, their cooperation with one another to those who have a similar training or interest in a particular subspecialty of the discipline. The norm of reciprocity transcends individual discipline interests, professorial rank, seniority, gender, race, or any other arbitrary boundary that may in less healthy climates create divisiveness among the faculty.

Effective communication

In a healthy department climate there is effective communication among all department members. Communication is all-inclusive in that no member of the department feels isolated or left out of the loop. All members receive relevant information that enables them to do the most effective job possible. Misunderstandings attributable to mistrust or paranoia are rare. For the most part, the members are candid and able to discuss difficult or potentially sensitive matters.

A healthy department climate sets the tone for conducting department business in a constructive manner and, therefore, facilitates effective department management. The benefits fall into one of two categories. The first category includes the advantages accrued because the faculty and staff in a healthy climate are less prone to become defensive. In an environment characterized by a high degree of mutual trust and effective communication, the faculty remain more open-minded and less resistant toward change. This includes changes in policy or procedure that would threaten faculty in departments with unhealthy climates. Conflict is easier to manage and more likely to result in a productive outcome when the department climate is healthy. The faculty are more receptive to constructive suggestions, which makes it easier to perform such difficult tasks as performance evaluation and merit pay review. Faculty who are not on the defensive are also less likely to misinterpret the chair's intent in such routine matters as course and committee assignments. The faculty in a healthy department climate tend to give department chairs and colleagues the benefit of the doubt when interpreting spoken or written messages and when assigning possible motives for decisions or actions. This same leniency is not present in departments with an unhealthy climate.

The second category of benefit accrues because all department members in a healthy climate contribute in a productive manner. The existence of mutual trust and respect, along with the norm of reciprocity, fosters productive working relationships among faculty and between faculty and the department chair. Problem solving tasks yield superior outcomes because every member of the department is able to express viewpoints without fear of retaliation. Consensus building is easier because faculty with a high degree of mutual trust and respect listen openly to colleagues' opinions. This more engaged listening, accompanied by the perception of constructive motives, is important to reaching consensus on salient issues, including the department mission and goals. The faculty can discuss how to absorb budget cuts or revise the curriculum without becoming defensive. Finally, faculty tend to be more productive in a healthy department climate. There is less skepticism regarding whether quality work is valued and, therefore, the faculty are more motivated to achieve.

The department chairs have much to gain by enhancing the department climate. Ironically, the benefits derived from a healthy climate are the very behaviors that continue to perpetuate a productive working environment. Faculty, for example, are less defensive when there is a high degree of mutual trust and respect. At the same time, the perception of a high degree of mutual trust and respect within the department reduces defensiveness and sustains a healthy department climate. The presence of a healthy department climate makes many of the administrative tasks performed by department chairs easier. Consequently, department chairs ensure their own success by enhancing the department climate.

Relevant Communication Concepts and Strategies

The department chairs hold tremendous power in enhancing the department climate. While the chairs may not have direct control over all the factors that help shape the department climate, they are in a position to greatly influence faculty perception. The department climate derives from the perceptions held by members. Collectively, these perceptions form the basis for the department's personality. It is this personality that influences how department faculty and staff respond to incoming information and perform their assigned duties. Department chairs derive the greatest benefit from a healthy climate in that it sets the tone for department activity. It is important for department chairs to understand how all of the following factors contribute to the shaping of the department climate.

Perception of department leadership

The department chairs are the primary source of faculty perceptions about the department, the administration, and the conditions that directly influence faculty morale and ultimately the department climate. The department chair is often the window through which faculty and staff view the campus. It is the department chair that interprets the actions and policies of the central administration. That interpretation carries a metacommunication that offers an assessment of campus policy and events. Take, for example, a department chair who tells faculty that "the administration doesn't understand our discipline." The chair is undermining the department climate. First, the statement makes clear that the chair is powerless in educating the administration about the discipline. The assertion does not give faculty confidence in the chair's ability to advocate department needs to the central administration. The statement also fuels a perception that the department will never be valued on campus. That perception can become a disincentive for faculty to produce at optimal levels. Department chairs are never off duty. Even candid, informal statements made to faculty outside the office represent the chair's opinion. Department chairs need to realize how much control they have in influencing faculty perceptions.

The department chair's leadership style also contributes to the department climate. The techniques and strategies that bolster a department chair's credibility also promote a healthy department climate. The faculty must have trust in the chair's competence. Does the department chair know campus policy? Does the chair have full knowledge and appreciation of all the curricular specializations within the department? Is the chair able to competently advocate the needs and mission of the department? It is important that faculty perceive the department chair as being fair and consistent in dealing with all members of the department. The perception of favoritism will both decrease the chair's credibility and damage the department climate. It is important to remember that faculty and staff must perceive the department chair as credible. A chair may make fair and consistent decisions across all department members, but only if the faculty perceive the chair as making fair and consistent decisions will the chair be credible.

Leadership is not neutral. A department chair can be a competent leader and administrator but must be perceived as such in order to be effective. The chair's credibility as a leader is an assigned attribute. In other words, a chair is a credible leader only if others perceive the chair's leadership as credible. It is the faculty's perception of a chair's ability that enables the faculty to trust the department leadership. The power to trust and be trusted is an essential prerequisite to enhancing the department climate.

Physical characteristics of the workplace

The chair's control over this category of factors will vary from one department to another. In some departments, faculty and staff do not work in the same building. Sometimes faculty share office space. The location of the department chair's office may be significantly closer to some department members than to others. Whatever the layout of a particular department, such physical characteristics contribute to the department climate. If, for example, the faculty in a single department are located in two or more buildings, those not housed in the same building as the department chair may feel out of touch with the department. While few department chairs have ultimate control over the physical facilities of the unit, they can compensate for misperceptions that might grow out of the physical characteristics. In the instance where the department faculty reside in two or more buildings, the department chair must take action to prevent the faculty from feeling isolated or separated from mainstream department activity. The chair might, for example, visit the offices located in other buildings on a regular basis. If the department celebrates birthdays, the location of the party site could rotate among the different buildings. Similarly, department committee meetings and, if possible, department meetings may rotate from one building to another. The chair's objective is to make certain that faculty not housed in the central building perceive themselves as tightly integrated with the whole department.

Symbolic aspects of the department

In each department there are physical aspects and tangible conditions that take on symbolic meaning for faculty and staff. These might include offices with windows or carpeting, committee assignments, or course and course time assignments. The specific physical aspects and their symbolic meaning may vary from one department to another. In some units, for example, the faculty view an assignment to teach the general education course as a demotion. In other units, the faculty perceive the assignment to teach a general education course as an indication of superior teaching capability. Similarly, the assignment of course times can carry symbolic meaning. Some faculty, for example, may perceive the assignment of 8:00 a.m. or 4:00 p.m. classes as a test of their ability to manage parenting alongside a career.

Whether or not these perceptions are valid is less significant than their existence. People act on their perceptions even when those perceptions do not mirror reality. Department chairs need to give careful consideration to the symbolic aspects of the department. How are course or committee assignments perceived by faculty? What does the chair communicate when the only minority faculty member is assigned to the least important committee year after year? Is there a symbolic significance to the assignment of office space? If so, is the symbolic significance one that communicates a sense of fairness? It is, for example, perfectly acceptable to give the prime office space to faculty with the most rank and seniority if this rule is consistently applied and all department faculty understand the guideline that governs the assignment of office space. Without this understanding, the chair may adversely affect the department climate unintentionally when assigning office space. Department chairs need to be aware of the symbolic meanings that the faculty assign to such physical conditions.

Campus conditions

Campus conditions can influence the department climate. These conditions include, but are not limited to, budget cuts, reductions in the total number of faculty, changes in central administration, increased or decreased accessibility to technical support, and increased or decreased availability of campus services. When conditions change on campus that affect the productivity of an academic department, they have the potential to influence the department climate. This does not mean that the department automatically inherits the campus climate. It is possible to have a department with a very positive climate on a campus where morale is generally low. The reverse is also feasible in that a department with a very poor climate can exist on a campus that is generally characterized by high morale. Department chairs cannot use the condition of the campus climate as an excuse for the status of the department climate without sacrificing their credibility.

The department chair has direct influence over how faculty and staff perceive external conditions. The department chair can minimize the destructive effect of campus conditions and other external forces upon department morale. Chairs can influence how faculty and staff perceive external events and forces. Even adverse conditions can be presented in a manner that encourages the department faculty to believe that they have choice and ultimately some control over their fate. It is one thing to communicate fiscal crisis as though all hope is lost and the department has no control over its future. It is another thing to present a fiscal crisis as a time for rethinking the department mission in order to guarantee a strong future. As the key interpreters of campus conditions, department chairs determine their influence on the department climate.

Department process for problem analysis and decision-making
There are numerous decisions and issues that legitimately involve all department members. The department chair has tremendous power in determining how the department engages in problem solving and decision-making. The chair can use those processes to reinforce the notion that all department members make a valued contribution. If department members become confident in knowing that they participate in making department decisions, they are less defensive and more trusting of the chair's leadership. When department members, however, perceive department deliberations as insincere, they become more defensive and less trusting of the chair's leadership.

Putting Theory Into Practice

Several internal conditions help to shape the department climate. The factors include the faculty's perceptions of the department leadership, the physical characteristics of the workplace, the symbolic aspects of the department, the department's interpretation of changing campus conditions, and the department process for decision-making. These factors are directly influenced by the chair's communication within the department. Case 2.1, The Inner Circle, describes how department decisions are made in a speech communication department. There are different faculty assessments of the chair's leadership. Those faculty who have confidence in the chair support the chair's action to initiate a search to fill a faculty position. The faculty who have less confidence in the chair distrust the chair's handling of the search process. Place yourself in the role of the department chair as you read the following case.

Case 2.1, The Inner Circle

The Climate
The speech communication department offers undergraduate and graduate course work in four areas: rhetoric and public address; interpersonal communication; organizational communication; and performance studies. Up until two years ago, the department was staffed with 12 full-time faculty, including the department chair. There were three faculty in each of the curricular specializations. The dean did not permit the department to replace the two faculty who retired three years ago because the dean determined that the department was overstaffed when a gradual, but steady, decline in student enrollment reached an all-time low. The retirements enabled the dean to downsize the department

to ten faculty. This left the rhetoric and public address and performance studies areas each short by a full-time faculty member.

Last summer when Dorothy Whitacker announced her intention to retire at the end of the current academic year, the department feared that the dean would also deny them an opportunity to replace Dorothy who teaches courses in rhetoric and public address, one of the more traditional areas of the communication discipline. Everyone was relieved when the department chair, Butch Harrison, announced that the college dean authorized a search to hire a new assistant professor on a tenure-track appointment to replace Dorothy Whitacker.

At the first department meeting of the fall term, Butch Harrison told the faculty that the department needed to draft a position announcement. If the department hoped to advertise the position at the national conference in late November, it needed to secure the administration's approval of the position announcement by late October. All position announcements must be approved by the college dean, the provost, and the campus affirmative action officer. Everyone agreed that it was in the department's best interest to advertise early so faculty could meet with applicants at the conference. Everyone also recognized that it would be difficult to reach agreement on the position description.

Faculty Perceptions

The faculty do not agree on how to fill Dorothy's position. Some believe that a person should be hired in the area of rhetoric and public address because that is what Dorothy taught and that area already lost one faculty member. Other faculty see Dorothy's retirement as an opportunity to shift resources away from rhetoric to one of the other areas of the department. Of course, these faculty do not agree on which area needs the most support.

Matt Morahan and Joe Wienhoff, two tenured full professors, are vocal in their opinion that the department should use the vacancy to add another faculty member in interpersonal communication. Rebecca Katz is the primary advocate for adding someone in organizational communication. Christine Edelmann and Juan Herrera believe that the greatest need is in performance studies. Herb Portz leads the crusade to keep the position in rhetoric and public address.

For months the faculty engaged in "sidebar" conversations about the issue. The key faculty opinion leaders are attempting to build coalitions in support of their view. Everyone knows that the department will have to reach a decision in order to draft a position announcement. While none look forward to the debate, everyone is anxious to get the position advertised in time to attract strong applicants.

The Department Chair

Butch Harrison is in his third year as department chair and his 12th year as a faculty member in the department. He teaches in the interpersonal communication area with Matt Morahan and Joe Wienhoff, who joined the department more than 15 years ago. The three enjoy national visibility for their research in interpersonal communication. They present numerous papers at professional conferences and take turns serving as committee chair for the interpersonal area of the discipline's national and regional associations.

The three are close friends as well as colleagues. In addition to sharing similar teaching and research interests, the three have a passion for golf. For years, they taught early morning classes so they could get to the golf course for a few hours most afternoons. After Butch became department chair, the three continued to caucus frequently in the department and often go to lunch together. The other faculty view these private meetings with considerable resentment. Butch rarely seeks out other faculty reaction or information. Most believe that Matt and Joe have the inside track in influencing the chair's decisions. Worse yet, once Butch reviews an issue with Matt and Joe, he proceeds as though he has full faculty input and concurrence.

When the former chair retired three years ago, the dean asked the department to select the next chair from within the department. This request disappointed many of the faculty, but especially Matt, Joe, and Butch who believe that a strong external chair brings a new vision and strength to a department. In self defense, the trio decided that one of them should apply for the chair's position. They decided that Butch was the strongest applicant. Matt and Joe feared that they were less likely to get the support of the faculty in rhetoric and performance studies. Before Butch was hired, Matt and Joe tangled with the other faculty on numerous issues as the department grew and changed during earlier decades. Butch was initially hesitant to seek the position but agreed that it was important for the interpersonal area to have a chair that supported its work.

Butch got the job, but the appointment left some hard feelings. Herb Portz perceives Butch as too young to understand the "true roots" of the discipline. Herb fears that Butch will cut rhetoric and public address in order to redirect more resources to interpersonal communication. Faculty in the performance studies area are less paranoid but do believe that their area holds no interest for Butch. Juan and Christine voted for Butch because they believe they can work with him as chair. They realize, however, that they need to educate him about performance studies and its place in the department curriculum. Neither forgets that Butch voted to eliminate performance

studies as a program specialization a few years earlier when the department faced a sizable budget cut.

Butch enjoys many of the duties he performs as chair but sometimes
experiences discomfort when handling difficult tasks with those faculty that
he knows did not support him for the chair position. Butch, for example,
dreads conducting the required annual performance evaluation with Herb
Portz, the most senior faculty member in the department. Butch also finds it
difficult to negotiate budget needs with the faculty in performance studies.
He knows that Christine Edelmann and Juan Herrera remember his outspoken opposition to retaining the performance studies area several years ago.
Butch is grateful for the counsel of Matt Morahan and Joe Wienhoff.

The Meeting

The department meets on the first Friday of each month. At the September
and October meetings, the issue of replacing Dorothy Whitacker was not on
the agenda. When asked, the chair explained that there were more pressing
issues to discuss, such as the teaching assignments for next fall. The chair
asserted that the position description was an important issue that should be
discussed only when there was ample time to consider all viewpoints. In his
words, "It would be unfair to tuck such a critical issue on a full agenda." The
faculty knew that they needed to make a decision about the position
description at the November meeting in order to advertise the position at the
national conference.

Butch Harrison began the meeting as usual with a long list of announcements. Buried near the end of the list, Butch announced that the position
description for Dorothy Whitacker's faculty line had been approved by the
administration and forwarded to the national association in time for the
national conference. The news surprised everyone except Matt and Joe.
Herb Portz interrupted before the chair could move on to the printed agenda.

Portz: "Run that past us again. Did you say that the position description
was approved and advertised?"

Harrison: "That's right. I know I waited until the 11th hour, but I wanted
to be certain that everyone had an opportunity to provide me with input on
this decision."

Herrera: "I thought that we were going to discuss it at a faculty meeting."

Harrison: "Time simply didn't allow that. I had to move so we could
recruit a strong applicant pool. We all agreed that it was important to have
an approved position description before the national conference. Well, it
was difficult, but we do have an approved position announcement for the

conference. I should tell you that we got tremendous support from the administration. The paperwork flew through channels at record speed. Obviously, the administration believes we made the right decision."

Portz: "We didn't make a decision. You did!"

Harrison: "Herb, you had the same opportunity as everyone to influence the outcome. It would be irresponsible for us to go to the national conference without an approved position description. You agreed with everyone earlier this fall when we made it a department priority to have an approved position description in time to meet with prospective applicants at the national conference in late November."

Edelmann: "Could we see a copy of the approved position description? It would be helpful to know what we hope to hire when we talk with our respective colleagues at the national conference."

Harrison: "No problem. I'll ask the secretary to put a copy in everyone's mailbox before we leave for the conference. I'm counting on everyone to beat the bushes so we get some strong applicants. It's important that we replace Dorothy with a strong person even if our search is limited to a new assistant professor."

Morahan: "Butch is right. We need to hire a strong person. It would be tragic if we allowed our individual interests to prevent us from hiring the strongest applicant."

Portz: "The strongest applicant in terms of what? We never reached a department decision as to what curriculum area most needs the faculty line. Are we hiring someone for rhetoric and public address to teach the classes that Dorothy taught or are we reducing our commitment to rhetoric and public address and redirecting those resources to another area?"

Wienhoff: "Let's not put the cart before the horse. We don't have any applicants yet. Let's wait and see where the strength is among the applicants."

Portz (becoming visibly agitated): "What does the position description stipulate as the qualifications? Are we advertising for a position in rhetoric and public address or for something else?"

Harrison: "I deferred to the majority who took the time to express an opinion. The ad asks for training and experience in any two of the following four areas: interpersonal, organizational communication, rhetoric, and performance studies. I believe that the position announcement will allow us full flexibility in recruiting and hiring the strongest candidate without squabbling over which area should get the faculty position."

Let's Analyze the Case

The chair believes that he spared the department a "squabble" over turf by listing all of the curricular specializations in the position announcement. The chair merely postponed the debate over turf until when the department screens the applicants. He also defers the department decision on how to best utilize the new hire to external forces, namely, the credentials of the applicants. No matter how uncomfortable the department discussion might be, it is unwise to allow the credentials of a single year's applicant pool to determine the department's direction and program inventory.

Butch Harrison may not intend to favor Matt Morahan and Joe Wienhoff, but he does communicate with them more frequently and more openly than he does with other faculty in the department. Matt and Joe may not be telling Butch what to do, but it is apparent to other faculty that they have the opportunity to do so. These observable communication practices fuel the perception held by other faculty that Matt and Joe have the inside track. Butch may spend less time with Matt and Joe than he did before becoming department chair. Chair duties, for example, probably take away the afternoon golf outings. Since becoming department chair, however, Butch's chats with Matt and Joe have a new symbolic meaning for the other members of the department. Because Butch tends to avoid one-on-one communication with the other faculty, he creates the impression that department decisions result from the chair's conversations with Matt and Joe.

More important, these observations contribute to the faculty perception of the department leadership. Butch is uncomfortable handling the tough issues because he senses that some of the faculty perceive him as incompetent to make some decisions or handle certain duties. Butch is grateful for the counsel of Matt and Joe, but his communication with them distances him from the other faculty. As long as the chair actively seeks the advice and support of only Matt and Joe, he will not win the trust and confidence of the other faculty whom he tends to avoid. It is a negative cycle in that the more Butch turns to Matt and Joe, the more estranged he becomes from the other faculty, which, in turn, is likely to increase Butch's dependence upon Matt and Joe for support. It is obvious that the department chair in Case 2.1 contributes to his own discomfort through his communication with faculty. Department chairs hired from inside the department may be tempted to carry existing friendships into the chair position. The transition from faculty to department chair, however, bears an ethical obligation to communicate with all faculty.

It's Your Turn

Imagine yourself as a new chair hired from inside the department and think through how you would manage the speech communication department described in Case 2.1.

1. What action could Harrison have taken when first appointed as department chair that would improve his rapport with the faculty from other curricular specializations? How might Harrison have earned the trust and support of the total faculty?

2. Now that three years have passed, what can Harrison do to earn the confidence of all faculty? How can Harrison demonstrate that he values input from all faculty? How might the chair structure the search process to ensure full participation of all department faculty?

Please Consider

In a healthy department climate, the faculty are generally less defensive and more receptive to change. These preconditions are essential to a department faculty's ability to reassess and revise the department mission. Deciding how to fill a faculty position is crucial to retaining or revising the department mission. In Case 2.1, The Inner Circle, the department strength was equally distributed across four curricular areas until the department lost two faculty members. The discipline expertise of the new hire will affect the department curricular offering. If, for example, the new hire does not take Dorothy Whitacker's place in teaching courses in rhetoric and public address, the department will have only one faculty member in that specialization. It is a shift in the department mission whether the faculty acknowledge it or not.

The current department climate is an obstacle to constructive discussion about the department mission and long-term planning. The poor climate prevents department members from presenting a coherent and positive view of the department to external publics. The faculty in the speech communication department described in Case 2.1 are not likely to perceive department strengths in the same way when speaking, for example, to prospective students, alumni, review teams, faculty in other departments on campus, potential donors, or community groups. The uneven and, in some instances, jaundiced view of the department creates a confused image of the department for the various external publics. In Case 2.1 the different perceptions may also pose a problem when individual faculty attempt to recruit applicants for the open position. Not only are the faculty likely to paint different pictures of the department, but their descriptions are likely to give evidence of the internal divisiveness and the mixed assessment of the chair's leadership.

The chair in Case 2.1 may avoid department discussions on certain issues to escape the confrontation that is inherent in the different views held by individual faculty. The faculty do not hold either shared values or shared perceptions. The presence of one would help create the other. Think about the relationship between shared values and shared perceptions in terms of the chair's tasks of structuring the department mission and enhancing the department climate.

1. What values might the speech communication faculty hold in common? Do they, for example, value teaching or a strong reputation in the discipline? It is especially important to identify shared values that cut across the existing divisions created by the curricular specializations.

2. Assume that everyone in the speech communication department values effective teaching and that all take considerable pride in community service and outreach activities. How could the department chair use those shared values to structure department discussion about how best to fill the open faculty position? Would acknowledging and preserving the core values help build the chair's credibility with all faculty?

Let's Recap

Take a moment and consider whether your approach to the speech communication department described in Case 2.1 would restore the characteristics of a healthy climate. If not, you may want to review the information presented earlier in this chapter. Does your approach contribute to

- a high degree of mutual trust and respect?
- an ability to openly air differences constructively without fear of retaliation?
- a norm of reciprocity?
- an effective communication?

While Matt Morahan and Joe Wienhoff enjoy effective communication with the department chair, they do not benefit from effective communication with their colleagues. Similarly, while there exists a high degree of mutual trust and respect between these two faculty members and the department chair, the same degree of mutual trust and respect does not exist between them and the other faculty or between the department chair and the other faculty. The climate in the speech communication department is unhealthy.

Does your strategy for how the department chair might enhance the department climate take into account those factors that contribute to faculty perceptions? If not, you may want to review the material presented earlier in this chapter. Does your approach

- foster a positive perception of department leadership?

- account for physical characteristics of the workplace?

- account for the symbolic aspects of the department?

- address relevant campus conditions?

- use a constructive process for department problem analysis and decision-making?

Putting Theory Into Practice

Butch Harrison, the chair of the speech communication department, has more problems than the one described in Case 2.1. Case 2.2, Making No-Win Decisions, illustrates the difficulty the chair has in pleasing faculty. The department chair feels pressured and bullied about issues that should be routine. Place yourself in the role of the department chair as you read Case 2.2.

Case 2.2, Making No-Win Decisions

An outgoing person, Butch Harrison, chair of the speech communication department, typically gets along well with most people. Since becoming department chair, however, Butch is experiencing an increasing uneasiness in dealing with his colleagues. He relies more and more on the counsel and friendship provided by Matt Morahan and Joe Wienhoff. Butch finds that he no longer has the friendly rapport with other faculty in the department that he had before assuming the chair position.

Butch isn't sure how to interact with these faculty who seem to watch and scrutinize his every move. They are quick to find fault with every decision. Responding to critical comments and suspicious inquiries consumes considerable time. Butch resents needing to explain clear-cut decisions to faculty who are not putting in near the same number of hours that he is to do all of the paperwork involved in chairing the department. Butch's annoyance is rapidly turning into anger. How can he handle the work if he must constantly explain his every move to faculty who could not do the chair's job?

He discusses the problem with Matt Morahan and Joe Wienhoff.

Wienhoff: "Forget it. You can't please everyone all of the time."

Harrison: "I don't seem to be able to please anyone ever."

Morahan: "That's far from the truth. You know that we believe you are doing a great job as department chair."

Harrison: "Sure, but you know that I can be trusted. I get the impression that none of the other faculty trust me to make fair decisions."

Morahan: "They're just paranoid. The entire department would be stronger if they would worry more about doing their own work."

Wienhoff: "That's the truth. Where does Herb Portz get off asking you to explain your rationale for allocating department travel funds. You'd think that as a full professor with one of the highest salaries in the department he could afford to pay more of his professional travel. Besides, he doesn't have the same need to make conference presentations that faculty seeking promotion and tenure have."

Harrison: "I agree–that's why I've always taken rank into consideration when awarding travel dollars. Since the dean keeps cutting our travel budget, I believe that it is more important to support faculty who are making conference presentations in order to meet promotion and tenure standards than to support travel for higher-paid faculty who attend conferences for their own enjoyment."

Morahan: "That's a sound decision. Don't worry about Portz. He is always self-centered in viewing department matters."

Harrison: "I know you are right, but Herrera raised a similar complaint about the allocation of travel funds."

Morahan: "You're kidding. Herrera rarely voices anything and certainly not a complaint."

Harrison: "I guess that's why it bothers me."

Wienhoff: "Well, what did Herrera say?"

Harrison: "He came right out and asked why I gave you and Matt each $800 for professional travel and he only got $400. He said that it was unfair because he is going to the same two conferences that you are attending. He seems to believe that since his expenses are the same as yours, he is entitled to the same travel support."

Morahan: "That's ridiculous. Did you tell him that when he starts doing as much as we do at professional meetings, you'll increase his travel support? Joe and I will present two papers each and serve on significant association committees. What's Herrera doing?"

Harrison: "I know that he is presenting one paper at the national conference. I'm not sure if he has a committee role or not. He's not very good at keeping me informed."

Morahan: "Well, you can't read his mind. What does he expect? Honestly, Butch, you're giving these idle complaints too much of your time. Shake it off. You're never going to please everyone. You just have to be content knowing that you are making good decisions."

Harrison: "I guess you're right."

Let's Analyze the Case

The department chair in Case 2.2, Making No-Win Decisions, believes that faculty are unfairly critical of his decisions. He is frustrated by their complaints that make clear that they do not trust him to treat all faculty fairly. Matt and Joe understand and agree with his rationale for allocating department travel funds. There is never enough money to cover all faculty expenses. The department chair allocates travel dollars, using criteria that to him best serve the total department. Butch Harrison's scheme for allocating travel funds gives more weight to faculty who are seeking promotion and tenure and to faculty who are making conference presentations. This department is not the first or only one to utilize such criteria, which helps to explain why the chair believes that the faculty are unduly critical.

The faculty are critical because they do not know the basis upon which the department chair makes travel allocations. Without a rationale for interpreting the differential travel allotments made to individual faculty, some of the faculty perceive the chair's decisions as arbitrary. Those faculty who believe that the chair holds their best interest trust the allocation as being fair. Those faculty who do not believe the chair has concern for their welfare do not perceive the allocation as fair. Most faculty do not know that the dean keeps cutting the department travel budget. That information would help explain individual reductions from one year to the next even though the faculty's need for travel dollars remains about the same.

The allocation of travel funds has a symbolic meaning in that it serves as a symbol of the chair's propensity to make unilateral and subjective decisions. By not sharing the rationale for making travel allocations with the department faculty and not involving the department faculty in the development of a department rationale for making travel allocations, the chair makes what could be a department decision a personal one. If the faculty discuss and understand the rationale for making travel allocations, then the chair is merely carrying out the collective wishes of the department when making travel allocations. Without faculty involvement, the chair makes a unilateral decision, which no matter how fair and prudent, will appear subjective.

It's Your Turn

Think through how the department chair in Case 2.2 should manage the allocation of travel funds.

1. How should the chair establish criteria for allocating travel funds? Should the faculty have a role in the process? If so, how might the chair structure department deliberations to minimize the pursuit of self-interest on the part of individual faculty members?

2. How would having the department faculty help develop criteria for allocating travel funds affect the chair's credibility? Would it influence the faculty's perception of the department leadership and alter the symbolic meaning currently assigned to travel allocations in the speech communication department? Would it influence the level of mutual trust and respect among department members and between the department chair and the faculty?

3. Should the chair keep faculty informed of reductions in the department travel budget? Should the chair disclose the budget total to all faculty? Would this information be helpful or hurtful in a department where the faculty understand the criteria used to make travel allocations?

Please Consider

The chair in Case 2.2 allocates travel dollars, using criteria that place a value on the purpose for the trip. Faculty who travel to present conference papers receive more than faculty who travel to attend conferences. It is important to note that the chair has no mechanism for assessing the reason for faculty travel. The chair is aware of Morahan and Wienhoff's conference activities but admits that he is not sure what Herrera is doing at the conference.

The chair credits this information void to the fact that Herrera doesn't keep him informed. Herrera is unaware of the criteria used for making travel allocations and does not know that information about conference activities will influence the chair's allocation of travel dollars. If Herrera is aware that his conference participation is equal to, or greater than, that of Morahan and Wienhoff, then his perception of receiving an unfair allocation has merit. Department chairs cannot expect the faculty to submit needed information when they do not know what information the chair uses to make various decisions.

Relevant Communication Concepts and Strategies

Cases 2.1, The Inner Circle, and 2.2, Making No-Win Decisions, illustrate the power of the department chair's communication. How department chairs communicate with faculty, both individually and collectively, has an enormous effect in shaping the department climate. From the analysis of Cases 2.1 and 2.2, we can deduce the following communication strategies that are essential for department chairs in any effort to build and maintain a healthy department climate.

Keep department members informed

Educate the faculty on state and campus issues. Explain the administration's perspective. Help the faculty and staff understand campus problems and the decisions of the central administration. Put isolated events and decisions in the larger context. Whenever possible, help the faculty interpret the potential effect of campus conditions and central administration decisions on the department. Do this with sensitivity and full awareness of the influence that the chair's presentation can have on the department. Rather than present only a message of gloom and doom, initiate a discussion about what the department's response or subsequent action to adverse conditions should be. It is important that department chairs be specific and not vague in describing relevant issues or in giving important information. The faculty should not be forced to fill in the blanks from their own information or by using their own imagination. They should not need to rely on the local media or the campus rumor mill for information.

Communicate with all members of the department

Department chairs, like most individuals, come to value the perspective of some people more than others. Time pressures are serious, and the chairs may only consult with a chosen few. This action is costly to the department climate. It is important that department chairs have equitable communication with all members. That means listening to the viewpoints of each and sharing information with all equally. This encompasses both formal and informal communication. The department chair that sends a formal memorandum to everyone but solicits the informal counsel of a chosen few does much to damage the chair's credibility and the department climate. The chair who communicates with some faculty through typed notes but takes the time to consult in person with other faculty undermines the chair's credibility and the department climate. This is true for professional as well as social communication. The department chair who has lunch regularly with the same department members communicates that the chair values some members more than others. That perception detracts from the chair's credibility and the department climate.

Remain accessible to all department members

Department chairs juggle a multitude of tasks, deadlines, and trivial activity. The chairs, perhaps more than any other administrator on campus, experience a high volume of walk-in traffic, including students, faculty, campus visitors, prospective students and their parents, businessmen, and anyone else who may show up without a scheduled appointment. Most faculty and staff understand that the chairs must guard their time carefully. It is important to distinguish between the chair's availability and the chair's accessibility. To be accessible to all department members, department chairs must do more than just maintain an open-door policy 40 hours each week. Department chairs must be approachable. All department members must feel comfortable approaching the chair about any issue. If faculty, staff, and students know that they can approach the department chair on any matter that concerns them, they perceive the chair as accessible. They will understand when the door is closed in order for the chair to meet a pressing deadline. They will also be more tolerant of the chair's need to spend time with those who do have concerns so long as they are confident that the chair will be equally approachable when they themselves present matters of concern.

Listen and comprehend incoming information

People tend to stop communicating with those who do not listen to them. There is a vast difference between hearing and listening. Listening implies an engaged audience who conscientiously attempts to comprehend and understand the incoming information. Often department chairs have a greater effect on others by how they listen rather than by what they say. Department chairs need to listen with the intent to understand instead of the intent to respond. Department chairs must offer tangible signs that they listen to faculty even when they disagree or choose to discount the incoming information. Evidence of active listening requires that department chairs acknowledge the receipt of information. This can be done by parroting back the viewpoint expressed before offering an opposing view. Chairs can demonstrate that they are listening by describing what they plan to do with the information. The department chair, for example, might tell someone that it is a significant issue and suggest that all department faculty discuss it at the next department meeting.

There is a bonus for department chairs who listen because every piece of incoming information also tells something about the individual sending it that may or may not be related to the message content. From active listening, department chairs learn more about department members. This information is useful when deciding how to approach faculty about a new or sensitive issue. Through active listening, chairs learn about the expectations of department members. This knowledge is essential to leadership that involves influencing the behavior of others.

Facilitate communication among department members

Let committee work and other department activities cut across discipline specializations, age, professorial rank, race, and other such classifications that might perpetuate internal divisions. When department chairs are unable to facilitate effective communication among department members, they become the gatekeeper for every communication transaction. This places a tremendous burden on the department chair. It negates effective consensus building and damages the department climate. Department chairs need all faculty to be able to work well together in subgroups without them. To do this, department chairs must demonstrate that every member is a valued contributor to department activity. The faculty are less likely to discount the opinions of certain colleagues if the chair includes and values the contributions of all faculty.

Putting Theory Into Practice

It is one thing to know how to communicate effectively and quite another to be able to communicate effectively on a daily basis. Department chairs juggle a multitude of tasks and interact with a number of persons everyday. Case 2.3, This Is Important, describes a department chair's reaction to a student concern. Using the communication strategies for enhancing the department climate, evaluate the department chair's interaction with the concerned students.

Case 2.3, This Is Important

The physics department enjoys a rather comfortable and stable existence. The department of ten faculty were immune to the budget cutbacks of the last decade because they are all tenured. When the institution reduced the number of faculty on campus, the physics department survived unscathed. The department lost a small portion of its operating budget but retained all faculty positions.

The physics faculty are a very cohesive group of men. They work well together, engage in a lot of team teaching, and socialize outside work. The department chair never worries about destructive conflict among the physics' faculty. The faculty have strong personalities, and each is able to express and argue his viewpoint. Although the faculty may engage in heated debate on an issue, they continue to respect and value each other as colleagues. The department climate developed over a period of two decades. Most of the faculty were hired as young assistant professors. They bonded early and coached each other through the tenure and promotion hurdles. Now all ten have tenure and all but two are full professors.

Twelve years ago, when the last department chair retired, the faculty voted to hire one of their own as chair. The college dean believed that a chair hired from the outside would bring a fresh perspective to the department. The college dean was particularly anxious to locate a qualified woman to assume the position of chair. With increasing numbers of women students in science, the dean is sensitive to the need for more women faculty who can serve as role models for young women who aspire to careers in science.

The department faculty disagree with the dean. They fear that a chair hired from the outside might upset the harmony in the department. At the dean's insistence, the department conducted a national search for a department chair. Campus policy stipulates that chairs hired from the outside can receive tenure when hired with a positive vote from the faculty. In two different national searches, the department faculty voted the final candidates as unacceptable for tenure in physics. The dean was not anxious to hire a chair who would not have tenure in the department. After months of discussion and two aborted national searches, the dean acquiesced to the wishes of the department.

Givos Galanos served as acting chair during the two years that the dean conducted the national searches for a physics chair. When the college dean abandoned his goal to hire a chair from outside the department, Dr. Galanos was the unanimous choice of the faculty. He is considered the "best friend" of virtually every member of the department. Without exception the faculty have tremendous confidence in Givos Galanos. Now having served as department chair for more than a decade, Dr. Galanos is very comfortable in the position.

Dr. Galanos practices a very informal management style. Department meetings are sometimes held over lunch or in someone's backyard. No minutes are kept, and faculty make department decisions by consensus without taking a formal vote. The faculty spend a lot of time together. The faculty organized a department bowling team that participates in a local league two nights every week during the fall and spring semesters. In the summer the department softball team competes against other community teams.

The Complaint

Dr. Galanos is confused about the next meeting penciled on his calendar. The department secretary made the appointment and entered the following note: "Jane Alexander & Company." Dr. Galanos knows Jane Alexander, a second semester senior with a 3.75 GPA. But what or who is the "company"?

Before he could give it much thought, Jane Alexander knocked on his open door. When Dr. Galanos invited her to come in, she led no fewer than 15 women students into the small and cluttered chair's office. Dr. Galanos is visibly thrown by the ensemble. Without thinking, he straightens his tie and reaches for his sports coat. Something about the dress and manner of this group of women tells Dr. Galanos that this is not an informal meeting.

As the women arrange themselves in the "standing room only" quarters, Jane Alexander takes out some typed notes. It is clear that she is the group's spokesperson and that they gave this meeting a lot of thought. All of this makes Dr. Galanos more uncomfortable.

Alexander: "Thank you for seeing us, Dr. Galanos. We are here to talk with you about something that is really important to us."

Galanos: "My door is always open to students. I'm sorry that there is not enough room for all of you to sit down. Perhaps we could set a time to meet in the department conference room. Right now it is being used by Dr. Sinah for a graduate seminar."

Alexander: "This is fine. We don't want to wait any longer. Actually, it took us some time to get up the nerve to approach you. Now that we're here, we don't want to reschedule this meeting."

Galanos: "That's fine. I just thought that the conference room might be more comfortable for all of us."

Alexander (staring at her notes): "Dr. Galanos, I'm a second semester senior so I hope that you'll recognize that I'm not here for any personal interest. I, or I should say we, have a serious concern about the department."

Galanos: "I'm afraid that I don't know all of you, but I'm always glad to hear the student's perspective on how we can keep our department strong."

Alexander: "Some of the women here are physics majors, and the rest are enrolled in other majors that require courses in physics. You probably noticed that there are no men students with us."

Galanos: "You're probably here to talk about the lack of women faculty in physics. I can assure you that this concerns all of us. The fact remains, however, that until we have a vacant faculty position to fill, there is no way that we can add a qualified woman to our faculty. The last time we had a retirement was 12 years ago when the department chair left. I ended up in this seat so we never hired a new faculty member. Please believe me when I tell you that hiring a qualified woman faculty member is a top priority for the department."

Alexander: "We agree that the lack of women faculty in physics is a problem, but that's not the reason for our visit. We're here to talk about Professor Remland. We owe it to the women who follow us to speak up. "

Galanos (sitting up taller in his chair behind the desk): "Dr. Remland! You do know that he's been in the department longer than I have. Just what concern could you possibly have?"

Alexander: "We're concerned about Dr. Remland's unethical treatment of women students. He–"

Galanos interrupted: "Unethical treatment of women students! You can't be serious. Dr. Remland was teaching before you were born. He has the full admiration of his faculty colleagues. I know him very well and am confident that Dr. Remland would never mistreat anyone, male or female. He is a dedicated teacher."

Alexander (sensing that she made the chair defensive): "Perhaps I used the wrong words. Professor Remland does not interact with women students in the same way that he does with men students. With us he is condescending. It is painfully obvious that Dr. Remland believes that women have no place in physics. He makes us feel unwelcome."

Galanos: "Listen to yourself. Dr. Remland, a respected and experienced instructor makes you feel 'unwelcome.' At the risk of being blunt, you're here for an education, not coddling."

Alexander: "We don't want to be coddled. We want to be taken seriously as a students who elected to study physics."

Galanos: "Well, if you want to be taken seriously, you need to focus on meeting class requirements, not criticizing the parenting skills of my faculty."

Alexander (taking a deep breath): "We do take class requirements seriously. That's why it is important that instructors treat us as serious students. Dr. Remland does not give women students the same mentoring or quality instruction that he gives our male counterparts."

Galanos: "I don't believe this. How can you waltz in here and make such empty accusations about one of our most respected and experienced instructors. I've known Dr. Remland a long time; I'm confident that he is an excellent instructor. He is not out to get women. I have to balance Dr. Remland's long and distinguished career against your assertion that he makes you feel unwelcome in physics. Jane, I used to rate you as one of our better students. When you stop and think about this, you'll realize that your hollow complaint is ill conceived. Ladies, I really believe that it is in your best interest if we terminate this discussion now and I forget that you made these spiteful charges."

Let's Analyze the Case

Dr. Galanos did not anticipate the student complaint about Dr. Remland. He reacted defensively. Dr. Galanos's bias keeps him from comprehending the complaint. He is more intent on responding than listening to the students' concern. Whether the women students' perception of Dr. Remland is accurate or not, the chair's defensive reaction does much to damage the department climate for these women students. The women will leave this discussion convinced that Dr. Remland's bias against women is shared by the department chair. They learn that their concern cannot be discussed with the department chair. This leaves the women students with only a few options. They can either forget the concern or raise it with someone else on campus. If they opt to forget their concern, they can decide to transfer to a different institution or stick it out until graduation. In either alternative, they do not leave the institution with a favorable impression of the department. As alumni they are less likely to contribute time or money to their alma mater. If the women decide to take their concern to someone else, the complaint becomes more widely known. The department chair, through his behavior, makes it someone else's conflict to manage.

Dr. Galanos does not help Dr. Remland by aborting the meeting with the concerned students. It is to Dr. Remland's advantage that the complaint be handled within the department. The chair is in the best position to expose false complaints; this requires that the women perceive the chair as neutral, not hostile. Only if the chair remains credible to the women students can he persuade them to abandon unfounded conclusions about Dr. Remland's treatment of women students. By taking sides early in the discussion, the chair surrenders his neutral posture that is essential to resolving the matter. It also increases the likelihood that the matter will be investigated and resolved by someone else outside the department.

Dr. Galanos claims that his door is always open to students, but he is not accessible to them. He feels the need to defend Dr. Remland before he hears the complaint. The case does not disclose the basis for the women students' perception because Dr. Galanos never pursues the matter. Dr. Galanos's defensive reaction reinforces the students' perception that women are treated less favorably than men. The manner in which the chair does not listen may actually confirm for these students that their perception is correct. If the women students' complaint is "empty" or "hollow," Dr. Galanos has a better chance of exposing that by listening carefully and pursuing the concern. Instead of asking the women to provide the reasons for their conclusion, Dr. Galanos terminates the meeting. Worse yet, he closes with what might be perceived as a veiled threat.

It's Your Turn

Assume the role of the department chair in Case 2.3 and think through how you would handle the meeting with Jane Alexander and the other women students.

1. Would you learn more about the reason for the appointment before the scheduled meeting time? Would your secretary know how to reach every person on your calendar?

2. In greeting Jane Alexander and the other students, would you engage in small talk or move right to the reason for their visit? Are there issues that you might raise initially to place them at ease and establish your credibility as a chair who is accessible to students? How would you accommodate the "standing room only" conditions of your office?

3. Review the dialogue in Case 2.3 and note when Dr. Galanos becomes defensive. Is it possible to listen without either becoming defensive or implying that you believe Dr. Remland is guilty of mistreating women students? Could the chair, for example, demonstrate his credibility as a neutral listener by asking for more detail or support for the assertions?

Let's Recap

Take a moment and review your approach for handling the meeting with Jane Alexander and the other women students. If your approach does not incorporate the characteristics of a healthy department climate, you may want to review the material presented earlier in this chapter. Does your approach exhibit

- a high degree of mutual trust and respect?

- an ability to openly air differences constructively without fear of retaliation?

- a norm of reciprocity?

- an effective communication?

Does your strategy for how the department chair might enhance the climate in the physics department take into account those factors that work to shape the department climate? If not, you may want to review the material presented earlier in this chapter. Does your approach

- foster a positive perception of department leadership?

- account for physical characteristics of the workplace?

- account for the symbolic aspects of the department?

- address relevant campus conditions?

- use a constructive process for department problem analysis and decision-making?

Putting Theory Into Practice

In Case 2.4, Equality, the chemistry department recruits its first minority faculty member. The chair begins the fall term with a true sense of accomplishment because the college dean made it clear that the department would lose the position if it was not able to recruit a qualified minority faculty member. The department chair's feeling of success is short lived as the new hire begins to encounter difficulty within the department. Place yourself in the role of the department chair as your read Case 2.4.

Case 2.4, Equality?

Craig Wilson, the long-time chair of the chemistry department, is preparing for the first department meeting of the new academic year. He is feeling optimistic about the start of the new academic year. His department met the dean's challenge to hire a minority faculty. The college dean threatened to take the open position if the department could not recruit a minority faculty member. The department hired two women faculty in the last six years, but each only stayed a couple of years. In earlier searches the department interviewed one minority faculty, but that applicant took another position before the department was ready to make an offer. With an increasing number of minority students enrolled in chemistry courses, the dean believes it is imperative that there be a minority presence on the faculty.

The department took the dean's prompting seriously. They cast a wide net, calling colleagues across the nation in an effort to encourage qualified minorities to apply. The department succeeded beyond everyone's expectations by hiring a young Hispanic woman, Maria Perez, for the tenure-track position beginning at the assistant professor rank.

It also pleased the department chair that the faculty were so strong in their support of Dr. Perez. The department practice is to have faculty vote the finalists for the open position as acceptable or unacceptable. The faculty were unanimous in finding Dr. Perez "acceptable" for the position. Not only do the faculty assess Dr. Perez as meeting the advertised position qualifications, but they are enthusiastic about hiring her. Craig Wilson recalls the department discussion of Dr. Perez's credentials. The descriptive language used by virtually all faculty was, in his view, extremely positive. Several faculty remarked about Maria's "boundless energy" and "zest for life." Even one of the more sober faculty members, Edwin Moses, commented on how "charming" she is. A few mentioned that Dr. Perez would be "a delightful addition" to the department. Most faculty commented positively on her "quick wit and personable manner." When one faculty member described Dr. Perez as having an "effervescent personality," the others quickly agreed.

Craig Wilson felt like the proverbial cat that swallowed the canary. He succeeded in meeting the dean's directive and finding someone that everyone loved. It promises to be a great year. He is excited as he takes his seat at the head of the table. He notes that the faculty seem extremely upbeat as they enter the conference room and take their seats for the first department meeting. Craig notices that Maria Perez seems to be the subject of the pre-meeting conversation.

Moses (turning to Perez): "Are you getting settled in our community? How's your family adjusting to the move? Have you picked a school for your children? Tell me again how old they are?"

Perez: "Yes, fine, yes, five and seven! There, I believe that answers all of your questions."

Moses (laughing): "I forgot how young your children are. How do they feel about having Mom at work all day?"

Perez: "I suspect about the same as I feel having them at school all day."

Moses (turning toward the chair): "Craig, have you set the date for the department fishing retreat? You know how I look forward to that trip."

Wilson: "No, I haven't. Do you have any suggestions?"

Wilson (looking at Maria Perez): "Edwin is talking about our fall fishing expedition. It's not really a retreat. Several of us like to fish so we tell our wives that we're talking shop. That way they don't grumble about our being gone."

O'Connor: "More important, they don't ask to go along!"

Moses (laughing and getting louder): "I don't have to worry about that. My wife won't even clean the fish that I catch."

O'Connor: "That's okay. I can't remember your catching many fish."

Moses (turning back to Maria Perez): "You can tell that we have a good time. Actually, we do talk some shop. It was on last year's fishing trip that we talked about how to advertise and fill your position so it's not all play."

Wilson: "If you men are through having fun, let's start the meeting. It's a short agenda so we should be able to adjourn to Mike's Pub by 5:00 p.m. Maria, that's another department tradition. We hold department meetings late in the day and then congregate at Mike's Pub. No matter what disagreements we have during the meeting, everyone feels better after the second round of drinks at Mike's Pub."

Moses: "So get on with it. Let's get through this agenda."

Wilson: "The main item of business is the committee assignments for the coming year. The department budget committee worked well last year so I'd like to retain the same membership on that committee."

Wilson paused to look for a few nodding heads before continuing: "That's great. I believe that continuity is important since the dean is talking more fiscal gloom and doom. That means that the department curriculum committee will have the same membership as last year. Are there any objections?" After a brief silence, he continues: "Good. I really appreciate your cooperation."

Perez: "Do you have a preference for which of the two committees I serve on? I have considerable experience with budget. Last year, I..."

Wilson (interrupting): "Don't worry, Maria. I'm getting to you. I propose that we add a new department committee that is responsible for student issues. I thought we would call it the student welfare committee. Maria, I want you to chair that committee."

Perez: "Sure, that's fine. Who else is on the committee?"

Wilson: "I haven't given that a lot of thought. Why don't you think about it and make some suggestions. I know that everyone is busy and this would mean a second committee assignment for a few of you. Maria, you might talk to those that you would like to have on the committee to ask if they have time to serve before giving me your suggestions. Can you handle that?"

Perez: "I believe so."

Wilson: "Okay then. This meeting is adjourned. I'll see everyone at Mike's Pub."

Let's Analyze the Case

Craig Wilson believes the hard part is done. The department successfully hired a minority woman faculty member. In reality, the department chair's most difficult task is just beginning. Dr. Maria Perez needs to become acclimated to the department climate. It is obvious that the department has many long-standing traditions, including a fall fishing trip and postmeeting gatherings at Mike's Pub. It is the department chair's responsibility to help Dr. Perez read and interpret the department climate. It is also the chair's responsibility to help Dr. Perez fit comfortably and productively into the department. That will involve helping other faculty adjust to and accept the newest department member. Should the department, for example, still conduct business on the fall fishing expedition? Should Maria Perez be invited (or expected) to join the fishing expedition? At a minimum, the chair needs to make certain that issues discussed do not reach closure at a recreational gathering when all of the department faculty are not present.

The department chair believes that everyone is pleased with the hire of Maria Perez. All faculty voted her as "acceptable" and were quick to describe her in positive terms. Review the evaluative terms used to described Dr. Perez. The faculty find her "charming" and "personable." They see her as having "boundless energy " and an "effervescent personality." None of these descriptors comment on her academic training or professional experience. The faculty selected someone with whom they feel comfortable, not someone that they necessarily perceive as an equal colleague.

Craig Wilson does not seem anxious to alter existing practice. Note that he creates a new committee for Maria Perez to chair rather than add her as a new member to either of the existing committees. This action communicates that the chair's priority is retaining the status quo. If this is the chair's posture, it is less likely that other members of the department will initiate any changes that might make Dr. Perez a more integral part of the chemistry department.

Department chairs have direct influence over how faculty treat and work with a new hire. During the short department meeting, Craig Wilson interrupts Dr. Perez as she is attempting to explain how her experience might be most beneficial to department committees. He also makes a light response to her question, saying, "Don't worry, Maria." If the chair interrupts Dr. Perez midsentence, isolates her from traditional committee assignments, and dismisses her comments with remarks that might be viewed as patronizing, then the chair authorizes others in the department to do the same by his example. Department chairs can help to assure that new hires are successful by demonstrating to other faculty that the chair values the new hire's contribution to the department. Craig Wilson does not do this.

It's Your Turn

Place yourself in the role of Dr. Craig Wilson, chair of the chemistry department, and think through how you would help Maria Perez become a fully contributing member of the department.

1. What can the chair do to demonstrate that he perceives Dr. Perez as a valued faculty member? Can the chair communicate a high regard for the professional capabilities of Maria Perez by assigning upper-level courses, appointing her to significant department committees, recommending her as the department representative on college or university committees, or other high-profile activities that have symbolic significance for department faculty?

2. Review the chair's dialogue in Case 2.4 and underline those comments that devalue Maria Perez's professional role. Rewrite the statements in a way that enhances Dr. Perez's credibility with her new colleagues.

3. Next, note the comments made by other faculty that indicate a disrespect for Maria Perez and her faculty role. How might the department chair intervene in these instances to bolster Dr. Perez without alienating the other faculty?

Let's Recap

The department climate represents the personality of the department. Because the department climate develops from perceptions, it is subject to change as conditions prompt new or altered perceptions. Department chairs have direct influence over the department climate because they are the primary interpreters of external conditions that affect department life. That is why the department climate does not automatically mirror the campus climate. The chair's influence on department climate is evident in all the cases.

A healthy department climate requires continuous maintenance. It cannot exist without the following key characteristics:

- High degree of mutual trust and respect

- Ability to openly air differences constructively without fear of retaliation

- Norm of reciprocity

- Effective communication

When these characteristics are present, the department climate sets a positive tone for conducting department business. Chairs benefit directly from a healthy department climate because the faculty in a department with a healthy climate are more supportive of department leadership and less resistant to change.

Department chairs need to understand how their communication within the department facilitates or impedes those factors that shape the department climate. Through their communication, department chairs can promote a positive perception of leadership. They can offset any disadvantage accrued from physical characteristics of the workplace. The chairs can use the symbolic aspects of the department to their advantage. As the primary interpreters of campus conditions, department chairs influence whether or not faculty adopt a constructive response to changing conditions. The chairs also determine whether the department uses a constructive process for problem analysis and decision-making.

Department chairs hold the key to enhancing department climate even when they do not have direct control over all the factors listed. If department chairs communicate equitably with all department members, keep them informed of campus issues, remain accessible to others, and practice meaningful listening, they will enhance the perception of their leadership, which, in turn, will improve the department climate. Department chairs also have the most to gain from a healthy department climate. The faculty in a positive department climate tend to be more accepting of leadership, less resistant change, and more collegial. Those are essential prerequisites to effective leadership.

3

DEFINING THE DEPARTMENT ETHICS

Department ethics refer to the generally understood (though perhaps unspoken) boundaries for acceptable behavior. They establish the framework for judging what is fair or unfair, responsible or irresponsible, considerate or inconsiderate, and other such bipolar descriptors of department and individual actions. Department ethics impose a conscience on department activity.

Department ethics are not the sum total of individual ethics practiced by department members. Rather, department ethics establish ground rules for the collective department membership. This may require some individuals to modify their personal ethics when performing department responsibilities. Ideally, department ethics supersede individual ethics on department business. For example, the person who may take shortcuts in filing an income tax return (an individual ethic) may not take shortcuts in preparing course materials (a department ethic).

Department ethics build on and reinforce department values. The existence of strong department ethics helps to create a positive department culture. When department members understand the ethical ground rules for behavior and can trust each other to comply with the common ethical code, there is greater respect among colleagues and between faculty and the department chair. Effective department chairs work to define department ethics that facilitate department management.

The Objective

One goal of this chapter is to help department chairs understand their responsibility for defining department ethics. This requires that department chairs model ethical behavior. It also requires chairs to encourage department members to engage in ethical conduct. Department chairs must convince department members that they expect and value ethical behavior. A second goal of this chapter is to help department chairs understand those factors that shape department ethics. Department chairs need to recognize how they may intentionally or unintentionally influence these factors. A third goal is to equip department chairs with an audit mechanism for assessing department ethics. This assessment tool helps chairs define (or redefine) department ethics so they have a positive effect on department operations and productivity.

Defining the Task

Department chairs help shape department ethics by exercising ethical leadership. The term ethical leadership refers to both the chair's leadership in securing compliance with applicable legal and professional ethical standards and in encouraging the traditional moral virtues of fairness and honesty in all dealings with faculty members (Higgerson and Higgerson, 1994). Ethical leadership requires that department chairs set an example of professional responsibility by being truthful, fair, and consistent in their relationships with faculty colleagues. Department chairs clarify by example what behavior is acceptable. The chairs also reinforce the limits for ethical behavior as they manage the interactions and dealings of department members.

Ethics must be integrated with day-to-day activity. Chairs must teach department members what they expect from them. Therefore, it becomes a management responsibility to encourage ethical behavior. That is done through personal example and through deliberate response to the actions of department members. If department ethics were solely the outcome of individual behavior, department ethics would be the sum of individual (and sometimes competing) ethics. Academic departments represent communities. As social structures, departments develop identities with central values and rules to govern behavior. Without these features, departments exhibit chaos and an "every person out for his or her self" mentality.

Most department chairs recognize that moral environments do not develop without some sense of community with shared values to guide individual behavior. Community members must work deliberately to support each other and uphold the values of the social structure. Chairs need to alter the perspective of department members from placing priority on what they want to do to giving first consideration to what they should do. This requires that department members place their personal interests in the context of the overall welfare of the department. Perhaps an example that illustrates this shift from a self-centered to an other-centered perspective is the presence of roller-blade skaters and cyclists on campus. It is not uncommon to observe persons on roller blades and bicycles who want to assume the roles of both pedestrian and vehicle as they navigate through traffic. They travel as pedestrian or vehicle, depending upon which definition suits their immediate need. A cyclist may travel in the right lane (as a vehicle) until coming to a four-way stop. Instead of stopping (as the law requires vehicles to do), the cyclist may turn sharply and pedal across the intersection in the crosswalk (posing as a pedestrian). If cyclists place the safety and welfare of everyone ahead of personal interests, they adopt behavior that reflects more what they *should* do than what they *want* to do.

In defining department ethics, chairs set the parameters for ethical behavior. Helping department members move from espousing department values to practicing department values requires that they develop a sense of community. Department chairs need to exercise ethical leadership on a daily basis to help department members know what they should do. When department ethics take priority over individual ethics, the department benefits.

Relevant Communication Concepts and Strategies

Leadership is an "influence relationship between leaders and followers who intend real changes that reflect their mutual purposes." (Rost, 1993, p. 154). Ethical leadership exists when department chairs use their influence ethically. Does the chair's influence intimidate? Does the chair's influence promise appropriate recognition and reward? Faculty, staff, and students form assessments of the chair's leadership that include an ethical dimension. This is evidenced in the language frequently used to evaluate department leadership. Faculty may, for example, say that the department chair was wrong to take action without department discussion. Faculty may report a chair's decision as disagreeable but *fair*. Sometimes faculty reference the department leadership as *self-serving* or *irresponsible*. Department members may describe the chair's action or decision as *biased*. Bipolar words used to describe behavior, such as right or wrong, fair or unfair, honest or dishonest, selfless or self-serving, and responsible or irresponsible, reflect the ethical dimension of the evaluative statement.

Department members assess the presence or absence of ethical leadership. This evaluation of the ethical quality in leadership derives primarily from observing the chair's behavior. How does the department chair behave toward faculty, staff, and students? How does the department chair interact with the dean and other important external publics? How does the department chair relate to other departments and offices on campus? How does the department chair protect and promote the department mission? In short, how does the department chair perform assigned duties? In discussing the ethical obligations for faculty performance, Steven Cahn (1986) asserts that professional ethics should be defined in terms of one's assigned duties and responsibilities. That also holds true for administrative positions. Typically, we evaluate administrative competence and skill in terms of how well an administrator performs assigned duties and responsibilities. Hence, department chairs who fail to perform one or more of their assigned responsibilities are likely to be judged as irresponsible. To the extent that the irresponsible behavior results in decisions that others perceive as unfair or dishonest, the chair's leadership is unethical.

Practicing ethical leadership and encouraging ethical behavior in others is a challenging task. As Mark Twain wrote, "Always do right. This will gratify some people, and astonish the rest." Ethical leadership is difficult because it requires the department chair to take positions that others will not perceive as neutral. For starters, department chairs need to understand what defines and contributes to ethical behavior. Rest and Narvaez (1994) describe the steps involved in evaluating alternatives and selecting an ethical course of action. Using the terms *moral* and *ethical* interchangeably, Rest and Navaez list the following four psychological components that determine moral behavior:

1. Moral sensitivity (interpreting the situation)

2. Moral judgment (judging which action is morally right or wrong)

3. Moral motivation (prioritizing moral values relative to other values)

4. Moral character (having courage, persistence, overcoming distractions, and implementing skills)

Consider these components in the context of the academic department and the responsibilities typically assigned to department chairs.

Moral sensitivity

This component refers to our awareness of how our actions affect other people. Moral sensitivity is the ability to empathize. Department chairs having moral sensitivity exhibit empathy for the roles and responsibilities of others (including the dean). Chairs must recognize how their actions affect others. To encourage moral sensitivity in other department members, the chairs must teach them to have empathy. Chairs need to communicate their expectation that all department members should consider the position of others in carrying out department business. The curriculum committee should, for example, consider the effect that its recommendation will have on faculty colleagues and students.

Empathy allows us to anticipate reactions. It guides the presentation of new information or decisions so we might minimize the potential negative ramifications of our behavior. It is particularly important to have empathy for those individuals affected by our actions. For example, sometimes faculty hold different opinions regarding the value of the various research orientations. In some departments, the faculty disagree on the relative merit of theoretical and applied research. Those faculty who do applied research may not command the respect of faculty who perform more theoretical research and vice versa. If the department mission encompasses both types of research, it is unethical for the chair or any department member to devalue either research orientation. Both research orientations need to be valued equally in thought, word, and deed. Department chairs must demonstrate their respect for both research orientations in day-to-day decisions as well as in their communication. It would, for example, be unethical to award faculty doing theoretical research more release time simply because the chair perceives theoretical research as having greater value. At the same time, it would be unethical to favor applied research efforts merely because they hold more opportunity for external funding. Through their own communication and actions, chairs persuade department members that acceptable behavior values both research orientations.

Moral judgment

This psychological component involves the process of judging which action is morally justified. What is right or wrong in conducting department business should be judged by department, not individual, ethics. There are those, for example, who believe that it is acceptable to cheat the government. That attitude and individual ethic is contextual in that it does not automatically follow that those same individuals cheat in other situations. Without clearly defined department ethics, department members must use individual ethics in determining what action is right or wrong. This threatens any sense of department community. It also poses an obstacle to department achievement unless all individual goals are similar and not in competition with department goals.

Department chairs help define department ethics by establishing the parameters by which department members judge the rightness or wrongness of a particular action. The department may, for example, stress the need for faculty to engage in research. That goal represents a department value. Research can be a recognized priority, but the department ethics help the faculty place that priority in the larger context of faculty responsibilities and the department mission. Department ethics help the faculty determine whether it is acceptable to pursue research while slighting their responsibility to teaching. Is it morally right or wrong to limit the time spent on teaching for the purpose of accelerating one's research program? Is it morally right or wrong to limit the time spent serving on committees and other service activities for the sake of pursuing research? The answer to those questions can vary with the department because not all departments have the same mission or ethics. As new faculty enter the department, the chairs need to help them understand the department ethics. Chairs also need to continually reinforce the department ethics for all department members. Without clearly defined department ethics, the department members will judge actions as being right or wrong on the basis of individual ethics. This produces conflict that threatens effective leadership and department achievement.

Moral motivation

Moral motivation refers to the importance given to moral values that may be in competition with other values. Faculty are responsible for delivering quality instruction. At research institutions, faculty also have responsibility for maintaining active research programs. It is, therefore, important that the faculty not spend so much time on teaching that research programs fail to make steady progress. It is not uncommon for department chairs to advise enthusiastic untenured assistant professors to guard their time. Well-intentioned department chairs may advise faculty to serve on fewer committees, spend two full days out of the office each week to work on research, or employ instructional methods that take less time. In giving this advice, the department chair places more importance on helping the untenured assistant professor succeed in receiving tenure than on promoting the instructional and service goals of the department.

Department chairs prioritize the moral values of the department through their actions. When persuading untenured assistant professors to devote more time to research than teaching or service, department chairs prioritize values that guide untenured faculty in knowing what decisions and actions are the right ones to pursue. The chair's behavior defines department ethics for the faculty member. It provides the untenured assistant professor with a framework for judging the rightness or wrongness of faculty performance.

Moral character

Department chairs who practice ethical leadership listen to others and encourage dissenting opinion. They also hold fast to convictions and exhibit true courage in overcoming petty distractions. They manage conflict on the basis of issue, not personality. They are able to articulate reasons for their decisions that demonstrate no self-interest. These qualities are essential to effective leadership. Moral character, however, is useless without effective communication skills. Communication skills enable leaders with moral character to communicate the boundaries for ethical behavior, to encourage others to behave ethically, to demonstrate their own ethical leadership, and to implement change when needed. Ethical leadership implies the ability to influence the behavior of others. This requires effective communication. Hence, effective and ethical leaders are also skilled communicators.

Department chairs need to encourage the moral character of department members. Chairs do this by reinforcing and rewarding others when they engage in morally right behavior. Chairs strengthen moral character in department members by making certain that none feel ostracized for pursuing moral actions. Finally, department chairs bolster those who engage in moral behavior by assisting their efforts to communicate with others. Department chairs control their department's decision-making process and, therefore, can make certain that the department does not vote on an issue before those articulating moral values are heard and understood.

Putting Theory Into Practice

Ethical leadership requires leaders to use, not abuse, the authority of their position to conscientiously perform assigned duties and responsibilities. The department chair in Case 3.1, Mixed Messages, has an excellent rapport with the faculty. The chair possesses strong interpersonal communication skills and takes pride in her ability to converse with every member of the department. The faculty are comfortable with the chair and candidly express their thoughts about colleagues and things that displease them. As you read Case 3.1, consider how the department chair defines her role and determine whether she fulfills the responsibilities of department chair. Assess whether this well-liked and well-intentioned chair is exercising ethical leadership.

Case 3.1, Mixed Messages

Frances Monet is the chair of biology at a middle-sized private university. She gets along well with virtually every member of the department. When interviewing for the position, Dr. Monet described her leadership style as "more friend and less boss." Faculty, staff, and students enjoy a relaxed and friendly rapport with the department chair.

Dr. Monet is organized and efficient. The department runs like clockwork. Dr. Monet prides herself on meeting deadlines and handling the day-to-day matters while keeping up with the endless paperwork. Dr. Monet replaced a retiring chair four years ago whose style was quite different. The former chair added a degree of chaos to department activity. The previous chair believed that he did his best work at the 11th hour, so faculty typically got short-notice requests for information and had to meet crunch deadlines to get proposals and applications in on time. The faculty watched administrative deadlines and helped manage department activity. The switch to Dr. Monet was a welcome relief. Things are done in a timely way without a lot of disruption. The faculty now give their attention to teaching and research.

Dr. Monet possesses strong interpersonal communication skills. She is confident in her ability to converse with every member of the department on an individual basis and takes pride in the fact that everyone likes her. She works hard to show faculty that she supports their activities and recognizes their individual and collective accomplishments. Faculty now look forward to annual performance evaluations, an activity that they once dreaded. Dr. Monet encourages the faculty to express any and all concerns. They talk candidly with the department chair. Often the department chair is the first person that faculty seek when needing to vent frustration.

Meet Dr. Charles Wisneski

Much of the faculty dissatisfaction focuses on Charles Wisneski. Dr. Wisneski is an untenured assistant professor in the department. Dr. Wisneski appears irresponsible to his faculty colleagues who believe that Dr. Wisneski's incompetence results in more work for them. For example, Dr. Wisneski didn't show up to teach on the first day of the current semester, and faculty colleagues had to cover his classes. When Dr. Monet called Charles Wisneski to find out why he did not come to class, he simply said that he didn't know he was teaching that day. In Dr. Wisneski's defense, he typically teaches on Tuesday and Thursday, but this semester he is to teach on Monday, Wednesday, and Friday. Most faculty find it incomprehensible that an assistant professor in his fourth year at the institution would fail to check the schedule of classes to learn the days and times of his courses.

The department coordinates the speaker's series for the college of science. The task of lining up speakers and mailing publicity about the series is one that rotates within the department. When it was Dr. Wisneski's turn to assume this task, he accepted the charge willingly. At the first department meeting in the fall, Dr. Wisneski invited his colleagues to forward ideas for the speaker's series so he could get moving on the year's program. That was the last anyone heard about the speaker's series. It was December before faculty began to inquire when word of the speakers for the current academic year would be available. When Dr. Monet broached the subject with Dr. Wisneski, he replied, "I'm on hold waiting for people to return my calls." When nothing was done by February, the chair asked another faculty member to pick up the task. Dr. Monet worried that the dean might cut the item from the next year's budget if the department failed to spend the resources allocated for the speaker's series.

These and similar instances result in faculty complaint about Dr. Wisneski. Dr. Monet listens patiently and finds that she must agree with the concern. She certainly cannot defend Dr. Wisneski's behavior. It is clear to Dr. Monet that Dr. Wisneski is not endearing himself to his faculty colleagues. From the annual performance evaluation sessions with Dr. Wisneski, Dr. Monet knows that his teaching evaluation ratings are solid but not excellent. Dr. Monet also knows that Dr. Wisneski's publication record is marginal. Typically, assistant professors have at least half a dozen peer-reviewed publications when they apply for tenure and promotion to associate professor. Given Dr. Wisneski's rate of productivity, he may have four or five publications at the close of his tenure probationary period. There is little doubt in Dr. Monet's mind that Dr. Wisneski will receive a negative vote for tenure and promotion.

Dr. Wisneski's Perception
Dr. Wisneski believes that he is making steady progress toward tenure. Each year he meets with Frances Monet and has, in his opinion, a pleasant conversation about his achievements. The sessions present Dr. Wisneski with an opportunity to explain whatever problems he encounters in trying to complete assigned duties. It was at the annual performance evaluation session, for example, that Dr. Wisneski showed the chair the list of possible speakers that he tried to contact. He explained that, as a new assistant professor, he is hesitant to become pushy with established scholars. Dr. Wisneski finds Dr. Monet to be very understanding and supportive. Dr. Wisneski does not sense that Dr. Monet is unhappy with his work. Following every evaluation session, Dr. Wisneski receives a kind letter from Dr. Monet that summarizes the content of their meeting and wishes him continued success.

Dr. Wisneski is unaware of the growing colleague resentment toward him. Since he opted to buy a house in the country, he comes in only on the days that he teaches. Hence, he does not spend a lot of time with other faculty in the department. When on campus, he teaches his classes, holds office hours, and attends committee meetings. That doesn't leave much time for socializing with faculty colleagues. As Dr. Wisneski smiles and greets people in the office lobby or in the corridors, he senses no animosity. Dr. Wisneski has no idea that many of his faculty colleagues report to the department chair when he misses a committee meeting or fails to measure up to their unspoken expectations for him.

Let's Analyze the Case

The biology chair, Dr. Frances Monet, describes her leadership style as "more friend and less boss." This self-assessment suggests that Dr. Monet perceives interpersonal skills as an important leadership trait. The chair also values efficiency and organization. The faculty recognize and applaud her interpersonal and organizational skills. Dr. Monet receives added recognition for these skills because her competence is a great improvement over the way in which the former department chair managed duties and related to the faculty.

The priority that Dr. Monet places on maintaining a friendly relationship with each department member undermines her success. It is important that department chairs cultivate productive interpersonal relationships with department members. Productive work relationships are professional but not necessarily friendly. The goal of maintaining "friendly" relationships with all individuals at all times and through all issues and situations can work against the honest airing of professional disagreements. That appears to be the situation in Case 3.1. Frances Monet's rapport with each faculty member grows out of her demonstrated support for his or her individual activities and accomplishments. The faculty perceive her as supportive of what they do and achieve. The chair uses performance evaluation sessions to review achievements and advise on faculty concerns. A goal to be supportive of faculty work does not ensure a comprehensive evaluation and does not provide a comfortable format to review areas of needed improvement. The chair fails to call attention to shortcomings in Dr. Wisneski's performance that are likely to result in a negative tenure vote. Dr. Wisneski perceives only the chair's warmth and support. He does not realize that his performance is not meeting the department standards for promotion and tenure.

Dr. Monet is also the hub of interpersonal relationships within the department. Because she is so accessible and receptive, the faculty take all matters to her. This places the chair in the middle on some significant issues. Dr. Monet knows how faculty in the department perceive Dr. Wisneski. She also knows that Dr. Wisneski does not sense that he is alienating his faculty colleagues. The faculty are less likely to address conflict among themselves when they believe that the chair knows and understands their individual viewpoints. The faculty who criticize Dr. Wisneski believe that the chair agrees with their assessment. They do not need to confront Dr. Wisneski because the department chair knows what happens and who deserves credit for covering Wisneski's mistakes. Dr. Wisneski believes that the chair understands the reason he was unable to finalize the speaker's series. From Dr. Wisneski's perspective, there is no need to offer an explanation for any failure to colleagues because the department chair understands what happened.

The department chair is not meeting her ethical responsibility for faculty evaluation and development. The chair recognizes that Dr. Wisneski needs to change specific aspects of his performance if he is to satisfy promotion and tenure standards. By not informing Dr. Wisneski of these shortcomings, the chair does not give him a chance to remedy mistakes. A negative tenure vote is likely to surprise Dr. Wisneski who believes that he is making steady progress toward achieving tenure. Further, Dr. Wisneski could grieve (or sue) if denied tenure, claiming that he was never told that his performance did not meet standards. Institutions cannot expect faculty to satisfy unknown performance expectations.

By allowing Dr. Wisneski to continue without proper notification, the department chair cheats the other department faculty. They accept the need to cover work not done by Dr. Wisneski. In the long run this communicates that some faculty are allowed to shirk assigned duties. To some, it may look as if the chair rewards Dr. Wisneski because every time he fails to do his job, he gets less work to do. The faculty may tolerate this in the case of an untenured faculty member knowing that the appointment will terminate after a negative tenure vote. The same practice, however, with a tenured faculty member, who decides to coast and not contribute in the same measure that other colleagues do will undermine the department climate and chair's credibility. The practice of rewarding poor performance by giving the work to someone else communicates inequity that will, in time, breed resentment toward the department chair as well as toward the negligent faculty member.

It's Your Turn

Place yourself in the role of department chair and think through how you would manage Dr. Charles Wisneski and the department faculty's reaction to him.

1. What is the department chair's ethical responsibility to Charles Wisneski? What is the department chair's ethical responsibility to the other faculty? How does the chair's responsibility for faculty performance evaluation relate to the overall welfare of the department? Does the chair demonstrate a moral sensitivity to Dr. Wisneski and the other faculty?

2. How would you handle Dr. Wisneski's failure to arrange the speaker's series? What would you do to help Dr. Wisneski learn and understand performance expectations for achieving tenure? Is it possible to be supportive while making suggestions for improving performance?

3. Does the chair exhibit strong moral character when listening to faculty complaints about Dr. Wisneski? How would you react when other faculty complain about Dr. Wisneski? Would you, for example, assume a neutral posture or promise to correct the problem? Would you encourage other faculty to talk with Dr. Wisneski? What is the chair's ethical responsibility for helping faculty work well together?

Please Consider

If a department chair fails to coach the faculty on performance expectations and fails to work with the faculty on ways to remedy unacceptable behavior, the chair is responsible for the faculty member's poor performance. When department chairs fail to carry out their assigned responsibilities, they frequently assume more liability for department shortcomings. In Case 3.1, the department chair knows but chooses to ignore that Dr. Wisneski believes he is making steady progress toward tenure when in fact he is not. Dr. Monet demonstrates moral sensitivity but no moral judgment, moral motivation, or moral character. It is unethical for the department chair to allow this misperception. Dr. Monet is more comfortable being supportive than confronting or initiating conflict. Yet, unless Dr. Wisneski recognizes and faces the conflict, he cannot possibly remedy his performance.

Conducting performance evaluation sessions with faculty who are not meeting performance expectations can be uncomfortable. Chapter Four of this text contains specific strategies for managing the task. You may want to revisit this case after reviewing the content presented in Chapter Four. For now, consider the chair's failure to communicate the truth to Dr. Wisneski in terms of ethical leadership. The chair's failure to exercise ethical leadership in this instance jeopardizes Charles Wisneski's chances for getting tenure, inconveniences other faculty who assume more work, and increases the institution's liability in the event that Dr. Wisneski should file suit if denied tenure.

Let's Recap

Consider how you would manage the situation described in Case 3.1 If your approach does not exhibit ethical leadership, you may want to review the material presented earlier in this chapter. Does your approach reflect a

- moral sensitivity in interpreting the situation?

- moral judgment, a sense of knowing what is morally right and wrong?

- moral motivation and an appropriate prioritizing of moral values?

- moral character by demonstrating your persistence in pursuing these moral values?

Relevant Communication Concepts and Strategies

Ethical leadership is not something that surfaces only when there is a crisis or obvious moral dilemma. Ethical leadership is an integral part of day-to-day management. Consciously or unconsciously, department members note whether the chair treats all faculty equitably, is accessible to all department members, is consistent in the application of department and university policy, and advances department interests. These observations establish the ground rules for individual behavior within the department. The old saying "Do as I say and not as I do" typifies the loss of credibility that occurs for chairs when faculty believe that a double standard exists.

Department chairs can assess existing department ethics. It is possible to determine whether department members behave ethically in carrying out their responsibilities and what factors induce current behavior. An ethics audit, like a bookkeeping audit, checks the record of current practice for discrepancies. Department chairs can influence the ethical behavior of individual department members by changing the outcome associated with unacceptable behavior. Suppose the department needs faculty to help with student recruitment, but the faculty fail to comply with this expectation. An ethics audit might show, however, that faculty who spend time on recruitment activities receive no recognition while faculty who guard their time more selfishly to do research receive larger merit pay increases. The chair needs to erase this discrepancy by rewarding faculty for work on student recruitment. That is more effective than merely telling department members that they must work on student recruitment when the reward system does not recognize the activity. To conduct an ethics audit, department chairs need to analyze the answers to the following queries.

Are department practices consistent with department and university policy?
Whenever department practice deviates from policy, there is at least the potential for unethical conduct. One possible area for such discrepancy is

the application of promotion and tenure standards. Suppose university standards stress teaching effectiveness as the primary criterion for tenure, but mediocre teaching qualifies for promotion and tenure when it is accompanied by a strong record of published research. Perhaps an excellent teacher is denied tenure because the applicant's record of research is marginal. Those decisions represent significant discrepancies between practice and policy.

The department ethics and chair's credibility suffer when the faculty and staff must follow department and university policy and the chair does not. For example, some department chairs are very careful with the expenditure of university funds. That is particularly important if the university is supported by public dollars. Well-meaning chairs may remind department members that phones should not be used for personal calls or that campus mail is not available for personal business, and other similar actions. These same chairs risk their credibility should they decide to announce a holiday gathering in their home by sending invitations duplicated on office equipment through campus mail. Some department chairs may perceive the examples as insignificant. However, it is not the significance of the activity in terms of resources used as much as the discrepancy in applying university policy equitably to everyone that shapes department ethics. The perception of a double standard whittles away at the department ethics and undermines the chair's credibility.

Are policies applied equitably across all situations and individuals?
Department chairs are sometimes surprised by how individual faculty learn the fate of their colleagues. Even in departments where the faculty don't seem to get along, they know who gets what in the way of assignments and rewards. The perception of fair treatment goes a long way toward establishing good will and trust within a department. A climate of mutual trust is fundamental to department ethics. This cannot exist if the chair does not apply policies equitably across situations and individuals. Most department chairs don't intend to favor one department member over another. Yet situations can develop that prompt an inequitable response. For example, the department and university policy may stipulate effective teaching as a criterion for tenure, but the benchmark for effective teaching may be lower for faculty who secure large sums of external grant funding. Department chairs may not intend to favor faculty who secure grants. Rather, it may be that some chairs are trying to compensate the extra effort that grantsmanship takes by discounting the standard for teaching. Circumstances exist that can prompt the most credible chairs to take action with good reason that others perceive as unfair.

Department chairs may give the impression of favoritism when handling personnel matters. Perhaps one of two department secretaries has an ill mother and requires considerable flexibility in work hours. A genuine effort to help a good employee through a difficult time could pose a problem for the department if the chair's action gives the impression that the secretary is receiving preferential treatment. This does not mean that the department chair needs to turn a deaf ear to the secretary with a real need for a flexible work schedule. It does mean, however, that the department chair cannot accommodate the request for flexible work hours without giving consideration to other secretaries and to faculty whose work needs to be done. It is also important that all department members realize that in the event they had a similar problem the department chair would be as accommodating.

Does the department leadership advance the department welfare over personal gain?

This is particularly acute for department chairs hired from within the department. One important transition for someone moving from the ranks of faculty to the position of department chair is the shift from discipline specialization to being the primary advocate for the total department program. The faculty expect the department chair to be equally knowledgeable about, and committed to, all discipline specializations represented in the department program. Any hint that the department chair uses the authority of the position to bolster the chair's own discipline specialization will win disfavor. The disapproval may not be obvious in that faculty, particularly untenured faculty, may sense the need to avoid voicing their disapproval to preserve a positive working relationship with the chair. Nevertheless, the perceptions of a bias toward the chair's own discipline specialization undermines the department ethics. Even if the chair's specialization is growing and warrants more resources, the decision to redirect funds to the specialization should derive from full department deliberation. The faculty are likely to perceive any unilateral action by the chair as an effort to safeguard the chair's personal interest rather than to pursue the department agenda. This is costly to both the chair and the department ethics.

Do actions uphold individual responsibility?

Ethical behavior must be considered in relation to the responsibilities of one's position. The roles of department chair, faculty, staff, and student all carry specific professional responsibilities. An important component of an ethics audit is to determine whether or not individual actions uphold individual role responsibilities. For example, the department chair is responsible for professional development and making certain that faculty know what is expected for tenure and promotion. Department chairs who duck a difficult performance evaluation session and fail to alert faculty to performance deficiencies are shirking that important responsibility. As the interpreters of campus policy, department chairs cannot assume that faculty understand promotion and tenure standards because they are written in the faculty handbook. One purpose for performance evaluation is to provide an assessment of faculty progress toward promotion and tenure. It is also the chair's responsibility to help new faculty become acclimated to the department. This means helping new hires learn performance expectations and ways to work effectively with faculty colleagues. Failure to help a new hire relate successfully with existing department members is unethical because it shirks this important responsibility. The department chair's leadership is ethical only when the chair performs all assigned responsibilities without abusing the authority of the position.

Do actions evidence respect for colleagues?

The department chair's evenhanded posture toward colleagues is important because failure to exhibit it licenses department members to mirror the differential treatment of colleagues. Department chairs cannot hold grudges, and they cannot exclude difficult faculty from department deliberations for reasons of comfort, convenience, or expediency. Also, chairs cannot allow department members to be nonprofessional in working with one another. Department chairs can, for example, make it clear that derogatory comments about colleagues are not heard or appreciated. If, on the other hand, the department chair makes snide remarks (humorous or otherwise) about individual department members, the chair encourages such destructive behavior in other department members.

Department chairs are never off duty. Even comments made outside the office on weekends continue to represent the chair's opinion. Think how we react when the president of the United States says, "Speaking as a citizen, not the president." Do we really perceive the comment as one made by John Q. Citizen? Often informal comments made outside the workplace are more believable to others. There is the perception that the chair is engaging in candid disclosure when out of office attire. Department members, the dean, and others do not separate the comment from the professional role of the chair. No matter when and where the chair speaks, others assume that the opinion expressed represents all that the chair knows and believes from the perspective of the chair's position.

Does the department chair selectively screen or withhold relevant information?

The old adage "What they don't know won't hurt them" is usually destructive in an academic department. The faculty are less likely to accept that the chair respects them as contributing department members if they believe that the chair does not trust them to have full information. This component of the ethics audit is particularly relevant today as more departments cope with adversity. Faculty become particularly disenchanted if they believe the department chair orchestrates department decisions by presenting partial or skewed information. Department members cannot behave ethically and responsibly if they do not have all of the information relevant to their task.

When department chairs withhold relevant information from department members, they prevent others from taking ownership of the issue and being committed to improving the department's position. Some chairs may decide that there is no point to full disclosure because the facts would confuse the issue. Some chairs might conclude that full information is irrelevant because the department has only a limited number of alternatives. This thinking denies the role of faculty and staff as creative resources for problem solving. The chair loses the advantage of hearing diverse viewpoints regarding important issues. The varied perspectives are likely to culminate in a more judicious review of available alternatives than any single view.

Does good work receive appropriate recognition?

Department chairs have more positive influence on the department when they give credit for department achievements to others. This practice also benefits the department climate if other department members follow the chair's lead in giving credit to colleagues. Rarely can one person honestly take full credit for a completed project. When chairs fail to recognize the efforts of others, they miss an opportunity to demonstrate a sense of fairness and ethical leadership. Worse yet, when department chairs take credit for the work of others, they appear to operate for self-interest. Chairs that do this will have a more difficult time convincing others that they put the welfare of the department ahead of their own personal interests.

Sometimes pressure to assert one's authority as chair or establish one's credibility as a capable chair encourages behavior that may be viewed as taking credit for the work of others. That places the chair's credibility in jeopardy. It is, for example, dangerous for chairs to give untenured faculty the impression that chairs control the tenure vote. Department chairs manage processes over which they have considerable influence but not always absolute control over the outcome. Similarly, letting the dean believe that the chair unilaterally determines the outcome of the department's vote is a mistake. That practice may build in the dean a false expectation for what the chair can guarantee regarding the department's action. It also is likely to get back to the faculty who may be less willing to participate and invest effort in future department matters.

Do department and institutional values make sense to everyone?
Department members cannot practice values that they do not understand. If, for example, the department mission includes a component for area service, it is important that department members have some understanding of that mission. They need to see how their training and expertise might lend itself to service activity. They need to understand how the service activity connects with their other faculty responsibilities. They need to know what types of service activities are valued and rewarded. Department chairs are the primary interpreters of department and university values. Chairs are responsible for making certain that faculty understand department values and recognize how they can contribute to the overall success of the department.

Typically, the institution has a policy on ethical conduct that usually appears in the faculty handbook. Frequently, campus policy on ethical conduct incorporates the Statement on Professional Ethics published in the *American Association of University Professors Policy Documents and Reports* (1990). Department chairs cannot assume that faculty will find, read, and understand the campus policy. It is the chair's responsibility to make certain that faculty are aware of the conduct rules, the expectation that faculty follow them, and the potential consequence to faculty if they do not. In addition, the faculty are subject to a number of laws and regulations regarding sexual harassment, research misconduct, drug-free standards of conduct, and conflict of interest. It is the department chair's responsibility to make certain that the faculty have a working understanding of these policies that govern individual behavior. Chairs who fail to make clear to faculty the expectation that the faculty must comply with both legal and institutional standards of ethical conduct increase the chairs' own as well as the institutions' liability.

Putting Theory Into Practice

We learn more about the biology department chaired by Dr. Frances Monet in Case 3.2, The Written Record. Charles Wisneski is one of two untenured faculty members in the department. The other untenured faculty member, Jonah Martin, does everything right. The contrast between Drs. Wisneski and Martin increases the odds against Dr. Wisneski's bid for tenure. The chair conducts annual performance evaluations of untenured faculty as required by university policy. As you read Case 3.2, consider the effect of the evaluations and whether the chair fulfills her ethical responsibility to the department, the institution, and these untenured faculty.

Case 3.2, The Written Record

There are two untenured assistant professors in the biology department. Both are in their fourth year of a six-year probationary period. We know from the information presented in Case 3.1 that Dr. Wisneski is not making satisfactory progress toward tenure and promotion. The other untenured faculty member is Dr. Jonah Martin.

Meet Dr. Jonah Martin

Jonah Martin is the complete antithesis of Charles Wisneski. He volunteers for extra committee work and conscientiously carries out all assigned tasks. He is proving to be a masterful teacher, and student ratings of his teaching are excellent. Faculty in the department find Dr. Martin a strong and supportive colleague. He is willing to tackle new course assignments, which allows a small group of faculty in the botany subspecialty of the discipline to trade off and team-teach some subjects.

Dr. Martin's work in developing a drought resistant strain of corn is important to area farmers. This is recognized by both the department and the granting agencies that award financial support for Dr. Martin's research. He already has more than the typical number of peer-reviewed publications needed for tenure and promotion to the rank of associate professor. The big worry with Dr. Martin is that other institutions might try to recruit him. Fortunately, Jonah Martin enjoys his colleagues in the biology department. Since his arrival, the department formed a softball team that plays against other departments during the spring and summer months. Last year, at Dr. Martin's suggestion, the department organized a bowling team. Both sport teams are purely recreational and include interested men and women in the department.

Performance Evaluation

Dr. Monet realizes that Dr. Martin's success works to the disadvantage of Dr. Wisneski. Even the few faculty who are more generous in rating colleagues will note the stark contrast between Drs. Wisneski and Martin and be more inclined to vote against Dr. Wisneski. Frances Monet doesn't look forward to the year when both Drs. Wisneski and Martin come up for tenure review. She realizes that Dr. Wisneski doesn't sense that he is in trouble, but she doesn't know what can she do about his inability to tune into the department culture. Dr. Wisneski seems totally unable to read the reactions of his colleagues, and Dr. Monet knows that she cannot control a tenure vote by faculty colleagues. Campus policy dictates that no administrator can overturn a negative tenure vote unless there is clear evidence of discrimination. That would be unlikely since Dr. Monet agrees with what she knows is the general consensus of the department faculty.

This year, Dr. Monet finds herself saying essentially the same things in the follow-up letters that document the performance evaluation sessions with each of the untenured faculty members.

Letter to Dr. Jonah Martin

Dear Jonah:

This letter serves to document that I met with you for the annual performance evaluation required of all untenured faculty. In that meeting we reviewed your achievements for the preceding year. As always, it was a pleasure to talk with you about your teaching, research, and numerous other activities.

It is obvious that you work very hard at teaching and with excellent results. Your student ratings remain good as you tackle new courses each semester. I'm not surprised that students enjoy your courses. Students appreciate the same personable quality that you bring to your colleagues in the department. I'm impressed with your continued progress in research. Congratulations on receiving yet another grant to support your work in developing a drought-resistant corn. You may consider making a presentation on your research as part of the college speaker's series. It is important for other faculty in the college to learn about your work.

Thank you for meeting with me. I wish you every continued success in your work for the coming year.

Sincerely,

Frances Monet
Professor and Chair

Letter to Dr. Charles Wisneski:

Dear Charles:

This letter serves to document that I met with you for the annual performance evaluation required of all untenured faculty. In that meeting we reviewed your achievements for the preceding year. As always, it was a pleasure to talk with you about your teaching, research, and numerous other activities.

It is obvious that you work very hard at teaching. I enjoyed my visit to your class and am confident that you will continue to work hard to provide quality instruction for our students. You made significant progress in research since the performance evaluation of one year ago. It is important that you see your research through to publication. Clearly, your work is in an area that is worth reporting. I regret the problem you had in managing the speaker's series. You contacted individuals who would be topflight speakers, and I cannot explain why they failed to return your telephone calls. I hope that you realize I had no choice but to move ahead with scheduling other speakers. This program is important to all of the faculty in the college.

Thank you for meeting with me. I wish you every continued success in your work for the coming year.

Sincerely,

Frances Monet
Professor and Chair

Let's Analyze the Case

The department chair already dreads the year when both Drs. Wisneski and Martin come up for tenure. The chair can predict the outcome but believes that she is helpless in altering what seems to be inevitable. She knows that the faculty will vote against Charles Wisneski, and campus policy does not allow any administrator to overturn a negative tenure vote unless there is obvious evidence of discrimination. The department chair does not recognize her role in helping faculty understand performance expectations. Interpreting campus policy for faculty is the responsibility of the department chair. The more general campus policy becomes operational at the department level. A campus tenure policy may stipulate that faculty demonstrate effective teaching. The department chair helps the faculty member know what types of evidence provide credible proof of effective teaching to those who will vote on the tenure application. Case 3.2 does not demonstrate that Dr. Monet fulfills this responsibility with either Charles Wisneski or Jonah Martin.

Dr. Monet's evaluation of the untenured faculty reviews only the faculty member's activities for the preceding year. The chair does not evaluate faculty activities in relation to tenure standards so there is no benchmark from which to determine deficiencies. When chairs consider faculty achievements in relation to tenure standards, there is a structure for discussing needed improvements. If the chair offered suggestions for improvement, they are not repeated in the letters documenting the annual performance evaluation. A neutral person reading the letters is likely to conclude that both untenured faculty are making acceptable progress toward tenure. The letter to Dr. Martin does not document his superlative performance, and the letter to Dr. Wisneski does not document the need for improved performance. Dr. Monet uses the same basic letter and alters only the paragraph that references the faculty member's activities. Hence, both letters start and end on the same positive note. This is unethical given that Dr. Monet believes these faculty members will have opposite outcomes in the tenure review process. Notice that both letters end with the chair's wishes for "every continued success." The closing certainly fails to suggest that there is any problem to be remedied.

The department chair exhibits moral sensitivity in that she is able to empathize with the plight of Charles Wisneski. The chair does not, however, exercise good moral judgment when she decides to ignore the suicidal path that Charles Wisneski is pursuing toward tenure review. It is clear that the faculty perceive Charles Wisneski as irresponsible. By not intervening to counsel Charles Wisneski regarding performance deficiencies, the chair actually helps to build a basis for the negative tenure vote. At the same time, the chair removes the opportunity for Dr. Wisneski to become a productive member of the department, which adversely affects all department faculty. By ignoring the obvious problem, the department chair is not being morally sensitive to either the needs of the department faculty or Charles Wisneski.

The chair's moral motivation places a higher priority on her overall rapport with individual faculty than on coaching them to success. The latter requires helping faculty confront deficiencies and offering suggestions for positive change. Those are tough tasks that might threaten the chair's rapport with individual faculty. In terms of the four psychological components that determine moral behavior, the department chair does not exhibit a strong moral character. While she recognizes the problem, she does not have the courage and persistence to implement desired changes that might improve Dr. Wisneski's chances for receiving tenure.

It's Your Turn

Place yourself in the role of the department chair and decide how you would morally fulfill your responsibility to evaluate faculty performance.

1. Do you agree with Dr. Monet's interpretation (moral sensitivity) of the situation? Is the department chair correct in her moral judgment? Is she morally right to remain supportive but allow both Drs. Wisneski and Martin to pursue their individual paths toward tenure review? If not, what is the department chair morally obliged to do?

2. What values should drive the department chair's moral motivation? How would you prioritize the following sets of values: faculty rights versus department need; individual professional development versus department objectives; and friendship versus leadership? Would you place the department's need for productive and successful faculty above the chair's need to maintain a friendly rapport with all department members?

Please Consider

Assume that Dr. Wisneski receives a negative tenure vote. He decides to grieve the outcome, claiming that he was never informed that his performance was in any way inadequate. Dr. Wisneski argues in his grievance that the chair praised his work and caused him to believe that he was making acceptable progress toward tenure. Given the chair's counsel, Dr. Wisneski argues that the faculty vote against his tenure is evidence of discrimination. Assume the role of the department chair and think through how you would respond to the grievance.

1. What is your ethical responsibility to the department in responding to the grievance filed by Dr. Wisneski? Do you have an ethical responsibility to Dr. Wisneski? Will the record document that you satisfied your ethical responsibility to Dr. Wisneski and your responsibility for faculty evaluation?

2. What is your ethical responsibility to the institution? Is the department leadership exercising the authority entrusted by the central administration? Is the department leadership satisfying the responsibility delegated by the central administration? What would you do differently?

Let's Recap

Take a moment and review the department ethics presented in Cases 3.1 and 3.2. Consider whether your approach would cultivate a more professional and productive definition of department ethics. If not, you may want to review the material presented earlier in this chapter on those factors that shape department ethics. Does your approach

- employ department practices that are consistent with department and university policy?

- apply policies equitably across all situations and individuals?

- advance the department's welfare over personal gain?

- uphold individual responsibility?

- evidence a respect for colleagues?

- selectively screen or withhold relevant information?

- give appropriate credit for good work?

- clarify department and institutional values?

Putting Theory Into Practice

Case 3.3, Reward or Punishment, explores the ethics of a political science department on two levels. First, the case discloses the chair's management of the merit pay review process. Second, the case describes how faculty tend to view and treat one specific department member. Given that ethical behavior requires department members to fulfill the responsibilities of their positions without abusing their authority, consider whether the faculty and the department chair behave ethically as you read Case 3.3.

Case 3.3, Reward or Punishment

Margaret Ingram, chair of the political science department, is dreading July 1. That is the date by which she needs to inform faculty of their salary increases for the coming fiscal and academic year. The state awarded an average salary increase of 2%, and Ingram knows that many faculty will be unhappy with their salary increases. In reality, a 2% salary increase is more problematic for Ingram than a zero salary increase.

The small pool of salary increase dollars must also cover awards for those faculty receiving promotions. The salary increase is $100 per month for promotion to assistant professor, $150 per month for promotion to associate professor, and $300 per month for promotion to full professor. In addition, the college dean uses 0.5% of the total salary increase dollars to make equity and market adjustments throughout the college as she deems appropriate. There is no guarantee that faculty in the political science department will receive any of the equity or market adjustments made at the college level.

The salary increase dollars received by Margaret Ingram for distribution among the political science faculty is roughly 1% of the department's faculty salary base. Campus policy requires that chairs distribute all salary increase dollars on the basis of merit. Consequently, Ingram's directive is to award all salary increase dollars only to faculty deserving merit.

Department Merit Plan

Four years ago when the central administration mandated that all salary increases be awarded on the basis of merit, it required each department to devise a plan for the distribution of merit. Faculty in the political science department drafted a statement stipulating performance standards and expectations for faculty work in the areas of teaching, research, and service. The procedures approved by the department faculty request individual faculty to submit a statement summarizing achievements for the preceding year. Each year the department faculty vote to elect five faculty to serve on the department personnel committee. The personnel committee reviews faculty achievement reports independently and rates each faculty member on the following scale: 0 (no merit), 1 (low merit), 2 (medium merit), and 3 (high merit). The department procedures stipulate that the recommendation of the personnel committee is advisory to the department chair, who makes the final recommendation with regard to faculty merit to the dean.

Chair Ingram's Recommendation

Margaret Ingram is not fully satisfied with the department's merit plan. The elaborate procedure does not satisfy the faculty, nor does it provide the chair with a comfortable rationale when explaining merit recommendations to individual faculty. Ingram cannot remember a year in which she didn't have several faculty complain about their merit rating and dollar increase.

For starters, there is a problem of rater reliability. While the department policy carefully details the standards for evaluating faculty work in the areas of teaching, research, and service, the plan offers no guidelines for how the members of the personnel committee should weight the various achievements. It is obvious in looking at the ratings submitted by the personnel committee members that everyone applies the standards in a different way.

Members of the personnel committee hold different perceptions of the importance and significance of specific activities. For example, a peer-reviewed publication in a national journal may impress some committee members but may be viewed by others on the committee as covering a topic that is not central to the discipline. Consequently, it is not uncommon for a faculty member to receive scores that range the full breadth of the merit scale. A faculty member might receive from the five members of the personnel committee, one "0," one "1," two "2's," and one "3." While this concerns Ingram, she doesn't believe that it is worth raising the issue with the faculty since the dollars assigned for merit increase are so small.

Margaret Ingram computes the average of the personnel committee scores to determine the final merit rating for each faculty member. Each year she reminds the faculty that she never disagrees with the outcome of committee's deliberation. Although the policy gives Ingram the responsibility for making final merit pay recommendations, she never varies her recommendation from the collective average of the personnel committee ratings. Dr. Ingram prefers to stand behind what she terms the "collective wisdom of the committee" than assert her personal rating as final, even though she frequently finds the averaged committee scores to be different from what she would recommend.

It is often difficult, however, to explain to disillusioned faculty why they receive particular merit ratings that represent the average of individual scores. There are instances when Ingram believes that the personnel committee ratings may not be objective. This is the case with Lance Richards, a full professor in the department of political science. Lance is a prolific writer with a strong international reputation as a scholar in the discipline. Yet, he typically receives below-average merit recommendations. This year, for example, the committee average resulted in a merit rating of 1.2 for Dr. Richards which translates into a 0.5% salary increase. The chair is certain that this outcome will anger Lance Richards.

Ingram isn't certain why the members of the personnel committee rate the achievements of Dr. Richards so low. Richards, a 15-year veteran of the department, is not friendly with his faculty colleagues. He is, nevertheless, extremely productive. His achievement report for the past year listed a new book, several peer-reviewed journal articles in national and international publications, strong teaching evaluations, another research grant, and the typical service portfolio of department and campus committees. In addition, Dr. Richards serves as editor for one of the more prestigious journals in the discipline. Dr. Richards is well aware of his strong reputation in the discipline and has an interpersonal manner that suggests he believes he is superior to his faculty colleagues. On occasion, Ingram hears remarks that suggest that some faculty believe Richards makes a lot of money from book royalties and consulting activities so, in their minds, he doesn't "need" a raise. Nevertheless, Ingram cannot deny that Lance Richards's accomplishments warrant more than a 1.2 merit rating. Ingram is certain that Dr. Richards will voice his dissatisfaction as soon as he receives word of the salary increase.

Let's Analyze the Case

The political science department has a merit pay review plan that displeases many department members. The department chair finds that the "elaborate procedure" fails to provide her with a comfortable rationale when explaining merit recommendations to individual faculty. Each year several faculty complain about the merit rating that they receive. The merit rating is the average of individual scores awarded independently by elected members of the department personnel committee. The outcome of the merit pay review is especially problematic for the department chair in the instance of Dr. Lance Richards, one of the department's more prolific scholars.

The chair's critique of the department merit plan demonstrates her moral sensitivity to the faculty who complain. The chair recognizes that the merit rating derived from the mathematical average of committee scores often varies from her personal assessment. There is little rater reliability among the elected personnel committee members who hold different values for the specific achievements of faculty. Hence, merit is not assigned equitably across all activities. The discrepancy results in a merit rating that does not correlate with achievement. Thus, the department practice is inconsistent with campus policy to award salary increases on the basis of merit.

Department values do not make sense to everyone. If everyone held a common understanding of those activities that have the greatest value to the department, there would be greater rater reliably in judging individual achievements. The department merit plan requires faculty to submit a list of achievements for the preceding year. The plan, however, does not prioritize faculty activities from a department perspective. As a result, the personnel committee members prioritize activities and assign values to faculty achievement based on personal values.

The department chair suspects that personal bias may result in some unfair ratings. The chair speculates that Dr. Richards's arrogance may cause colleagues to devalue his achievements. She also believes that some may be jealous of the extra money that Dr. Richards earns through consulting and book royalties. Clearly, the personnel committee members should not award Dr. Richards's merit rating on the basis of his personality or added income. If the department chair is correct in her speculation, then there is no clearly defined ethical standard for the personnel committee in completing this task. The committee members do not know how to assign value to specific achievements and do not understand that the merit rating is to be based on accomplishments rather than other more personal factors.

As the interpreter of university policy and the architect of department ethics, it is the department chair's responsibility to ensure that the department plan is consistent with university policy. It is also the department chair's responsibility to establish the parameters for ethical behavior in carrying out department business. Margaret Ingram, instead, views her task as computing the average of personnel committee scores. Dr. Ingram's moral motivation places a greater value on accepting and preserving what she terms the "collective wisdom" of the personnel committee than on ensuring that the committee members rate faculty achievements ethically from a department perspective.

It's Your Turn

Place yourself in the role of the department chair and think through how you would manage this situation.

1. Who has ethical responsibility for making merit pay recommendations? Is the department chair morally right to accept the average of committee scores as her merit rating for individual faculty?

2. What steps would you take to make the department merit plan consistent with university policy? What measures would you take to ensure that the department merit plan results in awarding salary increases on the basis of merit? Would you, for example, work with the personnel committee to develop a common orientation from which they evaluate individual achievements?

Please Consider

Margaret Ingram is more comfortable accepting the collective wisdom of the personnel committee than asserting her own assessment of faculty merit. Administrators at all levels of the university sometimes refer matters to committee. Used ethically, committee input serves a valuable purpose. Committees offer a fresh perspective on an issue. They also bring a variety of perspectives to bear on a problem. This can be useful information to an administrator in that committee deliberation can prevent premature closure on an issue. Committee deliberation guarantees a more comprehensive discussion of the issue than is likely to occur when an administrator makes a unilateral decision or seeks only the reaction of staff.

Sometimes administrators do not use committees ethically. Committees cannot free administrators from their assigned responsibilities. In Case 3.3, Margaret Ingram does not absolve herself from the responsibility to make merit pay recommendations by accepting the collective wisdom of the committee. Rather, Dr. Ingram makes the committee average her merit rating. This is particularly dangerous since Margaret Ingram has admitted that she cannot explain or defend the averaged merit ratings. The department chair trades her personal assessment that she can explain for one that she cannot explain. By using the committee average as the merit rating, the department chair sacrifices her credibility. She does not assume, without abuse, the responsibility assigned to her. She ducks the responsibility and, therefore, demonstrates a lack of ethical leadership.

It generally shows a lack of moral character to hide behind a committee's voice. In the face of difficult issues without easy answers, administrators may refer to a committee such important matters as deciding how to cut the budget or how to award salary increase dollars. While department members should participate in those decisions, the committee recommendation cannot free administrators from their responsibility. The faculty sense when the department chair uses a committee for an unethical purpose. The practice will anger most faculty.

Putting Theory Into Practice

We know from Case 3.3 that Margaret Ingram finds the department merit pay plan problematic. She expects a number of faculty complaints. Dr. Ingram finds it especially difficult to explain the merit evaluation outcome to Lance Richards, one of the department's most prolific scholars. In the instance of Dr. Richards, the department chair suspects that some members of the personnel committee may submit a biased and unfair rating. In Case 3.4, The Reaction, we observe the department chair's conversation with Dr. Richards. Pay attention to how the department chair assumes (or refuses) responsibility for the merit pay evaluation.

Case 3.4, The Reaction

As predicted, Lance Richards wants to talk about his merit rating and salary increase. Unlike previous years, this time Dr. Richards scheduled an appointment. In the past, he typically stopped in to vent his complaint as soon as he read the chair's letter. Dr. Richards made the appointment one full week after the chair mailed the letters announcing salary increases. Margaret Ingram hopes that the extra time will make the discussion with Lance more congenial. As Ingram waits for Lance Richards to arrive, she reviews the file of faculty achievement reports and double-checks her calculations of the merit ratings. Richards received ratings of 3, 0, 1, 1, and 1 from the five personnel committee members, which makes his merit rating 1.2. The chair takes solace in thinking that Dr. Richards does not see the achievement reports submitted by his colleagues.

The Meeting

Ingram is deep in thought when Richards knocks on the door. Before sitting down, Richards launches into the reason for his visit. "Well, I'm sure you know why I'm here. I want to know why you gave me such a low merit recommendation." Richards proceeds to take out a pen and paper with an obvious gesture that he intends to record his chair's response.

Ingram: "Now Lance, you know that the recommendation comes from the personnel committee's evaluation of your achievements. It's not my personal assessment of your work."

Richards (responding in a curt manner that evidences his annoyance): "We've discussed this before. The policy makes perfectly clear that the personnel committee's ranking is advisory only. You make the final recommendation regarding faculty merit pay increases."

Ingram: "I know, but the dollar amount that the department received for salary increases is so small that it is not worth making major adjustments in the committee recommendation."

Richards: "Are you saying that it would take a major adjustment to move the merit pay recommendation from the committee closer to the one you would give me?"

Ingram (sitting up taller in her chair): "Don't put words in my mouth. Instead, you might find it helpful to reflect on how your faculty colleagues perceive you."

Richards: "This is not a personality contest. The central administration directed that departments award salary increases on the basis of merit, and my record of achievement speaks for itself. Name one other person in this department who published a book last year or who serves as editor of the best journal in our discipline."

Ingram: "The best journal? That is exactly the attitude I'm talking about. Frankly, I can see why some of your faculty colleagues do not value your achievements as much as you believe they should."

Richards: "What do you mean?"

Ingram: "Well, you isolate yourself and exhibit an air of superiority. You rarely communicate with your faculty colleagues. Consequently, your colleagues don't know you or hear your discipline voice."

Richards: "My discipline voice! I'm published in every major journal. I'm also one of a very few in this department whose work is accepted, read, and valued in other disciplines. Who else in this department publishes in prestigious law review journals? They can read my contribution to the discipline."

Ingram: "Well, that may explain the lower evaluation of your achievements. You tend to publish in international and national journals that are not widely read by all the faculty in our department. Your research in political science is interdisciplinary in nature and, consequently, some of your colleagues may not perceive your work as mainstream."

Richards: "You mean that I'm punished for developing a scholarly reputation that takes me beyond our discipline and makes our discipline useful to theorists and practitioners in other fields?"

Ingram: "It's difficult to say. As you know, the members of the personnel committee vote without supplying reasons and submit their ratings to me anonymously. I'm really just trying to help you understand the rationale that may be present in the minds of the personnel committee members when they assign your merit rating."

Richards: "Are you saying that if I published only in mainstream political science journals, they would rate me higher?"

Ingram: "Of course, I can't guarantee that. I'm merely trying to help you understand what factors may influence the committee's merit evaluation of your work."

Richards: "Yes, and none of the factors you mentioned are listed as criteria for determining faculty merit. This is not fair."

Ingram: "Let's keep all of this in perspective. After central administration took off money for promotional increases and equity adjustments, the department only got 1% of its salary base for the total increase pool. Is that paltry sum of money worth all this excitement? You're still the highest paid faculty member in this department."

Richards (acting more outraged): "What? Now you're telling me that merit is awarded based on current salary levels and that for some reason higher-paid faculty shouldn't receive merit for their accomplishments."

Ingram: "Of course not. You're putting words in my mouth again. I wish I could give everyone in this unit a substantial increase."

Richards: "You're kidding. Surely you don't believe that we all have comparable achievements for the past year. How can you possibly believe that we all deserve the same merit increase? Pull out the achievement reports and let's see if anyone comes close to my record for the past year."

Ingram: "You know that I cannot show you the achievement reports submitted by other faculty."

Richards: "I don't know that. Last week I learned that campus policy stipulates that employees of this institution are entitled to see all documents that affect their personnel status at the university. My attorney believes that the achievement reports used by you to determine my merit rating is information that I can request."

Ingram (trying not to overreact to Richards's mention of meeting with an attorney): "I keep reminding you that it is not my rating, but the committee's rating."

Richards: "And I keep reminding you that department policy makes clear the committee only offers advice and you make the merit recommendation to the dean."

Ingram (moving to terminate the meeting): "This is getting us nowhere. You just don't understand. I do hope that you'll at least think about what I've said. Please consider how small the salary increase pool is this year. Even if you got a 3.0 merit rating, you would not get a large salary increase. Personally, I can't believe that you want to spend this much time and energy on such a trivial matter."

Let's Analyze the Case

Margaret Ingram is not willing to claim the merit rating as her own assessment of Lance Richards's achievement. The department chair becomes defensive early in the conversation when Dr. Richards states that he wants to hear why Dr. Ingram gave him such a low merit recommendation. Lance Richards is unwilling to allow the department chair to shift responsibility for the low merit rating to the committee. The department chair digs in deeper when she admits that her personal assessment is different from the committee average. At this point, Dr. Richards has the basis for a grievance.

The department chair attempts to change the issue by pointing out that the salary increase is so small that it is not worth getting upset. She also suggests that Dr. Richards give some thought to why his colleagues assign him low merit ratings. This response shifts the focus of discussion, but it also raises another issue that Dr. Richards can grieve. The department chair suggests that the personnel committee members rate Dr. Richards on criteria other than those stipulated for merit pay review. This is a serious admission, particularly since Dr. Ingram has no proof. If Dr. Richards discovers that the chair believes he receives low merit ratings for reasons other than his record of achievement, he has a basis to grieve the decision.

The department chair, unable to explain or defend the low merit rating, gets pushed into offering still other possible reasons for the committee action. The department chair suggests that Lance Richards's colleagues don't hear his "discipline voice" because Richards opts to isolate himself from department activity. The chair suggests that he publishes in journals that may not be read by many of the department faculty. It is a legitimate merit criterion if the department merit plan stipulates that publications in certain journals count more than articles in other journals. Even Dr. Richards's tendency to isolate himself from activity can be a legitimate merit criterion if he fails to engage in the types of department activity listed in the merit plan.

The last straw for Richards comes when the chair suggests that he shouldn't be upset over his salary increase because he is the highest paid faculty member in the department. This certainly deviates from campus policy for awarding salary increases on the basis of merit only. It becomes another issue that Lance Richards can grieve. Merit is relative, however, so it is important to know how Dr. Richards's achievements compare with those of other faculty. It came as a surprise to the department chair that Dr. Richards consulted an attorney and learned that campus policy may allow him to review the achievement reports submitted by the other department faculty. The chair believes that those documents are confidential.

The department chair brings the meeting to a close without resolving the issue. The conversation is likely to spur Lance Richards into taking further action. There is nothing in the conversation that provides a satisfactory answer to Dr. Richards's opening query. He never receives an explanation of why the department chair gave him such a low merit rating. Further, the chair's closing comments may feed Lance's anger. Dr. Richards is likely to take offense at being told he does not understand the situation and that this is a "trivial" matter.

It's Your Turn

Place yourself in the role of the department chair and decide how you would handle the conversation. Review the dialogue in Case 3.4 and underline the chair comments that you would change.

1. How would you demonstrate your moral sensitivity for Lance Richards's concern? What is your ethical responsibility to Lance Richards? Is Dr. Richards within his rights to question the merit review process and his merit rating?

2. Would you assume responsibility for the merit rating? If yes, what criteria would you offer for the 1.2 merit rating awarded to Lance Richards? If no, how would you explain the outcome? What is your ethical responsibility to the personnel committee?

3. Would you take any action following the conversation with Lance Richards? Would you alert the dean to the issue? Would you work with the department faculty to revise the merit plan? Would you implement orientation sessions or other clarifying mechanisms that would improve rater reliability among personnel committee members in future years? Would you contact the university legal counsel?

Let's Recap

Department chairs define department ethics through their own behavior and by encouraging moral behavior in others. Ethical leadership requires that department chairs assume full responsibility for their assigned duties without abusing the power of their position. When department chairs shirk or attempt to pass off assigned responsibilities, they sacrifice personal credibility and damage department ethics. To practice ethical leadership, department chairs must exhibit moral sensitivity, exercise moral judgment plus sound moral motivation, and demonstrate strong moral character. To define department ethics, department chairs must encourage those same psychological components in others.

A logical starting point for department chairs seeking to define (or redefine) department ethics is to do an ethics audit of the department. The ethics audit allows department chairs to locate the source of unethical conduct and improve department ethics. Chairs can conduct an ethics audit by asking the following questions:

• Are department practices consistent with department and university policy?

- Are policies applied equitably across all situations and individuals?
- Does the department leadership advance the department welfare over personal gain?
- Do actions uphold individual responsibility?
- Do actions evidence a respect for colleagues?
- Does the department leadership selectively screen or withhold relevant information?
- Does good work receive appropriate recognition?
- Do the department and institutional values make sense to everyone?

Department chairs benefit from the existence of clearly defined department ethics. When boundaries for ethical behavior are understood by all department members, the faculty behave professionally, which, in turn, facilitates effective leadership.

PART TWO

WORKING WITH FACULTY

In this section of the text, special emphasis is given to the interpersonal communication skills that department chairs need to work effectively with faculty and staff. Theoretical concepts and guidelines for effective communication are described in relation to three of the more difficult, but essential, tasks performed by department chairs: conducting performance counseling, managing conflict, and implementing change

Chapter 4: Conducting Performance Counseling
>   offers strategies for evaluating the performance of both tenured and untenured faculty

Chapter 5: Managing Conflict
>   includes information for making conflict management more comfortable and constructive

Chapter 6: Implementing Change
>   contains information about essential preconditions to change and describes communication strategies that help chairs to manage change more effectively

4

CONDUCTING PERFORMANCE COUNSELING

Performance counseling is an important task that is uncomfortable for many department chairs. Campus policy often mandates formal performance evaluation of at least untenured faculty in tenure-track positions. The purpose of the evaluations is to give untenured faculty some indication as to how their achievements measure against the promotion and tenure standards of the academic unit and the institution. At institutions where chairs conduct formal performance evaluations of all faculty, the purpose is to facilitate professional development of individual faculty. While most department chairs support the intended purpose of formal performance evaluation, the task of sitting down face-to-face with a faculty member for the purpose of evaluating that person's performance is an encounter that may be difficult and uncomfortable.

The discomfort experienced by department chairs when they find themselves placed in the position of evaluator is understandable for two reasons. First, department chairs find themselves "criticizing" a faculty colleague. For this reason, the task of conducting performance counseling sessions can be even more difficult for chairs who were promoted from within their home institutions. A department chair may think, "But we started here together. How can I criticize John? He's always been so supportive of me."

Second, there is the natural fear of confrontation. This apprehension is particularly present in department chairs who view performance evaluation as the process by which they must deliver bad news. Some chairs find performance evaluation comfortable, and even enjoyable, in those instances when faculty do not need to improve their performance but abhor the process when they must tell faculty that they are not meeting performance expectations. Chairs often expect faculty to become defensive, which is likely to lead to an uncomfortable confrontation.

The Objective

One goal of this chapter is to modify how department chairs perceive the task of conducting performance counseling sessions. Chairs need to recognize that performance counseling is an opportunity. It is a task that can accrue tangible benefits for the chair, individual faculty, and the department. When department chairs alter how they perceive their role and responsibility relative to performance evaluation, they become more comfortable with the task of conducting face-to-face performance counseling sessions. A second goal is to equip chairs with some specific communication strategies for conducting face-to-face performance counseling sessions. These strategies should help chairs become more comfortable and effective in fulfilling their responsibility for performance evaluation.

Defining the Task

The term performance counseling is more appropriate than performance evaluation because it describes the chair's role with a positive connotation. Department chairs who dread the task of "criticizing" faculty will be more comfortable with the notion of "coaching" faculty for success. Shifting the department chair's role from judge to coach makes the task of conducting face-to-face performance counseling sessions with individual faculty more comfortable for both the chair and the faculty. It helps to remember that performance counseling includes positive as well as negative elements. Too often, department chairs become focused on what needs to improve, and that makes the process of discussing faculty performance more difficult. Effective performance counseling reinforces those things that are being done effectively and offers suggestions for further improvement.

Performance counseling offers department chairs a vehicle for improving faculty performance. Through performance counseling, department chairs help to set the agenda for success. It also supplies a format for chairs and individual faculty to iron out role expectations by providing an opportunity to reinforce the specific expectations for faculty performance and to clarify what department support may be available. Further, it offers an opportunity to clarify the standards and expectations for promotion and tenure review. When the faculty understand the performance expectations and the boundaries for department support, they are better able to assess their own progress toward tenure and promotion. This serves to minimize grievances because faculty are less prone to grieve a personnel decision when it is predictable and consistent with their understanding of performance expectations.

Performance counseling also creates an opportunity for department chairs to build their credibility with individual faculty. No other single activity offers a better vehicle for demonstrating trust, support, and concern for faculty welfare. Through performance counseling, chairs can demonstrate their genuine desire to see faculty succeed. Effective performance counseling can help to establish a healthy department climate that is characterized by open and honest communication. The performance counseling session is a structured opportunity for opening the channels of communication in a constructive way. When the chairs and faculty engage in candid and professional discussions about faculty performance, they have a rapport that allows them to discuss other difficult issues.

Relevant Communication Concepts and Strategies

Unfortunately, these benefits are not guaranteed by merely conducting (or living through) performance counseling sessions. Department chairs need to know how to conduct performance counseling sessions so they realize a constructive outcome. The following strategies (Higgerson, 1994, 1995a) will help department chairs make performance counseling a positive and constructive activity.

Make performance counseling a year-round (not yearly) activity

By making performance counseling a year-round activity, department chairs can reduce the anxiety typically associated with an annual formal performance evaluation session. The more often faculty hear constructive evaluative comments regarding their performance, the less anxious they are about performance evaluation. Department chairs do not need to wait for the annual performance evaluation session in order to offer evaluative comment on faculty work. Imagine how much more comfortable both the chair and the faculty member become when the focus for evaluative comments is on helping that member succeed. By increasing the frequency of evaluation, it is easier for a department chair to keep performance counseling in a "coaching" mode. It is much harder to shed the role of "judge" or "critic" if once each year the department chair summons the faculty to a formal evaluation session and it is the only time in which they hear evaluative comments about their job performance.

Offer both formal and informal evaluations of job performance

Department chairs do not need a formally scheduled meeting in order to offer comments as to what is going right or what might be tried differently. As educators, we know that evaluative comments have more meaning if they are given in the context of the activity being observed. One chair, obviously proud of his organizational skills, explained, "I have a file for every faculty member in the department. Whenever I note some special accomplishment like a newly published article, I put a notation in that faculty member's file so I'll be sure to comment about it during the next annual performance evaluation session." Delayed praise is rarely effective. In the same manner, constructive suggestions for improved performance have less impact if the chair withholds them until the annual performance evaluation session. The faculty need both formal and informal evaluative comments on their performance. If the chair holds all informal comments until the annual meeting, the chair misses an opportunity for sustained and continuous performance evaluation that facilitates faculty development.

At the same time, evaluative comments made by the department chair can have an impact whenever and wherever they are made. Department chairs are never off duty. This fact was painfully illustrated during a department reaccreditation visit. The chair and all department faculty were meeting with the accreditation team. The department had lost several faculty positions, and the department needed to determine how to offer a quality program with the remaining faculty. The discussion was both candid and constructive. At one point, the department chair lamented, "If only we had someone who was qualified to teach the core methods course." As it happened, there was a faculty member teaching the core methods course. That person was the department's most junior (and untenured) faculty member. The person had accepted the assignment in order to help the department. Imagine how the faculty member felt on hearing the department chair make that evaluative comment in front of all the faculty colleagues and the accreditation team members. The department chair did appreciate the effort being made by the new faculty member to cover a course that required extra preparation because it was peripheral to the faculty member's teaching expertise. In fact, the department chair probably rewarded the faculty member on the next merit evaluation for making this generous and significant contribution to the department. Nevertheless, the evaluative comment made in the context of reaccreditation review had a negative connotation. Department chairs need to realize that they are never off duty, and both formal and informal evaluative comments will carry across various specific contexts.

Make job performance expectations clear

Department chairs must make certain that the faculty member understands job performance expectations before evaluating his or her work. The university standard for tenure may require "a record of peer-reviewed research." At the department level, the chair must help the faculty translate that more general standard into meaningful activities. For music faculty, peer-reviewed research may encompass reviews of performance. For radio and television faculty, it may include the selection of an original video for airing on national public television. For art and design faculty, the standard may include work accepted by jury for a national exhibit.

Faculty are more likely to become frustrated and fail when they do not know or understand the specific performance expectations that they must meet. For example, some untenured faculty accept so many committee assignments that they are unable to invest the needed amount of time in teaching and research activities. An important part of understanding performance expectations is learning the balance that faculty need to preserve among their various assigned duties. In face-to-face performance counseling sessions, the department chair can make certain that the faculty understand performance expectations and how best to invest their time.

Make performance goals specific and manageable

Performance counseling will be more effective if both the evaluative comments and the performance goals are specific and manageable. Avoid such comments as:

A. "You don't care about the department."

B. "You must work harder at teaching."

The statements offer no specific direction as to what performance goals faculty need to achieve. A faculty member could earnestly "care more" about the department or "work harder" at teaching and still fall short of the mark. The following comments are more helpful because they suggest specific and manageable performance goals:

A. "You are expected to participate in department governance by attending department meetings and serving on at least one committee each academic year."

B. "Prepare and distribute a course syllabus at the beginning of the term that informs students of the course objectives and grading criteria."

Those statements tell faculty what specific tasks demonstrate that they "care more" about the department or are "working harder" at teaching. Chairs miss the purpose of effective performance counseling when they end a performance counseling session with the following thoughts:

A. "He knows that I'm not pleased with his work."

B. "I made it clear that things have to change or she won't get tenure."

It's more important for the faculty to know what they need to do in very specific terms than to know merely that the department chair is displeased or that they are somehow missing the standard for tenure and promotion. The faculty cannot improve job performance unless they understand exactly what is expected and how to meet those performance standards.

Focus evaluative comments on a person's performance, not on a person's personality

There is a significant difference between the following two statements made by department chairs during faculty evaluation:

A. "You are totally insensitive to students."

B. "Students respond best to teachers who monitor their progress closely and provide frequent feedback regarding their academic performance."

The first statement is a personalized comment. It is more likely to increase a faculty member's defensiveness. It is also less informative because it does not help the faculty member know how to remedy performance that is unacceptable or inadequate. The second statement is directed at performance characteristics and not the faculty member's personality. Further, this statement implies that the chair making the comment believes that the faculty member has the ability to improve the performance outcome. The statement is less likely to increase defensiveness on the part of the faculty member and is more likely to result in positive change.

Link evaluative comments to specific examples

It is important that the criteria for evaluation be clear and consistent. The criteria need to be clear in order for faculty to understand what they must do. Remember the old joke where two faculty are talking about their prospects for getting tenure and one says to the other, "I know that you've got excellent student ratings on your teaching, a substantial list of publications, and served on every important committee on campus, but are you sure that the dean likes you?" This joke evidences why it is important for criteria regarding performance evaluation to be clear. If the criteria are unclear, faculty become frustrated because they can never be certain of the rules for success. This breeds an unhealthy department climate. It also reduces the trust that faculty have in the chair's ability to know and explain the criteria for tenure and promotion.

It is important that department chairs apply the criteria consistently across all faculty. To the extent that faculty have similar job descriptions, the criteria must be consistently applied across all faculty. If teaching effectiveness is considered absolutely essential for a positive recommendation on tenure, it cannot become less essential in the case of a faculty member who is extremely successful in securing external grant dollars. Such inconsistency in performance evaluation is very costly to the department climate and faculty morale. Chairs lose credibility with faculty when there is a perception of favoritism or inconsistent application of standards across all faculty. It does not mean that chairs cannot change performance criteria. A department seeking to revitalize instructional quality at the undergraduate level may want to alter the criteria used to evaluate teaching effectiveness. The chair must communicate and apply the changes clearly and consistently to all faculty.

Incorporate self-evaluation and goal setting

The faculty must participate in the evaluation of their performance and in setting their performance goals in order to have a commitment to achieving them. The chair might ask a faculty member to bring a written goal statement to the evaluation session. A faculty goal statement lets the chair know whether that person understands job performance expectations. Chairs might also require the faculty to prepare written self-evaluations of achievements and performance. This exercise typically reveals if faculty are able to assess their performance relative to the standards for promotion and tenure. Most chairs find it easier to offer evaluative comment on items initially raised by the faculty member. That allows faculty to be more in control of their own professional advancement. It also serves to reinforce the faculty's understanding of performance expectations and enables the department chair to make certain that the faculty have a realistic and manageable plan for achieving performance goals.

Offer specific suggestions for improvement

In an effective performance counseling session, the chair not only identifies areas of needed improvement but offers specific suggestions for how the faculty member can succeed. Phrases such as "have you tried..." or "what would happen if you..." are needed in order to move the performance counseling session from evaluation to remedy. Suppose a faculty member receives low student ratings on the following two items: makes criteria for grading clear and grades fairly. Those data might prompt the following evaluative comments from the department chair:

A. "You've got to explain your grading system to students."

B. "Be certain that students understand the criteria for assigning grades."

C. "How do you inform students about the grading criteria for the course?" Depending upon the faculty member's reply, the chair might add: "Are there other ways and times that you might repeat or emphasize this information?"

Comment A assumes that the instructor has not explained grading criteria. The statement invites the most defensive response from the faculty member. Comment B implies that the chair believes the instructor does inform students of the grading criteria, but the information is not clear. While this statement does not assign blame to the instructor, it does little to help the faculty member remedy the situation. Comment C begins by asking the faculty member to describe the current practice. It allows the chair to follow up with specific suggestions that are relevant to the particular situation. This comment is the most constructive one. It is also the one that best demonstrates the chair's genuine interest in having the instructor succeed.

Department chairs need to listen carefully to faculty responses during performance counseling sessions. Does the faculty member understand what is being suggested? Does the faculty member appear skeptical of the suggestions? Is the faculty member committed to trying alternative methods? Answers to these and similar questions let the chair know whether the faculty member accepts and understands suggestions for improvement. Job performance will not improve unless the faculty member understands what to do and agrees to implement suggestions.

Establish a time frame for achieving goals

Set a date for reviewing progress. A time frame establishes an expectation for continued performance counseling, which helps to keep performance evaluation in a coaching mode. The time frame should be realistic in terms of the remedy being tried but need not necessarily follow campus policy that may prescribe when performance evaluations should take place. A campus policy that requires a department chair to evaluate faculty performance each spring does not prevent the department chair from setting up other meetings during the year for the purpose of reviewing progress on specific aspects of that performance. For example, if a new faculty member is having difficulty getting acceptable student ratings on teaching, the department chair may schedule a meeting to discuss the newest set of student ratings at the close of each semester.

Recognize and reward positive achievement

Most department chairs recognize the value of rewarding faculty when they satisfy performance expectations. Despite the commonsense logic in this prescription, it is not always easy for department chairs to recognize and reward positive achievement. A faculty member may satisfy every performance expectation and still receive only an average or a below-average merit rating when his or her productivity is compared with the annual productivity of colleagues. It is particularly difficult when budget appropriations result in a salary increase that lags far behind the cost-of-living index. In such instances, faculty performance can be meritorious and go unrewarded.

Some department chairs find it difficult to recognize and reward positive achievement within the prescribed campus plan for awarding salary increases. Some plans dictate across-the-board salary increases, and some plans specify that chairs recommend salary increases on the basis of merit. Sometimes the campus salary increase plan calls for a combination of across-the-board and merit components. At those institutions where merit is the driving criterion for the distribution of salary increases, there is still the question of whether "merit" increases are awarded in dollar amounts or as a percent of base pay. Regardless of the pros and cons of each method, each distribution formula tends to discriminate against some subgroup of faculty. Fixed dollar allocations benefit faculty with lower salaries, and increases distributed as a percent of salary base favor faculty with higher salaries. When campus policy for distributing salary increase dollars works against recognizing and rewarding individual achievement, performance counseling offers the department chair a mechanism for bestowing specific and individual recognition. The ultimate reward from a coaching style of conducting face-to-face performance counseling sessions is the faculty member's individual professional advancement.

Efforts to recognize and reward positive achievement are frequently more difficult when the institution is responding to externally imposed conditions. For example, increased pressures to make higher education accountable for the quality of instruction have resulted in mandated assessment initiatives, productivity reports, faculty work studies, surveys of faculty roles and responsibilities, and other documentation of faculty effort and effectiveness. Increasing numbers of faculty spend long hours designing and implementing assessment measures or responding to productivity surveys. Those tasks are not always counted as part of the faculty workload or integrated into the existing reward system. Yet, the time spent on those activities takes faculty away from the very performance expectations on which they are recognized and rewarded. Consequently, some faculty are penalized for participating in such campus initiatives. Through performance counseling, department chairs can assess faculty workloads as well as faculty achievements.

Putting Theory Into Practice

The strategies suggested for conducting performance counseling sessions will make intuitive good sense to many department chairs. On an intellectual level, most chairs see the advantage of such prescriptive advice as linking evaluative comments to specific examples or making performance goals specific and manageable. It is quite another matter to put these guidelines into practice.

In Case 4.1, Superstar or Naive, a well-intentioned chair helps to promote performance activities that are not consistent with the institution's standards for promotion and tenure. The chair now faces the task of reversing a trend in performance activity that is suicidal for the individual faculty member. Place yourself in the position of the school of music's director as you read the following case.

Case 4.1, Superstar or Naive

Background Information

Two years ago, the director successfully recruited a talented oboist, Igor Pryor, to join the school of music faculty. With the school's commitment to building a strong performance faculty, the director deemed this to be an important hire. Professor Pryor's appointment also filled an opening in the school's woodwind quintet, a group that has enjoyed an international reputation. The dean was apprehensive about making an offer to Pryor because he did not possess the traditional academic credentials. After weeks of heated debate, the director finally persuaded the dean to accept Pryor's vast experience as a professional musician as equivalent to the requisite graduate degrees and to approve the hire of Igor Pryor.

During his first two years, Professor Pryor managed to win the acclaim of the other members of the woodwind quintet as a talented musician. In addition, he exhibited considerable expertise in his efforts to promote the quintet's professional reputation. It was Professor Pryor who orchestrated the quintet's booking for a one-month tour of Europe last semester. Professor Pryor has maintained a rigorous performance schedule as a member of the area symphony orchestra. In the area of performance, Professor Pryor has proved to be even more impressive than anyone had anticipated.

The Problem

Unfortunately, Professor Pryor pays little attention to anything other than performance. During the past two years, the director has received numerous complaints from students who report that Professor Pryor is hard to find and does not keep office hours or scheduled appointments with students. Some of the complaints suggest that his classes are not well prepared. Students report that Professor Pryor does not distribute a course syllabus, and the basis for assigned grades is never clear. Only three of the six students originally enrolled in oboe instruction for credit remain. From this group, the director has heard complaints that Professor Pryor often cancels scheduled lessons without notice.

The one time that the director assigned Professor Pryor to teach a theory class that has a large enrollment, he protested on the basis that his travel schedule, as dictated by his membership in the woodwind quintet, would cause him to miss too many classes. After several meetings on the matter, the class was assigned to another faculty member. Professor Pryor believes that he should only engage in small group or one-on-one instruction that can fit into his performance schedule.

Professor Pryor's performance in the area of school and university service has lacked commitment and effort. He accepts committee assignments willingly but then fails to take an active role. This lax attitude toward all committee assignments has been noticed by others. Professor Pryor is the school's only representative on the college advisory council, but the dean has indicated his disappointment that the school's elected representative only attended one of six meetings held during the past semester.

Current Situation

University policy requires that the director meet at least once each year with every untenured faculty member to review his or her progress toward meeting the standards for promotion and tenure. The meeting is to be documented with a written record of what was discussed. Last year the director opted to soft-pedal the criticism of Pryor's teaching and service because the director believed that Pryor needed one year to become acclimated to the school and the university. The director is about to have the second annual meeting with Professor Pryor. The director now believes that Pryor has had ample time to become acquainted with the teaching and service components of his appointment.

While the director recognizes the tremendous benefit derived from Professor Pryor's strong performance record, the director also realizes that without documentation of effective teaching and service Professor Pryor will not be able to obtain tenure or promotion at the university. Furthermore, the director recognizes that unless Professor Pryor qualifies for promotion and tenure, the school will not be able to sell the dean on the hire of any other performance-oriented individual. The director is preparing for the second annual evaluation session with Professor Pryor.

Let's Analyze the Case

Professor Pryor is superbly able to support the school's commitment to building a strong performance faculty. His achievements in the area of music performance are exemplary. The director of the school of music would prefer to retain Professor Pryor, especially since it was so difficult to convince the dean to hire a professional musician who lacked the customary academic credentials. At the same time, the director realizes that Pryor will only secure tenure and promotion if he demonstrates his effectiveness as a teacher and takes his service assignments seriously. The director's responsibility is to clarify the performance expectations for promotion and tenure with Professor Pryor. The director must help Professor Pryor establish acceptable and manageable goals for his performance in all areas, including teaching and service. Particularly since Professor Pryor is new to university life, it is imperative that the director's evaluative comments be linked to specific examples. Without a clear understanding of the activities that are acceptable and valued, Professor Pryor will not know how to satisfy performance expectations. For example, a course syllabus is considered routine in preparing to teach any course. Yet, it is possible that Professor Pryor is unaware of that expectation. Furthermore, Pryor may not know what a course syllabus is or how to prepare one.

The director's approach to Professor Pryor must account for Pryor's personality. The information presented in Case 4.1 suggests that Professor Pryor is motivated to pursue any and all performance opportunities. There is a clear sense of Pryor's strong self-esteem in the area of performance. It is unlikely that one performance counseling session will be sufficient to help Pryor comprehend and respond positively to suggestions for improving his performance in the areas of teaching and service. The director contributed to the problem by not addressing the need for improved performance sooner. Pryor has no idea that anything is wrong. From Professor Pryor's perception, the first-year review went smoothly, and since then he has continued to focus on the same activities and accomplishments. For that reason, the director will want to establish a time frame for achieving specific goals in the problem areas.

It's Your Turn

Think through how you would approach Professor Pryor in the second annual performance evaluation session.

1. Be specific in delineating the arguments that you would make. How would you substantiate the assertions? Give some thought to the language that you would use. Would you, for example, reference the problem behavior as "our problem" or "his problem"? Would you begin the meeting by complimenting Pryor on his exemplary record in the area of performance or first discuss the areas in which Pryor's work needs the most improvement?

2. Would you address the needed improvement both in teaching and in service during one session? Anticipate Pryor's reaction and decide how you would handle his immediate response. Is Pryor likely to deny the student complaints or be crushed by them? Which response is most in keeping with Pryor's personality? What method would you use for follow-up with Pryor? What time frame would you establish for each issue? How would you monitor Pryor's efforts to improve his performance?

Please Consider

The fact that the director had to sell the dean on hiring Professor Pryor adds to the complexity of this situation. Obviously, the director perceives a need to hire faculty who are superbly skilled in music performance whether or not they possess the terminal academic degree. In the event that Professor Pryor fails to meet the standards for promotion and tenure, it will be more difficult to sell the dean on hiring music professionals for continuing, tenure-track faculty positions. Nevertheless, the director has a potential personnel problem. Your answer to the following questions will influence how you approach Professor Pryor.

1. Would you apprise the dean of Pryor's inadequate performance in teaching? If so, how much would you tell the dean? Remember that the dean is already aware of Pryor's lax attitude about serving on the college advisory council. Could such a discussion prejudice the dean against Pryor's application for promotion and tenure? Could the dean be helpful in orienting Professor Pryor to the expectations for faculty performance?

2. What are your ethical responsibilities to Professor Pryor? Do you have

ethical responsibilities to the other faculty in the department, to the students, and to the dean? How can you meet your ethical responsibilities to all parties involved?

Let's Recap

Take a moment and finalize your notes for your meeting with Pryor. Highlight your main objectives and be certain that the strategy you outlined will serve the purpose that you've set for the performance counseling session. If your approach does not incorporate the characteristics of effective performance counseling, you may want to review the material presented earlier in this chapter on how to effectively conduct performance counseling. Does your approach

- make performance counseling a year-round activity?
- offer both formal and informal evaluation of job performance?
- make job performance expectations clear?
- make performance goals specific and manageable?
- focus evaluative comments on performance, not personality?
- link evaluative comments to specific examples?
- incorporate self-evaluation and goal setting?
- offer specific suggestions for improvement?
- establish a time frame for achieving goals?
- recognize and reward positive achievement?

Putting Theory Into Practice

Once you are prepared for the meeting with Pryor, you are ready to read Case 4.2, The Encounter. Does the director of the school of music manage the performance counseling session as you would?

Case 4.2, The Encounter

The Setting
The annual performance evaluation session required by university policy takes place in the director's office. The director is going over some notes for the meeting as Professor Pryor arrives. Obviously looking forward to the

meeting, Pryor bounds into the room with the energy and enthusiasm that he exhibits in his performance activities.

The Conversation

Before the director can stand up, Professor Pryor is in front of the desk with his arm extended for his usual firm, cordial handshake. "Thank you for meeting with me. I always look forward to our conversations. You have been so wonderfully supportive of my work."

Director: "Well, you've done a lot to bring acclaim to the school. I'm proud of your achievements as a performing musician, but that's not the sole reason for this meeting. As you know, university policy requires that I meet at least once each year with every untenured faculty member to review individual achievements in an effort to..."

Pryor (interrupting): "I know. I know. And I love any excuse to talk about the progress I'm making with the woodwind quintet and my many achievements in other performance opportunities."

Director: "Of course, this annual evaluation must address all the duties assigned to individual faculty. In your case, it is time that we talk specifically about your work in the areas of teaching and service. Before we get into that, however, I want to commend you on your superlative work in the area of performance. You have far exceeded everyone's expectations both as a musician and in your skill for booking prestigious tours for the school's woodwind quintet. You certainly helped to advance the school's international reputation."

Pryor: "That's what you hired me to do, but thank you for your kind words."

Director: "How are your classes going? Do you enjoy teaching?"

Pryor: "Everything is fine. I have no problems and no complaints. I enjoy working with the oboe students very much."

Director: "I noticed that we lost three of the six students originally enrolled in oboe instruction."

Pryor: "Yes, finally. It wasn't easy, but I am pleased to report that I was able to help a few of our misplaced students make a difficult decision."

Director: "What do you mean?"

Pryor: "To be perfectly honest, not all of the six students originally enrolled in oboe instruction were sufficiently skilled and talented to be serious oboe performers. In my professional judgment, three of them should not have been permitted to enroll. I merely helped them face the truth."

Director: "But we are not running a conservatory of music. Not all students enrolled in oboe plan to be professional musicians. Perhaps..."

Pryor (interrupting again): "Well, those students do not need to take my time and the school's resources."

Director: "I see. Well, I've also got to tell you that I received some complaints from your students. They report that you are not distributing a course syllabus and that you frequently cancel individual lessons without notice."

Pryor (sitting taller and looking a bit outraged): "That is not true! Who would say such a thing? I demand to know who is spreading these lies."

Director: "That's not really important. It is important that you understand that there is an expectation that students enrolled in any course for credit will receive a syllabus. Have you thought about preparing a syllabus for the courses you teach?"

Pryor: "It cannot be done. I do not know what students need to learn until I meet them. How could I possibly do a syllabus for any course in advance?"

Director: "I think perhaps we should schedule another meeting in which we look at some sample syllabi and talk about how you can do that in a way that meets the school's expectation for instruction."

Pryor (shrugging his shoulders and shaking his head): "I'm really not sure that I see the need to spend time on unnecessary paperwork."

Director: "I realize that you don't have much experience in university teaching, but I believe it is important to your success at this institution. What time would you have next week to meet with me to talk about writing a syllabus? Could we meet at this time next week?"

Pryor: "I guess so if you feel it's really that important."

Director: "I do. There is one more issue that I need to discuss and that is your participation on the college advisory council. This is an important service assignment because you are the school's only representative on the council. The dean tells me that you have only attended one of the six meetings scheduled during the last semester."

Pryor: "I'm glad you brought this up. I meant to talk with you about it sooner. At the beginning of each semester, the dean asks the council members to submit their work schedule so he can decide on the best meeting time. I dutifully report my teaching and performance schedule complete with information on when I will be out of town on tour. The dean insists on scheduling council meetings when he knows that I am unavailable. Could it be that he doesn't want the school of music represented at the council meetings?"

Director: "I seriously doubt that since he has called to my attention your lack of attendance."

Pryor: "Why does he insist on holding the meetings on days and at times when he knows that I cannot be there? This seems to me to be an obvious case of discrimination either against the school of music or against me personally. I hope that you can remedy this situation."

Director: "Your faculty colleagues in the school expect you to take seriously your service assignments and your teaching responsibilities. When faculty members do not satisfy performance expectations in the areas of teaching and service, it has a negative impact on how their colleagues perceive them. In this case, your refusal to teach a theory class with a large enrollment suggests to your colleagues that your performance commitments are somehow more important than their performance commitments. This does not ingratiate you with your colleagues."

Pryor: "The truth is that most of my colleagues do not have a performance reputation that rivals mine. However, I do think I know what you are talking about. I have sensed some resentment toward me on the part of my faculty colleagues. You are confirming this. I guess it is to be expected that there would be some professional jealousy on the part of faculty who do not have my international reputation in performance. Do you think this jealousy will cause them to vote against my promotion and tenure?"

Director: "I'm not ready to say that there is professional jealousy. I do believe that faculty take exception to favoritism, and when you are exempted from teaching a theory course with a large enrollment, it appears that you are receiving preferential treatment. It is important that you uphold your responsibility as a teacher in the school as well as a performing artist. Your teaching adequacy will be determined by whether or not you assume your share of the teaching load as well as your effectiveness in instruction, which will be measured by both student and peer evaluations."

Pryor: "If my colleagues and students are honest, there should be no problem in substantiating my teaching effectiveness!"

Let's Analyze the Case

The conversation in Case 4.2 provides a more complete picture of Professor Pryor's personality. We know that Pryor has a strong ego, particularly in regard to his reputation as a performing musician. We sense that his ego is not linked with his work in the areas of teaching and service. We do not know, however, why Pryor does not approach teaching and service with the same zeal that he approaches performance. This is the key to understanding what may motivate Pryor to pay more attention to his work in the classroom and on campus committees.

The director needs to identify the reason that Professor Pryor takes less pride in his success and reputation as a teacher or as a colleague involved in service activities. It is possible that the academic world is so new to Professor Pryor that he is uncomfortable in the role of teacher. Perhaps Pryor does not know how to write a syllabus. Most people prefer to spend their time working on those aspects of their job description that are familiar and enjoyable. If Pryor's inattention to teaching is due to his unfamiliarity with and resulting discomfort in that activity, it is best remedied by a careful orientation as to the specific expectations and tasks associated with effective teaching.

It is also possible that Professor Pryor is attempting to rewrite his position description. While Pryor applied for a position that specified faculty duties in the areas of teaching, research or creative activity, and service, he may seek (intentionally or unintentionally) to renegotiate his assignment to 100% performance. If that is the case, one way to remedy the problem is to help Professor Pryor realize that such a reassignment of duties would be detrimental to his success, given that institutional policy requires all faculty to demonstrate a professional contribution in all three areas. The performance counseling session described in Case 4.2 suggests that Pryor may be unaware of the tasks typically associated with effective teaching. It does not, however, rule out the possibility that he is attempting to renegotiate his position description.

When department chairs are uncertain as to what motivates the problem behavior, they will likely need several conversations before they can recommend a solution. Before a chair can motivate faculty to change their behavior, the chair needs to know first why the present deficiency exists. If the deficiency exists because the person doesn't know what is expected, then the remedy must center around helping that faculty member understand performance expectations. If the deficiency exists because the faculty member prefers to avoid certain activities, then the remedy must center on making clear that avoidance will be counterproductive.

It's Your Turn

1. Was the director successful in getting Pryor's attention on the problem areas that need improvement? How would you approach a follow-up meeting with Professor Pryor? How would you make performance expectations clear? What specific evaluative comments would you make?

2. Script your next conversation with Professor Pryor. Would your language change? Would you use different information or examples to

document the need for improving Pryor's work in teaching and service? How might you incorporate self-evaluation and goal-setting effectively? What specific suggestions for improvement would you offer? What time frame would you establish for achieving goals and monitoring Professor Pryor's progress?

3. What are the ethical considerations involved in balancing individual faculty assignments with the needs of the overall unit and the expectations of the institution? What are the ethical considerations for balancing the professional activities of faculty members seeking national and international reputations for their work and the needs of students?

Please Consider

It is not clear from the information presented in Case 4.1 that Professor Pryor received helpful performance counseling as a new faculty member. The director's decision to soft-pedal criticism in Professor Pryor's formal first-year evaluation suggests that the director did not discuss how Professor Pryor's performance was not fulfilling expectations. Consequently, there is no reason to believe that Professor Pryor was aware of his shortcomings. Chairs cannot expect faculty to change or improve performance if they do not inform them that there is a problem to remedy.

Department chairs can influence the long-term success of new faculty through performance counseling. Especially with new faculty hires, effective performance counseling is essentially professional mentoring. Department chairs cannot relax after processing appointment papers to hire the top candidate. The department chair should begin performance counseling immediately to help new faculty hires understand and adapt to the department culture. This includes helping new faculty understand department and institutional standards for faculty work and helping to ensure that department colleagues accept the new faculty.

It is particularly beneficial and cost-effective to acclimate new faculty to the department culture in those disciplines where the department must work hard to recruit an underrepresented gender or minority. Department chairs can do this through their conversations with the new faculty members and through their actions within the department. The department chair must make certain that a new hire accurately understands the department culture and is fully cognizant of performance expectations. The faculty handbook may state that faculty seeking tenure must demonstrate a "substantial record of peer-reviewed research." The chair can help the new faculty member understand what specific research products will be recognized by the department and the institution as proof of meeting this standard for tenure. For example, will the production of an original training video be recognized as research in a department of radio and television? The chair can also help the new faculty member's transition into the department culture by demonstrating respect for his or her role and contribution. For example, a new minority hire is less likely to be seen as a preferential hire by colleagues if the department chair appoints that person to significant department committees and solicits his or her opinion on issues discussed at department meetings.

The same need for informal performance counseling exists with any unique or nontraditional hire. Depending upon the demographics of each department, this may include women, racial minorities, term appointees, and adjunct or part-time faculty. In all of these instances, new faculty hires are likely to enter the department culture more successfully if they understand specific performance expectations, and if the department faculty value their contributions. The department chair is in the best position to serve as the interpreter of department standards and as the facilitator for expanding the membership of the department culture.

Putting Theory Into Practice

A second performance counseling challenge for department chairs is tenured faculty. In some instances, tenured faculty are long-time colleagues who may hold more seniority in the department than the chair. Occasionally, the long-time colleagues may even be former mentors of the department chair. In still other instances, the tenured faculty may no longer be among the department's more productive faculty. Whatever the specific situation, it is a special challenge to engage in performance counseling with tenured faculty. Yet, department chairs must assume a leadership role in providing performance counseling for senior faculty.

In Case 4.3, The Self-Centered Team Member, the department chair must take action to change the perception and performance of a tenured full professor. The problem behavior threatens the welfare of the department in several ways. Place yourself in the position of the department chair as you read the following case.

Case 4.3, The Self-Centered Team Member

Meet Professor Wright

Professor Wright, an established and prolific scholar, was influential in building interest in a unique research area that at one time was considered trivial to most members of the professional association. Wright was a pioneer in transforming this initially slighted research subject into a recognized subspecialty of the discipline that is now able to support a new journal in the discipline.

In the department, Professor Wright teaches 500-level courses in his research specialty. Even though the department boasts a healthy graduate enrollment, the number of students seeking to pursue a master's or doctorate in this subspecialty is small, and Dr. Wright's seminars typically enroll 2 or 3 students. Three years ago the institution established a general guideline that 500-level courses should only be taught with enrollments of 5 or more students. This guideline is not strictly enforced by the central administration, but course enrollment and credit hour generation data are frequently used by the dean as a basis for justifying budget reductions. Dr. Wright is unconcerned. He perceives budget worries as "the administration's problem." He feels no shame in his low enrollments because, as he explains, his field is a difficult one that can only be pursued by the very brightest graduate students.

The Department Chair's Perspective

The chair perceives the low enrollment as a significant problem but is uncertain how to manage the situation. Last semester, the department chair insisted that Dr. Wright teach an undergraduate course enrolling 30 students with disastrous results. The chair spent considerable time listening to student complaints. The student drop rate for the course was 40%, which created a backlog of students who need to take the course before graduation.

The undergraduate student complaints are consistent with the department chair's perception of Dr. Wright. Students complain that Dr. Wright refuses to explain the course content. Furthermore, students that persist in seeking a clearer explanation for course material are chastised in front of the class. According to the students, Dr. Wright is quick to conclude that bright and hard-working students do not have difficulty, and therefore, those students in need of help are either dumb or lazy.

Faculty Colleagues

Dr. Wright exhibits the same air of superiority in working with other faculty in the department. He uses dissertation and thesis committees as a forum to interrogate faculty colleagues on their "narrow" or "inadequate" grasp of the discipline. Consequently, faculty are not anxious to serve with Dr. Wright on graduate student committees. Graduate students who are aware of the tension do not seek to add Dr. Wright to their committees. The few students who add Dr. Wright to a committee chaired by another faculty member find their degree completion in jeopardy. Typically, Dr. Wright follows his attack on faculty colleagues with assertions about the inferiority of their student's research. In these instances, Dr. Wright refuses to sign off on the final thesis or dissertation. When Dr. Wright serves as a student's graduate advisor, the other faculty on the committee complain that the committee never meets until the final defense and then Dr. Wright seeks approval through intimidation tactics. For the most part, graduate students either study with Dr. Wright, or they study with the rest of the department.

Dr. Wright's alienation from his colleagues extends to social gatherings in the department, which he refuses to attend. The more estranged Dr. Wright becomes, the more he seems content to view the rift as evidence of his superiority. Dr. Wright reasons that his colleagues are inferior and jealous of his intellect and standing in the discipline.

Other Issues

As a tenured full professor in the department, Dr. Wright votes on all applications for promotion and tenure. Dr. Wright has not voted in favor of a colleague's promotion or tenure for more than five years. This causes the department to submit dossiers that contain a split vote. Split votes are interpreted by the central administration as an indication that the faculty candidate does not clearly meet the standard.

It is also apparent to the central administration that the department members disagree. To those not familiar with the discipline or the nature of the conflict, the department appears to be divided between the productive researcher and the other faculty. Because the institution has a strong research mission, the central administration gives Dr. Wright more empathy than the department chair would like. This perception is fueled by Dr. Wright who takes every opportunity to write lengthy letters detailing his numerous accomplishments, despite the lax standards of his colleagues, to various members of the central administration.

The Department Chair's Challenge

The institution does not require formal performance evaluation of tenured full professors. It is clear, however, that Dr. Wright's current behavior is jeopardizing the welfare of the department. The department chair must convince Dr. Wright to exercise more productive behavior that contributes positively to the general health of the department.

Let's Analyze the Case

The department chair in Case 4.3 is in a difficult position because there isn't an established rapport that facilitates performance counseling with Dr. Wright. The facts presented suggest that Professor Wright has been allowed to function independently of the department. A rift exists between Dr. Wright and the other faculty in the department. There is little evidence of previous efforts to bridge this rift or ease the tension that exists among faculty in the department. Furthermore, Dr. Wright has evolved a rationale for the rift between himself and the other faculty, one that further bolsters his self-esteem. If Dr. Wright truly believes that the tension is attributable to his superior intellect and professional reputation within the discipline, then reducing the tension disputes Dr. Wright's high opinion of himself.

The behavior exhibited by Dr. Wright threatens the welfare of the department in several ways. First, the confrontational and public manner in which Dr. Wright challenges his colleagues hampers professional collegiality within the department. Second, the fact that disagreements are typically aired during graduate student committee meetings jeopardizes the graduate program. This type of conflict among faculty hurts graduate student recruitment, degree completion rates, and distribution of graduate student supervisory duties among the department faculty. All of these observable outcomes are often used by the central administration and other external agencies in assessing department productivity. Third, there is evidence to suggest that the low enrollments in Dr. Wright's classes contribute to reductions in the department's budget. It is difficult for the department chair to argue, for example, that the unit is understaffed if the department can afford to offer underenrolled seminars. Fourth, the conflict between Dr. Wright and the other faculty creates a negative image of the department. The central administration is aware of the in-house fighting, and the tension would likely be apparent to a program accrediting or review team.

The department chair cannot ignore the problem. Somehow, the chair needs to change Dr. Wright's perception and behavior. Simultaneously, the chair needs to convince the other faculty to alter their response to Dr. Wright. For the benefit of the department, the chair needs to establish a productive working relationship among all the department faculty. The chair must consider the perceptions held by graduate students and the central administration in planning a strategy for managing the situation. For example, if Dr. Wright has the ear and sympathy of the dean, the chair will need an approach that does not prompt the dean to intervene on Dr. Wright's behalf. It is important that the strategy not place graduate students in an uncomfortable or adverse position. There are many interests to consider in detailing a plan of action.

It is important that the department chair focus evaluative comments on specific work-related behaviors, not on Dr. Wright's personality. The department chair needs to demonstrate a neutral posture in listening to Dr. Wright's assessment of the evaluative comments. To acquire Dr. Wright's genuine effort in reconciling with the other faculty, the chair must help Professor Wright realize some advantage in doing so. That requires some assessment of Wright's motives and priorities. Would Wright be motivated to change if a productive alliance with other department faculty resulted in higher esteem within the department? Would Wright, for example, be convinced to stop sending lengthy letters to central administrators that describe the department in an unfavorable light if he knew that this negative press resulted in a lower budget that, in turn, forced the chair to reduce travel support for Dr. Wright? Answers to these and similar questions help the department chair know how to approach Dr. Wright.

It's Your Turn

Review the facts presented in Case 4.3, and decide how you would manage the situation.

1. What possible motives exist that might be used to persuade Dr. Wright to behave in a more collegial manner toward other department faculty? How might the department chair float some trial balloons to learn which of these motives is most salient to Dr. Wright? In what way is the department's reputation on and off campus important to Dr. Wright? Does the existing tension between Dr. Wright and the other faculty harm Dr. Wright? How could the department chair help Dr. Wright realize the personal and professional liability of his actions?

2. Where would you as the department chair begin in working with Dr. Wright? Would you schedule a formal meeting or write a letter? Are there informal steps you would take to improve the climate or rapport with Dr. Wright before getting to the central issue? If so, what would

you do? Should you seek support from sources external to the department? How would you encourage other faculty to seek a more collegial relationship with Dr. Wright?

Please Consider

Case 4.3 illustrates the reason for not treating performance counseling only as an annual or formal activity. It is difficult to conduct performance counseling of tenured faculty unless a rapport exists for providing evaluative comments. When performance counseling is a year-round activity that encompasses both informal and formal comments, the faculty are more accustomed to accepting the chair's assessment. Year-round performance counseling for all department faculty can exist with or without a formal campus policy. An established practice of performance counseling makes it more comfortable and possible for chairs to offer constructive criticism before faculty performance goes too far astray and tensions become too great.

The department chair has a responsibility to help senior faculty with continued professional development. Professional growth should not stop once faculty clear the tenure and promotion hurdles. Instead, the goal shifts from standards needed to secure tenure and promotion to professional objectives for further growth and recognition within the department and the discipline. With a clear understanding that the primary objective is continued professional development, tenured faculty can appreciate the chair's counsel.

Let's Recap

Review your strategy for managing the situation described in Case 4.3. Will your approach to Dr. Wright demonstrate that your primary concern is the department's welfare and the continued professional development of all faculty? All of the guidelines described earlier in this chapter for making performance counseling effective apply when working with tenured faculty. If your approach does not incorporate the following characteristics of effective performance counseling, you may want to review the material presented earlier in the chapter on how to effectively conduct performance counseling. Does your approach to Dr. Wright

- make performance counseling a year-round activity?
- offer both formal and informal evaluation of job performance?
- make job performance expectations clear?

- make performance goals specific and manageable?
- focus evaluative comments on performance and not personality?
- link evaluative comments to specific examples?
- incorporate self-evaluation and goal setting?
- offer specific suggestions for improvement?
- establish a time frame for achieving goals?
- recognize and reward positive achievement?

Change takes time. It is critical, therefore, that the chair continually reinforce progress as it occurs. All of the parties need reinforcement if they are, in time, to alter their perception and behavior.

Relevant Communication Concepts and Strategies

It is helpful to maintain a written record of performance counseling sessions. Such a record is valuable in making personnel decisions about promotion, tenure, and salary increases. Most institutions that require performance evaluation stipulate some method of documentation. Sometimes this is a standardized form that is completed by the department chair and placed in the faculty member's personnel file. On other campuses, the faculty member and the chair co-sign a statement summarizing the content of the evaluation session. Sometimes the faculty member writes a summary that the chair signs. At still other institutions, the department chair writes a letter to the faculty member summarizing the content of the performance counseling session. Campus policy also varies greatly on whether or not chairs forward copies of such documentation to the academic dean or other administrative offices.

Even when campus policy does not require documentation, it is a good idea to prepare a written record of every performance counseling session. In a constructive way, this documentation serves as a blueprint for faculty as they continue to improve performance and work to satisfy performance expectations. Chairs must make certain that faculty understand the constructive purpose for documenting performance counseling sessions. A faculty member need only follow the advice summarized in writing to have a solid case for tenure and promotion. A letter from the department chair to the faculty member provides considerable flexibility in tailoring the content to each individual faculty member. Chairs should incorporate the following guidelines (Higgerson, 1995b), whether using a prescribed form or drafting a letter.

Accurately reflect the content of the performance counseling session
The letter should accurately reflect the substance of the meeting both in terms of the description of the issues discussed and the weight given to each issue. If 75% of the meeting was spent discussing ways to improve teaching, then the letter should indicate that. There is a tendency in many people to soft-pedal suggestions for improvement that might be construed as criticism when putting those suggestions in writing. Department chairs who have very candid and serious discussions about performance that needs improvement may be tempted to gloss over the needed improvements in the written documentation. They may see the rehashing of substandard performance in a written form as "rubbing it in" or "belaboring the obvious." This is counterproductive and indeed detrimental to the ultimate success of the faculty member. Further, should the faculty member not improve in performance, the written documentation will suggest that the faculty member was not adequately apprised of the changes that were needed. That could prove problematic in the event the faculty member is denied tenure or promotion and wishes to file a grievance or a lawsuit.

Avoid giving mixed signals
Mixed signals typically occur when we attempt to preface suggestions for change with praise. Sometimes a mixed signal occurs when a chair decides to soften the written documentation of a problematic evaluation by burying the need for improvement in the middle of a letter that begins and ends with praise. Sometimes a mixed signal occurs within a single sentence. The following statements are examples of mixed signals:

A. "No one in the department works harder at teaching even though your student ratings are somewhat disappointing."

B. "The department was fortunate to recruit someone with your research expertise even though it's taking longer than anticipated for you to get your lab set up to do research."

These statements don't extend unqualified praise. Nor do these statements identify a problem. The reader is left with the task of interpreting what they mean. The benefit of documenting a performance counseling session is lost when the summary of what was said during the session is so ambiguous.

Be specific in summarizing evaluative comments
The written documentation should list in detail the evaluative comments made during the face-to-face performance counseling session. Include both the positive and the negative evaluative comments. Not all persons are

skilled listeners who can remember the details of a conversation. Evaluative comments are especially difficult to remember when they represent new information or information that is, for any reason, difficult to hear. A written summary of evaluative comments is a resource for the faculty member in between evaluation sessions.

Reiterate specific suggestions for improvement

Every suggestion made during the face-to-face performance counseling session should be included in the written documentation. This serves as a guide to both the faculty member and the chair. All concerned can refer to an accurate listing of the suggestions. It is particularly helpful to the chair who may have a difficult time getting a faculty member to follow through on the suggestions. It gives the faculty member a guideline for monitoring progress until the next performance counseling session. Imagine how difficult it would be to build or assemble a complex machine if the directions were only given orally and the mechanic was expected to remember and use everything mentioned. Most people are better able to comply with suggestions for change when they have both a verbal explanation and a written statement of the steps to be followed. Reworking the examples of mixed signals presented earlier, a chair might make the following specific suggestions for improvement:

1. "Since students rate you lowest on 'grades fairly' and 'sets clear objectives for the course,' I suggest that you add information on course objectives and grading criteria to your course syllabus. Discuss these issues with students on the first day of class."

2. "Your work in revising the core methods course must be completed for department review by the close of this semester."

3. "It is imperative that you get your research lab operational. Please prepare a written statement of the remaining obstacles and a time frame for accomplishing this task. I will review the list to determine what other support the department might offer toward this end."

Write with third-person clarity

For documentation of performance counseling to be effective, it must be written in a way that a third party not present during the meeting can read and understand what happened during the performance counseling session. This means that department chairs should avoid "just between us" phrases such as those contained in the following statements:

A. "We are in agreement as to what you need to do."

B. "I'm certain that you understand what needs to be done without my reiterating it in this letter."

C. "I'm confident that you can make the changes we discussed before next year's evaluation."

Those statements do little to document what has happened in the face-to-face performance counseling session. In fact, the statements do not offer evidence that the music director fulfilled her responsibility for evaluating faculty performance.

Putting Theory Into Practice

Review the conversation with Professor Pryor that unfolds in Case 4.2. What information should the director of the school of music put in a letter to Professor Pryor to document the performance counseling session. Read the sample letter in Case 4.4, The Follow-up, and determine if it includes the elements that you believe should be in the letter to Professor Pryor.

Case 4.4, The Follow-up

Professor Igor Pryor
School of Music
East Campus

Dear Professor Pryor:

Without question, you have maintained an extensive performance schedule both as a member of the woodwind quintet and as a solo performer. I am pleased with your numerous and significant accomplishments in the area of performance. Your work to earn international visibility for the woodwind quintet and the School of Music is exemplary.

I recognize that you work hard teaching oboe to the three students that remain in oboe instruction. I look forward to talking with you further about how to design a course syllabus that accommodates specific instructional objectives for students with varied levels of performance skill. Also, I wish that more students could benefit from your vast experience and talent in musical performance.

You continue to serve the School of Music in several important ways. Certainly, your work as manager of the woodwind quintet was integral to the success of that group's European tour. You serve as the School of

Music's only representative on the College Advisory Council. This is a significant contribution even though your attendance at committee meetings is disappointing.

I was surprised to learn that you believe that some of your colleagues are jealous of your achievements. I sense that you fear this could result in an unjustified negative vote on your tenure. I cannot point to anything that might substantiate your fear. Indeed, I've seen several music faculty with distinguished performance records promoted and/or tenured over the past several years with a strong endorsement from their faculty colleagues.

I enjoyed having an opportunity to review your numerous activities and accomplishments. I hope that next year is both productive and rewarding.

Sincerely,

Hope Samuels
Director

Let's Analyze the Case

The letter in Case 4.4 does not evidence the criteria for effectively documenting a performance counseling session. First, the letter does not accurately reflect the content of the performance counseling session described in Case 4.2 either in terms of the issues discussed or in terms of the weight given to each issue. The letter in Case 4.4 embellishes the positive assessment of Professor Pryor's performance and minimizes the discussion of needed improvements in the areas of teaching and service.

Second, the letter offers many mixed signals. It is not clear from the letter that Professor Pryor needs to make any change in his work in order to satisfy the standards for promotion and tenure. The last statement in the third paragraph regarding Professor Pryor's service as a member of the college advisory council reads: "This is a significant contribution even though your attendance at committee meetings is disappointing." As written, this statement does not offer any specific suggestion for improvement. Nor does it reflect the seriousness of the missed meetings. Consider the statement: "I wish that more students could benefit from your vast experience and talent in musical performance." The statement does not offer any assessment as to whether teaching performance is acceptable or effective. It does not indicate that Professor Pryor refuses to teach large enrolled classes. Rather, it can be read to imply that Professor Pryor is working with as many students as possible.

These mixed signals are not helpful to the faculty member because they confuse rather than clarify performance standards and expectations.

Third, the letter does not provide a clear summary of evaluative comments. It does not summarize specific suggestions for improvement but actually endorses the status quo. Review the following statements that appear in the letter:

A. "I recognize that you work hard teaching oboe to the three students that remain in oboe instruction."

B. "You continue to serve the school of music in several important ways."

These statements do not suggest that change is needed. Rather, the statements offer a collective sense that Professor Pryor is making good progress toward tenure and promotion. The statement that comes close to suggesting that change is needed is: "I look forward to talking with you further about how to design a course syllabus that accommodates specific instructional objectives for students with varied levels of performance skill." The statement, however, does not communicate the serious nature of the suggestion. It does not, for example, make clear that Pryor does not distribute a syllabus and resists doing so.

The letter does not contain any specific suggestions for improvement. There is no mention, for example, that the director stressed the need to distribute a syllabus in each course. There is no mention in the letter of student complaints or the fact that student enrollment in oboe dropped dramatically. Instead, the letter implies that Professor Pryor's teaching is such that the director's only regret is that more students cannot "benefit" from Pryor's "vast experience and talent in musical performance."

Fourth, the letter in Case 4.4 does not indicate with third-person clarity that Professor Pryor is appropriately apprised of the standards for promotion and tenure. The letter does not offer any evidence that the director met her responsibility to assist Pryor in meeting university standards for tenure and promotion. There is virtually nothing in the letter to suggest that Pryor is being counseled on how to improve job performance in order to successfully satisfy university standards for promotion and tenure. A faculty member with a file of letters that reads as this one does has a basis for grieving a negative decision on tenure and promotion.

It's Your Turn

Review the evaluation session described in Case 4.2 and list the specific issues that should be summarized in the written follow-up of the meeting.

Draft a letter to Professor Pryor that documents the performance counseling session detailed in Case 4.2. The following questions will help you determine if your letter meets the guidelines for documenting performance counseling that were described earlier in this chapter.

1. Does your letter accurately reflect the content of the performance counseling session? Does it reflect the content of the meeting in terms of issues discussed and the weight given to each issue? Does your letter contain mixed signals? Does your letter summarize the evaluative comments? Does your letter reiterate specific suggestions for improvement? Does it reference the need to meet again?

2. Could a neutral person read and understand your letter? Have someone read your letter and tell you whether Professor Pryor is making satisfactory progress toward tenure and promotion. Ask the person who reads your letter to summarize the main issues addressed. Did you succeed in writing with third-person clarity?

Let's Recap

Regular and constructive evaluation of faculty performance is the responsibility of the department chair. Chairs will be more comfortable with this important task if they assume the role of a coach rather than a critic. In a coaching mode, the chair and individual faculty are on the same side. Both want the faculty member to meet department and university performance expectations in order to achieve promotion, tenure, and other tangible rewards. Both want the individual faculty member to perform well those activities that will earn professional visibility and respect.

Performance counseling is more effective as a year-round activity. To reap maximum benefit from performance counseling, department chairs must make job expectations clear and set specific, manageable, goals for individual performance. Performance counseling encompasses both informal and formal comment made by the chair. To be most helpful, evaluative comments should focus on job performance, not the individual's personality, and should be linked to specific examples and specific suggestions for improvement. Effective performance counseling incorporates self-evaluation and goal setting. It also establishes a timetable for achieving goals. Finally, effective performance counseling recognizes and rewards positive achievement.

Effective performance counseling fuels and sustains continuous faculty development. It also provides a solid foundation for a productive working relationship between chair and faculty. The task of performance counseling equips the department chair with an opportunity to build credibility with faculty. Through performance counseling, chairs demonstrate their competence as evidenced in their understanding of campus policy and what it takes to be successful. Through performance counseling, chairs exhibit their interest in having faculty succeed. This overt demonstration of good will does a lot to bolster a department chair's credibility with faculty. Department chairs need an ongoing program of effective performance counseling for faculty whether or not campus policy requires periodic evaluation of faculty performance.

5

MANAGING CONFLICT

A 1990 survey (Gmelch, 1991) of roughly 800 department chairs from 100 research institutions identified the primary sources of stress among practicing department chairs. The second most frequently mentioned source of stress was confrontation with colleagues. This category included conducting performance evaluation, making decisions that affect the lives of faculty colleagues, and resolving differences between faculty colleagues. Conflict is possible, if not probable, in many of the duties and responsibilities assigned to department chairs. Those duties that might lead to conflict include, but are certainly not limited to, assigning courses and course times, offering summer contracts, recommending salary increases, assigning office space, recommending promotion and tenure, filling open positions, stipulating the use of student workers and secretarial support, determining access to computers, allocating long-distance telephone privileges, awarding travel support, and making committee assignments.

The opportunity for conflict increases when department chairs must manage with declining human and fiscal resources, but conflict can erupt even in instances when there is (or should be) no real disagreement. Readers of Gary Larson's "Far Side" may recall the cartoon that pictured two identical desks, each equidistant from the only window in the room. The man seated behind one of the desks is pointing at the other desk while he shouts, "Someday that desk will be mine!" Whether logical or not, conflict will develop among people who work together. Sometimes department chairs must manage conflict that exists among others, including disagreements between faculty members or between faculty and students. At other times, department chairs must manage conflict between themselves and others, such as disagreements with faculty, students, or central administration. The fact that confrontation with colleagues surfaced as the second most often mentioned source of stress in a survey of some 800 chairs may be indicative of both the discomfort of managing conflict and the frequency with which department chairs encounter conflict. Department chairs need to know how to manage conflict effectively.

The Objective

One goal of this chapter is to illustrate the difference between resolving and managing conflict. Too often, chairs assume responsibility for resolving conflict when the goal should be to manage conflict. Department chairs need to reconceptualize the task of managing conflict and adopt proactive strategies for managing conflict. A second goal of this chapter is to demonstrate how department chairs can develop a repertoire of communication strategies for managing conflict. The art of managing conflict is a skill that can be learned and improved. The case studies presented in this chapter allow chairs to practice and sharpen their skills in managing conflict.

Defining the Task

It is important to recognize the difference between resolving conflict and managing conflict. The goal of conflict resolution is conflict elimination. Conflict resolution is often an impossible task and not always a desirable goal. Department chairs who accept conflict resolution as their ultimate objective will undoubtedly fail. Conflict management is directed toward reducing destructive conflict but allows for the existence of constructive conflict. Department chairs who accept conflict management as the objective realize that all conflict cannot or should not be eliminated. It will help to understand some basic facts about conflict.

Conflict is inevitable

Conflict is a natural outcome of human interaction. Conflict exists whenever there is disagreement and derives from differences in attitudes, beliefs, and expectations. Conflict can result from differences in perception as to what has happened or what needs to be done. Whenever two or more people disagree about a decision or action, conflict exists. Conflict is inevitable because not all persons think alike. Not all persons hold the same values or priorities. Not all persons react to situations in the same manner. Those facts make conflict resolution virtually impossible.

Conflict can be positive

It is important to remember that conflict is not inherently destructive. In fact, some conflict is desirable. In a constructive mode, conflict can improve problem solving, clarify issues or expectations, increase participant involvement and commitment, and result in a better decision or outcome.

If all faculty held the same views on every issue, final decisions and recommendations would not account for the full range of ramifications. If all faculty thought alike, departments would experience little change. Change that results in improvement typically grows out of conflict.

Conflict can be managed

Conflict that is allowed to run its own course is more likely to be destructive. Department chairs need to be ready to manage conflict. However, two precautions must be noted. First, how a department chair responds to a conflict affects the conflict. Even when a department chair opts to ignore an existing conflict, his or her silence affects the conflict. Second, the department chair's response is never static in that a chair brings to each conflict a personal set of beliefs, perceptions, and expectations. Chairs need to remember that their perception of the persons involved or the situation may not be congruent with reality. Everyone, including department chairs, views conflict from his or her own biases despite the best of intentions.

Conflict resolution is not always the goal

Conflict management, unlike conflict resolution, acknowledges that human interaction is dynamic and that people do not always think or act alike. Because conflict results from differences in attitudes, beliefs, and expectations, a conflict-free environment would be one that is so homogeneous that it could not be optimally innovative or productive. The goal becomes maximizing constructive conflict and minimizing destructive conflict. Conflict management includes those times when chairs need to initiate or encourage conflict to achieve a positive outcome.

Relevant Communication Concepts and Strategies

The task of managing conflict is not limited to those moments when confrontation is apparent. A department chair's role in managing conflict includes preconflict and postconflict communication. A chair's daily communication with faculty, staff, and students can do a lot to minimize destructive confrontation and set the stage for more effective conflict management when differences surface within the department. The following communication strategies (Higgerson, 1991, 1992b) prescribe a proactive posture for department chairs in managing conflict.

Establish and maintain a healthy work environment

Much has been written about the importance of the work environment (sometimes termed the department climate) to the overall morale and productivity of the unit. A healthy work environment is characterized by open and effective communication. In a healthy environment, faculty discuss differences of opinion in a candid and constructive manner without fear of retaliation. There is a high degree of mutual respect and trust within the department.

The presence of a healthy work environment gives the department chair an advantage in managing conflict. The work environment sets the tone for conflict and conflict management. If mutual respect and trust exists among colleagues, and faculty air differences openly and constructively, there is less opportunity for destructive conflicts to escalate because individuals are less prone to perceive differences of opinion as personal attacks or components of some hidden agenda.

It is important to realize that individual academic departments can have a climate that, though vulnerable to the total campus climate, can be very different from the campus environment. For example, a department with very low morale can exist on a campus that generally has high faculty morale. It is also possible to have a department with very high faculty morale on a campus that is characterized by a dismal climate. Department chairs need not inherit a poor or destructive campus climate. Instead, chairs need to cultivate a healthy work environment that is conducive to effective management. Specific suggestions for enhancing the department climate are presented in Chapter 2.

Be clear in communicating your goals and expectations for the department and faculty performance

Conflict is more likely to occur when communication is not clear and when there is confusion about what is valued and rewarded. It is the responsibility of the department chair to make goals and expectations clear. It is imperative that the chair help faculty translate the more general university expectations into activities and achievements that are discipline specific. For example, the university may have as part of its mission a commitment to service. The faculty handbook may stipulate that faculty seeking tenure and promotion have a documented record of professional service. The department chair is responsible for making certain that individual faculty understand what specific activities count as evidence of professional service. Does professional service encompass volunteer activities within the community such as working on blood drives or teaching Sunday school? Is professional service limited to positions held and activities performed within the professional associations of the academic discipline? Perhaps professional service includes volunteer activities in the community, but only if the work draws upon the faculty member's discipline expertise. It is the department chair's responsibility to make certain that faculty understand specific expectations for faculty work. The chair must also advise faculty on how best to invest their time and energy in acceptable activities in order to meet department and university standards in the areas of teaching, research, and service.

Department chairs must also be consistent in recognizing and rewarding faculty who meet department and university standards. If campus policy requires faculty to demonstrate effective teaching, this standard cannot be lowered for some faculty. That is sometimes difficult because we tend to evaluate individuals on the basis of their total effort. A chair may want to be more lenient in interpreting teaching effectiveness for a faculty member who is outstanding in securing external grant dollars. Such a double standard, no matter how well-intentioned, is costly to the department climate and the chair's credibility.

The department chair can effectively defuse potential conflict if the department goals and expectations for faculty performance are clear and consistently applied. When the faculty understand department goals and expectations, they have an underlying logic for many of the department chair's decisions and actions. For example, if the faculty recognize that the department has a priority for professional travel that accrues recognition for the department, they understand why a faculty member who presents a paper at a national meeting receives more travel support than the faculty member who merely attends the same meeting. The chair can defuse potential conflict that might result from a perception of favoritism (or discrimination) by equipping faculty in advance with the logic underlying the chair's decision.

Establish ground rules for airing disagreement

The task of managing conflict becomes easier if chairs establish ground rules for airing disagreements. For example, a ground rule might dictate that different opinions will be heard and respected or that abusive language will not be tolerated. Such ground rules help to establish boundaries for airing disagreements in a constructive (and professional) manner. Department chairs can establish as many ground rules as they believe necessary for maintaining an environment that is conducive to effectively airing disagreements. The specific ground rules imposed in a particular department will, to some extent, be a product of the chair's personality and management style. Ground rules also respond to the specific personalities within the department. While there is no standardized list of ground rules, some guidelines that the chair might establish include the following:

- Abusive language will not be tolerated.

- Derogatory comments that represent personal attacks on colleagues will not be tolerated.

- Differences of opinion will be discussed and everyone will be heard.

- Department members can express their views without interruption or fear of retaliation.

- Unsubstantiated assertions will not influence the vote or outcome.

- Issues, not personalities, are subject to debate.

- Tears or emotional outbursts do not derail discussion of substantive issues.

- Department issues will be discussed and decided at department meetings, not by any subgroup of faculty.

Ground rules are most effective if they apply to all members of the department and are enforced across all situations. Department chairs cannot expect to preserve a ground rule of hearing and discussing differences of opinion in a professional manner if they tolerate verbal outbursts from even one faculty member. Ground rules only help a chair manage conflict if they are applied uniformly across all members of the department. When applied consistently, however, ground rules increase the chair's credibility within the department.

Ground rules help a department chair keep the conflict on the issue of disagreement, which is important to effective conflict management. Crying is one behavior that tends to shift a conflict situation away from the issue of disagreement. A department chair may switch from the issue of disagreement to a more supportive role when confronted with tears. This shift changes the agenda from one of airing the disagreement to nurturing or mending a broken spirit. Crying is one behavior that some persons may use to avoid an issue of disagreement. If that becomes the case, a department chair needs to establish a ground rule for managing those situations. For starters, the chair must make it clear that crying is not rewarded and that the issue of disagreement will be discussed. When the faculty member breaks into tears, the chair might abort the discussion and say, "Obviously, you're not able to discuss this matter at this time." The chair may offer to leave for a few moments while the faculty member regains composure. The chair might tell the faculty member that upon the chair's return the faculty member can indicate whether he or she can continue the conversation or another time needs to be scheduled to discuss the matter. This response makes clear that the issue of disagreement will be discussed and that any amount of crying will not alter that fact.

Anticipate conflict areas and be ready to intervene when needed.
Intervention does not need to wait until a conflict erupts. Intervention is most effective when it prevents or defuses a conflict. For example, a department chair might anticipate conflict following the hire of the first minority member of the department. The department chair may fear that other faculty will not accept or value fully the first minority hire. To minimize this potential conflict, the department chair needs to intervene and clearly establish the new faculty member's value within the department through the chair's rhetoric and actions. The chair may, for example, solicit the new faculty member's opinion of a salient issue during a department meeting. The chair can appoint the new faculty member to one of the more significant department committees. Another form of chair intervention is to include the new hire in informal and social activities such as lunch groups or the department's softball team. The potential conflict will be minimized if it is clear that the department chair values the new hire's contribution to the department.

Successful early intervention requires that chairs notice and accurately interpret communication cues that signal a brewing conflict. Chairs should pay close attention to the following cues.

Changes in behavior. The chair should note when a talkative person becomes silent or when a quiet person becomes vocal, when a person who is prompt and responsive becomes lax and lethargic, and when a department member alters his or her routine behavior (or dress) in any way. Noticeable changes in verbal and nonverbal behavior typically evidence changes in attitude. When those changes occur, the chair can anticipate that the relationship among faculty and staff in the department will be altered.

Changes in policy. It doesn't matter whether a new policy is imposed by the central administration, an accrediting body, or by vote of the department faculty. New policy represents a change and, as described in Chapter 6, change is uncomfortable for many people. New policy (even when wanted) can transform reasonable and confident faculty into irrational and insecure human beings.

Change in the department. This might be a new chair, a new faculty member, a retirement, a significant increase (or decrease) in enrollment, office relocation (or renovation), the integration of new computer equipment, curriculum revision, or a change in any aspect of the department that

affects faculty. Changes in the department typically require the chair's intervention. (Chapter 6 includes strategies for when and how the department
chair should intervene to effectively implement change.)

Know when and how to confront conflict

There are times when it is necessary and advantageous to confront conflict.
A department chair, however, must remain the manager of conflict rather
than a participant in a destructive confrontation. The following four conditions help determine when and how to confront conflict.

Timing. The worst time to confront a conflict is when the conditions
are such that the department chair will be less able to manage the confrontation. This includes those moments when voices are raised and participants
are not thinking rationally. It is a difficult concept to internalize because
most chairs tend to believe that they must do something immediately when
others in the department are engaged in a heated argument. Chairs who
attempt to resolve or manage heated discussions when the participants are
exercising more emotion than logic will discover that the most they can do is
referee. Few disputants are ready to see reason or be open-minded during a
heated argument. By waiting, the department chair can create an opportunity for each disputant to relinquish his or her original position privately.
Department chairs need to be proactive and more calculating in deciding
when and how to confront conflict.

That does not give chairs license to turn a blind eye to a heated discussion between two faculty members in the department lobby. Obviously, that
behavior is inappropriate and cannot be permitted. There is, however, a difference between stopping inappropriate behavior and managing the conflict.
A chair may, for example, terminate the heated discussion by saying, "Both
of you should realize that this is not an appropriate place to air this disagreement. I suggest that the three of us sit down and talk this through tomorrow
at 3:00 p.m. in my office." That strategy terminates the inappropriate
behavior and allows the parties involved to cool off before addressing the
issue of disagreement. It also makes clear that the difference of opinion will
be aired for the purpose of reaching some workable solution.

Know the facts. Perception is not always reality. If department chairs
know the relevant facts, they can distinguish reality from perception. This is
the key to remaining neutral when confronting conflict between faculty
members or between faculty and students. It is also critical to the chair's success in confronting a conflict that the chair may have with a faculty member,
a student, or the dean.

Chairs should make an effort to gather relevant facts. For example, if one student complains that a professor discriminates against women students, the chair will want to gather some information before acting on the complaint. The process includes some reflective analysis of any previous complaints that may or may not substantiate the student's claim. The chair may recall positive comments that other students offered regarding this professor. The chair may remember personal observations of the professor's interaction with women students. The chair can also solicit the professor's assessment of the complaining student's academic performance. Collectively, this additional information creates a context within which the chair can more accurately separate fact from perception and assess the merit of the initial complaint.

Depersonalize the issue. When confronting conflict, it is important to focus the discussion on the issue and not the personalities involved. There is, for example, a significant difference between telling someone that "the department needs your commitment and support" and asserting that "you only look out for yourself." The first statement depersonalizes the conflict and describes a behavior or performance expectation. The second statement personalizes the issue of disagreement and attacks the personality of the person. By personalizing the statement, the chair implies that the objectionable behavior is the result of some character flaw and does not suggest that the person can change the unacceptable behavior.

Unfortunately, not everyone seeks to minimize destructive conflict. Some people want to escalate a conflict and often do so by personalizing the issue. Take, for example, the faculty member who hates to lose an argument but typically holds a minority viewpoint. Such a person, sensing that most of the faculty disagree, is likely to resort to shifting the discussion from the issue being debated to the personalities involved. He or she may assert, "I don't understand why you can't get this," or may blurt out, "You never could understand the larger issues." Such statements bring out defensive behavior in those who believe that they have been personally attacked. A department chair managing such conflict needs to intervene and depersonalize the exchange. It is particularly helpful if the chair's intervention can precede any defensive response from the person who's been attacked. The chair's intervention needs to redirect the discussion to the substance of the issue and dismiss the personalized comment. For example, a chair might say, "Does anyone have anything to add regarding the substance of this issue?" Over time, consistency in the chair's response will help to establish a new ground rule that personalized attacks will not be heard when the department discusses an issue on which there is a difference of opinion.

Don't prolong the confrontation. Department chairs cannot afford to carry a grudge. Once the chair confronts the conflict and makes it clear what behavior is unacceptable, the chair should drop the issue. This is important to the chair's overall relationship with each faculty member. Department chairs cannot allow a disagreement over one issue to shape their relationships with individual faculty. The faculty (and even the dean) need to know that the department chair holds them in high regard and respects their contribution even when the chair disagrees with their thinking on one particular issue. Typically, the faculty will be relieved and grateful if normal communication on more harmonious issues can place the disagreement in a larger, more productive context. As a general rule, the more heated the disagreement on a particular issue, the sooner the chair should initiate a discussion with that disputant on a different and more agreeable subject.

Know when and how to initiate conflict

Sometimes a conflict that remains below the surface can be destructive to department productivity and faculty morale. Differences of opinion can become larger than the original issue of disagreement if allowed to fester and build. Chairs can release potentially destructive tension by initiating conflict and allowing the disagreement to be aired in a constructive and controlled manner.

There are two instances when it is particularly useful to initiate conflict. The first is when the offender doesn't realize that his or her behavior is contributing to a department conflict. For example, the secretary who is always late for work may not realize that coming late creates a problem because faculty need access to locked files and supply cabinets before going to first-period classes. The secretary may be conscientious about making up the missed time at the end of the day and unaware that her tardiness poses a problem for anyone. By intervening and pointing out that a conflict does exist, the department chair can prevent the conflict from escalating.

A second instance when a chair may need to initiate conflict is to help facilitate decision-making. This could occur when evaluating a faculty member's progress toward meeting the standards for promotion and tenure. Sometimes untenured faculty get so involved in committee assignments that they neglect achievements in the areas of teaching and research. The chair can prevent a larger problem by initiating conflict early in the probationary period by making it clear that the faculty member is not likely to be recommended for tenure because he or she is ignoring two of the three standards for tenure. Done early enough in the probationary period, a faculty member has the opportunity to remedy the investment of his or her time and succeed in meeting all of the standards for promotion and tenure. If the chair does not initiate the conflict, the faculty member may not face the important decision of how to invest energy and time and the result could be a denial of tenure and promotion.

Recognize which conflicts are yours to manage

Fortunately, some conflicts are not the business of the department chair. One easy guideline for determining whether a conflict is the department chair's to manage is to ask the question, "Does the conflict affect the overall productivity or morale of the department?" If the answer is yes, management of the conflict is the responsibility of the department chair. A chair may have two faculty members who are also neighbors and who happen to be feuding over the location of a fence between the two properties. That conflict is not the chair's to manage unless it escalates to a level where one or both faculty begin bad-mouthing the other to students. When the dispute damages department productivity, the conflict becomes the chair's to manage. It does not mean that the department chair becomes accountable for working out a solution to the placement of the fence between the two properties. It does, however, mean that the department chair must make clear that a neighborhood disagreement cannot jeopardize the academic department or interrupt the professional contributions of individual faculty to the department.

Putting Theory Into Practice

In Case 5.1, The Accusation, the department chair must manage a conflict between two faculty members. Dr. Marie Zaleznik, a tenured associate professor, demands that charges of unethical conduct be brought against Dan Peterson, an untenured assistant professor. Place yourself in the role of Dr. Ronald Schmidt, chair of the marketing department at Southern Hills University, as you read Case 5.1.

Case 5.1, The Accusation

Schmidt (outraged): "Those are serious charges you are making against Dan Peterson. You could be sued for slander."

Zaleznik: "I can only be guilty of slander if I am lying. I am not lying, and I can prove it. Nor am I making these charges lightly. Dan has consistently padded his credentials in a fraudulent way. You're not willing to look at the facts because Dan's the department's favorite son. You and the other members of the 'old guard' have always protected him."

Schmidt: "That's not true. Dan has done very well here despite having to contend with some overzealous colleagues. What possible basis could you have for making such an outrageous accusation?"

Zaleznik: "I'll tell you what I have found. As you know, this is my third year on the department's personnel committee, which means that I review the achievements submitted by every faculty member each year. The accomplishments forwarded by Dan Peterson each year contain fraudulent exaggerations. In the past he has claimed to have been a "guest lecturer" in classes where he was merely one of several faculty invited to attend a class to field questions. This year Dan reached an all-time low."

Schmidt (clearly uncomfortable): "I am not going to enter a discussion over semantics."

Zaleznik: "Dr. Schmidt, this is not a matter of semantics. It's a matter of ethics and accurate reporting. Dan also claimed that he made a presentation at national conferences when, in fact, his only role was to attend a meeting as a member of a caucus group. He's been doing these things for years, but now he's gone one step further. This year he claimed that he had a manuscript accepted for publication that I know for a fact was not accepted."

Schmidt: "How in the world would you know that?"

Zaleznik: "I'm a reviewer for the journal he listed as having accepted the publication and I checked with the editor. His manuscript was reviewed and rejected."

Schmidt: "What right do you have to check on something like that? Besides, maybe Danny intends to revise and resubmit it."

Zaleznik: "Maybe so, but he should not list the manuscript as having been accepted. You better look at the information I've compiled and be ready to take some action. If you're not prepared to restore an ethical standard in this department, I'll take this to someone who will."

Let's Analyze the Case

The conflict described in Case 5.1 is multidimensional. There is the obvious conflict between Marie Zaleznik and Dan Peterson. From Zaleznik's perspective, Peterson fraudulently presented his professional accomplishments. A second conflict exists in Dr. Zaleznik's perception of the "old guard" and their favoritism toward Dan Peterson. Depending on the validity of the charges made by Dr. Zaleznik, the chair may also discover that Dan Peterson's actions are in violation of the campus policy on ethical conduct. That would pose a conflict for the department chair who is responsible for upholding university policy and preserving a sense of professional ethics within the department. It may also pose a problem for the department in complying with ethical standards set by the professional accrediting body.

The language used by Dr. Zaleznik suggests that the work environment in this department is not healthy. Zaleznik, and perhaps other faculty, perceive the existence of a double standard for evaluating and rewarding the accomplishments of faculty. Zaleznik clearly perceives the existence of subgroups within the department and the presence of favoritism toward at least one person. That makes the chair's task of managing the conflict more difficult because Zaleznik does not view the chair as objective. If the work environment were such that Zaleznik believed that the chair treated all faculty equitably, the chair could more easily manage the immediate conflict.

The chair's response suggests that Schmidt observed the growing rift between Peterson and some of the other faculty. Early in the conversation, the chair quips: "Dan has done very well here despite having to contend with some overzealous colleagues." If the chair perceived the growing animosity between Peterson and some of the other faculty, he could have intervened by demonstrating his objectivity in dealing with faculty. This might include course assignments, release time for research, committee assignments, allocation of travel support, and other decisions affecting faculty. Depending on the level of resentment, the chair might hold one-on-one conversations with those faculty who appear to be most convinced of a bias toward Peterson. The chair might also counsel Peterson on how to behave in the department and the importance of not giving colleagues an opportunity to perceive him as exercising any advantage. The chair in this case does not manage the encounter with Dr. Zaleznik very well. When Dr. Zaleznik accuses Dan Peterson of unethical conduct, the chair becomes defensive. By defending Dan Peterson without reviewing the information presented by Marie Zaleznik, the chair escalates the conflict. The chair is not objective about the complaint, and Dr. Zaleznik leaves the encounter with the impression that the chair will not investigate the charges fairly. The chair's defensive rhetoric actually substantiates Marie Zaleznik's belief that Dan Peterson is the old guard's "favorite son."

It is possible that Peterson doesn't understand the performance expectations. It is also possible that Peterson feels somehow pressured into making bolder exaggerations of his accomplishments. The chair may need to counsel Peterson on what is acceptable in listing accomplishments. If Peterson has overstated his achievements for three years with nothing but positive response in the form of praise and salary increases, he has little reason to do things differently. The chair's early intervention would have benefited Peterson and perhaps prevented the immediate conflict.

The chair must manage more than the immediate conflict. The chair's credibility with Marie Zaleznik and perhaps other faculty will be influenced by how he handles the charges made against Dan Peterson. In the event that the chair opts to protect Dan Peterson at all costs, he loses credibility with at least some of the faculty. To the extent that Dan Peterson is the "favorite son" of the senior faculty, the chair could lose credibility with the old guard should he fail to protect Dan from what may be perceived by them as a vicious and unwarranted attack. The chair's objective is to appear neutral as he reviews the facts and applies university policy regarding the standards for ethical conduct by faculty.

It's Your Turn

Review Case 5.1 and think how you would handle the initial meeting with Dr. Zaleznik.

1. How would you handle the accusation? What nonverbal action would you take to defuse Dr. Zaleznik's anger? Would you spend time in small talk, allowing her to cool off before the discussion continued? Would you remain seated behind your desk or take a chair nearer Dr. Zaleznik? Would you allow Marie Zaleznik to vent all of her thoughts and frustrations or interrupt the harsher statements?

2. How would you handle the conversation with Dr. Zaleznik? Underline the statements made by the department chair that you would rewrite. Anticipate Dr. Zaleznik's reaction to your rhetoric and the altered scenario. Would Marie Zaleznik leave your office believing that the matter would be reviewed objectively?

Please Consider

Probably the first deletion you made was the chair's statement, "You could be sued for slander." Marie Zaleznik could perceive this statement as a threat. At a minimum, it creates a barrier for a candid and open discussion. The statement implies that the chair does not wish to hear negative comments about Dan Peterson. When Dr. Zaleznik persists, the chair asserts that Dan has succeeded while contending with some "overzealous colleagues." That assertion escalates the conflict because it indicates that the chair is taking sides. Further, by labeling Marie Zaleznik's charges as an "outrageous accusation," the chair makes clear his disbelief of the information presented by Dr. Zaleznik. The chair demonstrates that he cannot be objective regarding the charges being brought against Dan Peterson. This only confirms Zaleznik's perception of favoritism.

Once Dr. Zaleznik presents some facts, the chair attempts to dismiss the entire discussion by saying, "I am not going to enter a discussion over semantics." The statement suggests that the information presented by Dr. Zaleznik will not get an objective review by Dr. Schmidt. The conflict continues to escalate when the chair blurts out that Dr. Zaleznik has no right to "check on" the accuracy of information presented by Dan Peterson in his annual achievement report. The fact that the chair follows this assertion with an inadequate rationale on Dan's behalf is further evidence of his bias. The chair knows that a rejected publication should not be listed as accepted even if the author intends to revise and resubmit it. At this point in the dialogue, the chair refers to Dan Peterson as "Danny," which further confirms Dr. Zaleznik's suspicion of the favoritism shown Dan Peterson.

Did you identify these comments as those that you would rewrite? Now that you've had some practice in neutralizing the conflict, let's make the case more interesting. Continue to assume the role of department chair, but add the following facts:

1. University policy allows for a faculty member to bring charges of unethical conduct against another faculty member with or without the chair's support.

2. Dan Peterson earned his baccalaureate and master's degrees in the marketing department at Southern Hills University.

3. Dan's grandfather was dean of the business college at Southern Hills University. The building that houses the marketing department, Peterson Hall, was named for Dean Peterson upon his retirement.

4. The Peterson family endowed a special speaker series and established a substantial scholarship fund.

5. Peterson was hired ABD (all but dissertation) on a contingency contract. The contingency clause stipulated that Dan Peterson must complete his doctorate before the end of the first nine-month contract to be retained on a continuing tenure-track appointment. Dan did not finish his doctorate, but the chair renewed his appointment without department discussion.

How would those facts alter your handling of the situation? Would the facts cause you to change your initial response to Dr. Zaleznik? Does the additional information alter how you would approach Dan Peterson? Would you inform the dean of the charges made by Dr. Zaleznik?

Let's Recap

Review your strategy for managing the situation described in Case 5.1. If your approach does not incorporate the communication strategies for minimizing destructive conflict, you may want to review the material presented earlier in this chapter on how to effectively manage conflict. Does your approach

- help establish and maintain a healthy work environment?

- clearly communicate your goals and expectations for faculty performance?

- establish (or follow already established) ground rules for airing disagreements?

- anticipate conflict areas and allow for intervention when needed?

- give consideration to when and how to confront conflict?

- give consideration to when and how to initiate conflict?

- recognize which aspects of the conflict are the chair's to manage?

Putting Theory Into Practice

Dan Peterson did indeed exaggerate his accomplishments. Since learning of the charges, Peterson openly apologized for his actions. He even offered to take a pay cut in order to demonstrate to his faculty colleagues that he does not wish to benefit from work not done. Dan Peterson hopes that all may be forgiven. He enjoys living in his hometown and would like to retain his faculty appointment at Southern Hills University. However, sensing Marie Zaleznik's strong conviction that such unethical conduct should be punished, Peterson decides to apply for other positions.

Dan Peterson left a note in the chair's mailbox asking for a letter of recommendation. The position announcement attached to Peterson's request specifies that the applicant possess "professional integrity sufficient to serve as a role model for first-generation college students."

Dr. Schmidt elects to write a letter of recommendation for Dan Peterson. It is a difficult decision. He sincerely wants to help Peterson but doesn't know how to approach the task. Schmidt decides to write on behalf of Peterson because he believes that Peterson is an excellent teacher with a bright future. The chair believes that Peterson's career should not be ruined because of one isolated misunderstanding. Schmidt's letter of recommendation for Dan Peterson appears as Case 5.2.

Case 5.2, Letter of Recommendation

Dr. Kuei-Ning Lin, Chair
Department of Marketing
Superior College
Townsend, Utah 57802

Dear Dr. Lin:

I am writing this letter at the request of Dan Peterson whom I have known since he was a young child who would occasionally visit his grandfather, the former dean of our college. I was pleased when Dan enrolled at Southern Hills University (SHU) as a freshman in marketing. The faculty who had Dan in class remember well his excellent work as an undergraduate student. The department is proud that Dan also completed his master's at SHU.

Dan went to State University for his doctorate, returning each summer to teach for us at SHU. He is very loyal to this institution. Dan and his family have been both faithful and generous in their support of the department and the college. We were fortunate to recruit Dan for a tenure-track position as he neared completion of his doctorate.

For the past three years, Dan has taught full-time in the department. Students enjoy his classes. I have observed Dan teach on numerous occasions and find him to be an excellent teacher. He is very ambitious and takes great pride in his work.

In all candor, I sincerely wish that Dan Peterson did not need to leave SHU. I and many of my colleagues will miss him.

Sincerely,

Ronald Schmidt
Professor and Chair

Let's Analyze the Case

Let's evaluate the letter presented as Case 5.2. The chair decides to write an evaluation without reference to the charges made by Marie Zaleznik.

Instead, the chair mentions how long he has known Dan Peterson. It is clear that the chair likes Dan Peterson. It is also clear that the chair believes that Dan is an excellent teacher. This assertion, however, would be more credible if it were substantiated with some specific information that describes Dan Peterson's method of teaching. For example, the letter might mention some special ability such as his skill in fielding student questions or in teaching large lecture classes. The general way in which the chair praises Peterson's teaching does not provide the search committee with an assessment that enables them to determine if Peterson is the type of teacher needed at Superior College. As presented, the high regard expressed for Peterson's teaching is not sufficient to persuade the search committee that he is the best choice for the available position.

The overall tone of the letter suggests that the chair intends to be supportive of Peterson's application. However, the letter fails to cover many of the issues usually addressed. For example, there is no mention of how Peterson interacts with colleagues. There is no progress report on Peterson's dissertation and no explanation as to how the appointment at Southern Hills may have slowed Peterson's progress in completing the doctoral degree. There is no comment on Peterson's work in the areas of research and service. While Superior College may not have an expectation for published research, Southern Hills does. Hence, the search committee at Superior should want to know of Peterson's accomplishments in all three areas of faculty performance required at Southern Hills University.

Perhaps most damaging is the fact that the chair makes clear Peterson's longtime association with Southern Hills University. The search committee at Superior College will no doubt wonder why Peterson is seeking a position elsewhere. The chair's letter raises the question without providing an explanation. The chair elects to avoid mention of the charges made by Marie Zaleznik. However, the chair's letter of recommendation raises a serious red flag by indicating that Peterson encountered some problem at Southern Hills that caused him to submit an application to Superior College. The closing paragraph admits that the chair wishes that Peterson did not "need to leave" Southern Hills University. If the search committee remains serious about Peterson's candidacy, they will want to pursue the reason he needs to leave Southern Hills. We are left to wonder how the chair would handle a telephone call seeking some follow-up comment on the letter of recommendation.

It's Your Turn

Think through how you would handle Dan Peterson's request for a letter of recommendation.

1. What is your ethical responsibility to Dan Peterson? What is your ethical responsibility to the department and the institution? What is your ethical responsibility to other programs in your discipline who might hire Dan Peterson?

2. Is it possible to write a letter that benefits Dan Peterson without selling short your ethical responsibility to the discipline, the department, and the institution? What can you say about Peterson that would be helpful in his search for another position?

3. Draft a letter of recommendation for Dan Peterson. Review it and determine whether what you have written would be helpful to Peterson's application. Does your letter fulfill your ethical responsibility to Peterson, the discipline, the department, and the institution? What follow-up questions might you be asked in a telephone call from a member of the search committee, and how would you answer them?

Putting Theory Into Practice

Case 5.3, Self-Interest, describes a difference of opinion held by two faculty members regarding how merit pay should be awarded. In this case, Katherine Sullivan, chair of the department of philosophy, has heard the opposing points of view so often that she can anticipate the dialogue that will unfold at an upcoming meeting. Place yourself in the department chair's role as you read the following case.

Case 5.3, Self-Interest

The Characters

Katherine Sullivan, chair of the department of philosophy, dreads the upcoming department meeting. The first item on the agenda is a review of the department procedures for awarding merit increases. Over the years, the department has become fairly proficient in its evaluation of faculty merit. The one remaining source of disagreement is how merit awards should be translated into salary increase dollars. Each year, the department receives a pool of money that is based on a percent of the total salary base of the academic unit. Hence, faculty at the rank of professor with larger salaries contribute more to the salary increase pool than faculty at more junior professorial ranks who earn lower salaries.

For the past three years, the department awarded merit as a fixed dollar amount rather than as a percent of an individual faculty member's salary base. Faculty are rated on a scale from zero to three and everyone receiving the same numeric score receives the same dollar increase. When translated to percent of salary increase, an assistant professor has a higher percent of salary increase than a full professor with the same numeric merit score. In fact, a professor deemed to be highly meritorious might receive a below-average salary increase.

Katherine recognizes that the current practice discriminates against senior faculty who in many instances have served the department and institution for 20 or more years. Further, it creates a salary compression problem in that the salaries of untenured junior faculty are rapidly catching up with the salaries of faculty who have 20 or more years of service in the department. The senior faculty carry the weight of directing graduate theses and dissertations so untenured faculty can devote more time to completing the research necessary for successful tenure and promotion review. Because the department cannot reach consensus on the issue, the matter is typically decided by vote. With faculty voting self-interest, the outcome is decided by the fact that the department is composed of seven untenured assistant professors, two tenured associate professors, and three tenured full professors. Katherine can predict how the discussion will go.

The Meeting

It didn't take long for the conflict to surface at the faculty meeting.

Sam Harris, a full professor, is the first to break the ice. "I believe it's time to consider another method for awarding salary increases. We have used the fixed dollar allocation for three years with great penalty to senior faculty. I propose that we begin using a combination model in which half of the salary increase awarded by the state would be allocated as a percent of salary base and the other half would be distributed as a dollar amount. A combination model is the only fair salary increase plan because it does not penalize either senior or junior faculty."

"I'm opposed to distributing salary increases in any method other than a straight dollar allocation," snapped Jessica McClellen, one of the untenured faculty members.

"Won't you at least consider a plan that doesn't discriminate against either junior or senior faculty?" asked Sam.

"My merit should count the same as your merit. If you and I each receive a merit rating of three, we deserve the same dollar amount. It's only fair. There is no reason why your merit should count more," retorted Jessica.

"My 26 years of service should count for something." added Sam.

"Absolutely not! Why should you be paid for being older? Besides, your higher salary eats more of the summer budget so it all balances out. When it's your turn to teach in the summer, there are fewer summer appointments for the rest of us," Jessica added defiantly as though she had uncovered a serious inequity.

"But the years of experience possessed by senior faculty enable us to contribute in a different dimension. For example, we bear the brunt of directing graduate students, a selfless activity that takes us away from our personal research and..."

Before Sam could finish his sentence, Jessica interrupted, saying, "If I do the work assigned to me in a meritorious way, it doesn't matter what I do. My merit pay in dollars should equal yours. I contribute just as much as you do and my merit should not be worth one penny less than your merit."

By this time, Jessica is sitting taller in her chair and appears somewhat triumphant. She hastens to add, "I support a socialistic philosophy. I disapprove of any system that promotes classes among us."

"But the salaries of the senior faculty contribute more to the total salary increase pool. With the average salary increase of 4.5% this year, a full professor making $50,000 will contribute $2,250 to the department salary increase pool and an assistant professor making $30,000 will only contribute $1,350. If they both get the same numeric merit rating and a dollar increase of $1,500, the professor's merit will represent a 3% salary increase, whereas the assistant professor's merit will represent a 5% salary increase. You benefit from the large contribution that the senior faculty make to the department salary increase pool. How is that fair?" asked Sam.

"It's perfectly fair in a socialistic system where there is not a caste system that separates. My contribution is as important as yours and should be worth as much as yours. It's quite simple," replied Jessica.

Sam ventured one more thought, "I firmly believe that any model other than a combination model is divisive to the department because it is a model of self-interest. If Dr. McClellen was motivated only by her self-professed belief in socialism, she would also want all new assistant professors to have starting salaries that are not one penny less than the salaries of other more experienced assistant professors. Yet, I suspect that Jessica would oppose any plan that did not preserve her status over other more junior assistant professors."

Jessica retorted: "I realize that the current practice of awarding merit in dollars benefits me because I'm a new faculty member, but that's not a reason to switch to a different system." Then with a chuckle, she added, "I may change my vote when I'm a full professor, but right now this is the right way to do it."

Let's Analyze the Case

The department chair dreaded the department meeting because she could anticipate the dialogue that she would hear. It was no secret that there were at least two opposing points of view among department faculty about the awarding of merit salary increases. The chair is uncertain how to confront this conflict other than to have it rehashed periodically at a department meeting. As expected, the strong viewpoints regarding the issue surfaced during the meeting. All of the usual comments were made, and again the faculty could not reach a satisfactory solution or compromise. It seems that the only way to settle the matter is to take another vote, and the outcome is predictable. The faculty are unable to engage in a discussion about the method for awarding salary increases without advocating their own self-interest. Sam Harris suggests a compromise by using a combination model. Even this "compromise" alternative represents a method that would benefit Sam Harris more than the current practice.

Worse yet, the sentiment expressed by faculty becomes more acerbic every time they revisit the issue. The language used by the assistant professor, Jessica McClellen, indicates a deeply felt bitterness toward senior professors that extends beyond this one issue. McClellen perceives the senior faculty as limiting her opportunity for a summer employment. In her opinion, the senior faculty receive unfair benefit and the fixed dollar method of awarding salary increases helps to balance other inequities. It is not clear from the case whether there are legitimate reasons for McClellen's belief that inequity exists between the senior and junior faculty. It is possible that this one issue has been allowed to fester to the point where it has produced a rift between the senior and junior faculty.

The discussion presented in Case 5.3 gives us reason to conclude that the work environment is not as healthy as it might be. The faculty do not share a common vision of the department mission or priorities. Consequently, the faculty make decisions and vote from a personal bias to preserve self-interest. If the attitudes expressed are representative of those held by the group, then faculty at each rank are only aware of their own contribution to the department. Sam Harris mentions the extra time that the senior faculty invest in supervising graduate students, but this fact fails to convince Jessica McClellen who asserts that the more junior faculty work just as hard and senior faculty salaries take up a disproportionate share of the money allocated for summer teaching appointments. From Sam Harris's point of view, the heavier graduate student advisement load carried by the senior faculty gives the untenured faculty more release time for research activity. Each group believes that they are working hard to the advantage of the other group. This suggests that at least some faculty believe that the goals and expectations for faculty performance are not the same for all faculty.

The department chair allows the discussion to unfold as she predicted it would. Sullivan opts not to intervene in that portion of the discussion detailed in Case 5.3. The chair is not sure how to manage the conflict. She recognizes that the current method for awarding salary increases is unfair to senior faculty but cannot think of any way to initiate a change in the status quo. The chair's posture suggests that she believes that it is an issue that must be decided by the faculty. The chair could have intervened before the meeting. It is easier to change attitudes on salient issues in a one-on-one format. This does not mean that the chair should persuade all faculty to vote a certain way on an issue. Rather, a chair can intervene by helping individual faculty understand the perspective held by other faculty. The intervention can heighten sensitivity about how individuals interpret and assess the various viewpoints. The conversation might also explore the cost of the conflict to individual faculty and the department. That would help individual faculty put a single issue in the larger context of the department mission and priorities.

This department lacks ground rules for airing differences of opinion. The chair's silence through a lengthy disagreement suggests that the operating ground rule is that all can say whatever they please. One may be struck by how free at least one faculty member is to express personal opinion and prejudice. Particularly since the chair was able to predict the way in which the discussion would unfold, ground rules could have been used to break the destructive pattern. The chair, for example, might introduce the issue by acknowledging the frequently heard arguments and challenging all faculty in this year's discussion to move beyond arguments of obvious self-interest. The chair could stress the need for a department discussion and vote that is more responsible. The chair might also speak first on the issue and educate the faculty on the pros and cons of the current practice such as the growing problem of salary compression or the need to retain faculty. That would help the faculty consider the salary increase plan within the larger context of department priorities.

It's Your Turn

Assume the role of the chair and decide how would you manage this conflict.

1. What would you do in advance of the meeting to make the conflict more manageable? Review the discussion in Case 5.3. At what point would you intervene in the discussion? What would you say and to whom would you address your comments? Could you structure the meeting in a way that prevents a repeat of the dialogue that tends to fuel a larger conflict?

2. Does the dialogue impact the overall department climate? Should such differences of opinion between junior and senior faculty be decided by a vote? Is there more at stake than the issue of merit pay? Will the manner in which you manage this conflict influence your credibility with the faculty? How might this issue affect other department priorities?

Please Consider

The department chair will influence the outcome of this disagreement. Chairs cannot remain neutral on such disagreements. In Case 5.3, the department chair allows the disagreement to unfold as she knew it would without intervention. When managing conflict, the decision to remain silent is a response to the conflict and one that the faculty are not likely to perceive as neutral. It is clear from the dialogue presented in Case 5.3 that the faculty are unable to resolve the conflict on their own. Consequently, it is irresponsible for the chair to allow the conflict to continue to fester until it does further damage to the department climate and professional rapport among faculty.

Chairs can also prejudice the outcome of an issue through their management of the conflict. In Case 5.3, the chair recognizes that the current practice of awarding salary increases favors the more junior faculty who earn lower salaries. The chair, however, is unwilling to articulate her opinion. A credible chair could probably sway department opinion by offering the chair's view of what would be most fair. Without the chair's inserting a logic for weighing the pros and cons of the possible salary increase plans, the self-interest escalates in a way that can damage long-term professional relationships among faculty and destroy a positive work environment. The language used by Jessica McClellen, for example, illustrates a general disrespect for opposing points of view and an arrogance about arguing self-interest.

The dialogue in Case 5.3 depicts the department culture and offers some insight on the chair's management style. The chair is prone to let faculty decide issues, which is not inherently a poor management style. A chair, however, cannot let faculty decide the issue without managing the conflict. It is the chair's responsibility to ensure that faculty present their various viewpoints in a professional manner and that faculty separate this one issue of conflict from their overall assessment of a colleague's worth. It is the chair's responsibility to help faculty advance substantive arguments that allow the department to weigh all sides of the issue. Only then can the department reach a workable solution or at least cast an informed vote. The chair in Case 5.3 permits the same disagreement to unfold repeatedly, thus increasing the likelihood that the issue of contention will escalate and absorb other feelings of resentment and ill will among faculty in the department.

It is virtually impossible for a chair to remain neutral while the faculty decide such serious issues as the one described in Case 5.3. Even when chairs prefer not to disclose their personal views on a particular issue, they need to manage the conflict so the faculty are more likely to reach a constructive outcome that does not harm the department by creating unnecessary animosity among faculty or toward the department chair. Please consider the impact that department chairs have on department conflict as you read Case 5.4.

Case 5.4, The Chair's Bias

Unofficial Meetings

Since the last department meeting, many of the faculty met with Katherine Sullivan to express their personal views on the issue of how salary increases should be awarded.

The first one to visit the department chair was Sam Harris. Sullivan discloses that she is uncomfortable with the current practice of awarding salary increases because it discriminates against the more senior faculty. Sullivan adds that it is unlikely that a faculty vote will enable her to change the current practice because senior faculty are outnumbered in the department. Sam suggests that the discussion might improve if the chair demonstrates the economics of a specific case, using each of the three possible salary plans: fixed dollar amounts, a percent of salary base, and a combination model. Sam hopes that this will help a majority of faculty understand that the combination model is the fairest in that it is the only plan that doesn't discriminate against either junior or senior faculty. Katherine agrees to present a hypothetical case to the faculty before further discussion of the issue. Harris leaves the chair's office believing that Sullivan empathizes with the senior faculty. Sam Harris informs the other tenured faculty of his conversation with Katherine Sullivan.

Katherine is also visited by almost all of the untenured faculty in the department, each pleading the case for using the current practice. The rationale presented by each ranges from the cost of groceries to why no-one's work should count less than someone else's effort. Katherine Sullivan enjoys a good rapport with the untenured faculty. In fact, Sullivan is more comfortable working with the untenured faculty than she is with the more senior faculty. While Sullivan enjoys the respect of both groups, the untenured faculty are in general less critical of the chair's management of the department. Also, Sullivan feels closer to the untenured faculty. She hired them and counsels them on their progress in meeting the department and university standards for tenure. Katherine listens to each untenured faculty member in the same supportive manner that the untenured faculty experience during performance evaluation sessions.

Round Two

The next department meeting moves along smoothly until the last item on the agenda, the salary increase plan. The department chair initiates the discussion by announcing that she has promised to bring an example of what each of the three possible salary increase plans would do to a specific salary. Sullivan quickly adds that she "dropped the ball" on this and just wasn't able to get it done.

The chair proceeds by offering a verbal summary of the three plans. "I believe that we are all familiar with the provisions of each plan. When salary increases are awarded by fixed dollar amounts, there is some benefit to the lower-paid faculty because the dollar amount of the increase typically results in a higher percent of salary base. If salary increases are awarded as a percent of salary base, then higher-paid faculty get more dollars. The combination model actually washes out the effect of merit because it cancels the benefit of either of the other two plans."

With that brief overview, the chair invites faculty comment. None of the faculty are quick to discuss the issue. Sensing the silence, the chair quickly adds, "If there is no discussion, I don't have any reason to change the current practice for awarding salary increases."

At this point, Sam Harris ventures a comment, "As you all know, I support the combination model because it doesn't 'wash out' merit but rather allows for the distribution of merit in a manner that does not penalize any particular subgroup of faculty. That seems to me to be a worthwhile goal in the interest of preserving good will among faculty in the department."

Jessica McClellen retorts, "How is my good will going to improve if I lose money? Any change from the current practice is taking money out of my pocket and I can't vote for that. After all, we are all expected to produce so why should we have a salary increase plan that favors high paid faculty?"

With this comment, many of the faculty sigh. Sullivan knows from her individual conversations with the faculty that many untenured faculty are uncomfortable with the way in which Jessica McClellen insists on turning the discussion into a personalized attack on senior faculty. Few of the untenured faculty really believe McClellen's appeal to socialism or her charge that the other salary increase plans creates a caste system within the department.

Dave Johnson, the newest untenured faculty member, adds, "Well, what type of combination model would we use?"

The chair replies, "That is another issue. We could use any number of combination models between the fixed dollar amount and a percentage of base. We would have to look at the factors and decide how to weight each. If we end up weighting the percent of salary base more heavily than the portion that might be awarded as a fixed dollar amount, we have in reality shifted from the current practice to the percent of salary increase plan."

Sam Harris couldn't believe what he was hearing. He felt betrayed by the department chair and concluded that it was hopeless to make further comment. Obviously, the chair altered her position on the issue. Not only did she elect to renege on the promise to present some concrete examples, but she no longer expressed any empathy for the plight of senior faculty.

With no further comment, the chair closes discussion by saying, "Well, it looks as if there is no consensus to change the present practice."

Let's Analyze the Case

The question of what method should be used to award salary increases has been decided. The department will continue to award salary increases as a fixed dollar amount, the plan that favors faculty with lower salaries. The department chair predicted that this would be the outcome of the faculty deliberation because, as she reminded Sam Harris, the untenured faculty outnumber the senior faculty.

The outcome, however, is not the result of reasoned faculty deliberation. The faculty discussion never gets past self-interest. McClellen's self-interest is obvious. It is doubtful that many, if any, of the faculty accepted her rationale as a bias toward a socialistic perspective. It is interesting to note that McClellen makes at least one untenured faculty member uncomfortable. We recognize the desire to dissociate ourselves from a certain position that we might otherwise endorse to avoid being grouped with those who are championing the position in an unflattering or unprofessional manner. As it turned out, Jessica McClellen did not have to say much because of how the chair presents the issue. Had McClellen needed to advance her position, she might have effectively altered the outcome by forcing some of the other untenured faculty to dissociate themselves from McClellen by voting for a compromise salary plan.

The department chair presents the issue in a way that places the need for advocacy with those faculty who want a change in the current practice. That leaves it to Sam Harris and other senior faculty to persuade the larger group of untenured faculty that the current plan that benefits lower-paid faculty most should be changed. The chair prejudices the outcome by framing the discussion this way. The department chair could present the issue as a need to examine the present system, giving full consideration to both benefits and liabilities. That would allow for a more even comparison of all possible salary increase plans. It also would distribute the need for advocacy to both proponents of the current practice and champions of change. In this discussion format, the department chair then would need to keep the discussion focused on substantive issues rather than personalities.

The department chair further influences the outcome by providing editorial comment about the three possible salary increase plans. There is never a clear comparison of the plans because the chair, as she said, "dropped the ball" and didn't prepare a hypothetical instance that would demonstrate what happens to a specific example under each of the possible plans. Instead, the chair offers an editorial comment on the three plans. Sullivan discounts the combination model when she asserts that it "washes out" merit. Without a concrete example, that statement is difficult to disprove or verify during a department meeting.

The chair also limits sincere debate and prejudices the outcome by signaling personal bias. The chair's intention is not clear. In both Case 5.3 and Case 5.4, Sullivan insists that it is an issue that must be decided by the faculty. Yet the issue was decided by the chair. Even at the close of the discussion, the chair insists that she is obliged to continue the current practice since there is no consensus for change. Everyone recognizes that it is an issue on which there is no consensus. By stating that it would take a consensus to change the current practice, the chair determines the outcome.

It's Your Turn

Assume the role of the department chair and think through how you would manage this conflict.

1. How would you handle the individual conversations with faculty members that took place between the two department meetings? What is your ethical responsibility to individual faculty when they are divided on an issue of department concern? What is your ethical responsibility to the overall department mission? Is the chair's ethical responsibility limited to casting a personal vote to break a tie when department faculty are split on an issue?

2. How would you frame the discussion at the department meeting? Review Case 5.4 and underline the comments made by the department chair that you would change. Substitute your language in the case and speculate how your approach would alter the outcome. Would your approach alter the attitudes held by faculty? Would your approach alter your rapport with faculty?

Please Consider

There is more at stake than whether or not the department retains the current practice for awarding salary increases. One precondition to the chair's ability to effectively manage conflict is a healthy work environment. The outcome of the current issue helps to preserve or alter the work environment that will, in turn, affect the chair's ability to manage the next conflict. If the senior faculty in Case 5.4 leave the department meeting believing that the chair betrayed them and prejudiced the outcome, their perception will influence future behavior. It is, therefore, less significant to know whether the department chair in Case 5.4 intended to prejudice the outcome than it is to understand how the chair's actions were perceived. Each conflict management task can either improve or weaken the chair's ability to effectively manage the next conflict.

The chair's credibility with the faculty is inevitably linked to how the chair treats them. In Case 5.4 it is understandable that Sam Harris felt betrayed. Harris would not be surprised by a faculty vote that upheld the current practice for awarding salary increases. In fact, Harris probably expected the outcome that was realized. What Harris did not expect was the chair's action. The chair had promised to prepare and present a concrete example that demonstrates what each of the possible salary plans does to a specific salary. In the meeting, the chair dismisses the promise in a blithe and casual manner that implies the request was somehow unimportant to the discussion. Further, by waiting until the department meeting to dismiss the need for concrete examples as unimportant, the chair prevents Sam from generating the examples.

Review your plan for managing the department meeting in Case 5.4. Would your approach preserve or enhance your credibility with individual faculty? Would your management of the department meeting preserve or bolster a healthy work environment within the department?

Let's Recap

Conflict is inevitable because it is a natural outcome of human interaction. If the department chair effectively manages conflict, the department actually benefits from the existence of differing viewpoints. The chair's objective is to manage rather than resolve conflict. Department chairs want to maximize constructive conflict and minimize destructive conflict.

The most effective way to manage conflict is to establish and maintain a healthy department climate. Faculty in healthy work environments are generally more supportive, cooperative, and accepting of change than faculty who work in negative department climates. Destructive conflict is less frequent in a positive work environment. Department chairs also facilitate the sometimes uncomfortable task of managing conflict by clearly communicating the goals and expectations for faculty performance and by establishing workable ground rules for airing disagreements.

The task of managing conflict involves more than arbitration. Chairs need to know when and how to intervene in order to prevent or minimize destructive conflict. Chairs sometimes need to initiate conflict in order to facilitate effective decision-making and preempt larger, more troublesome disagreements. The task of managing conflict is essential to maintaining workable and productive interactions and relationships within the department. Once department chairs understand the full benefit of managing conflict, the task becomes more comfortable.

6

IMPLEMENTING CHANGE

For most department chairs it is more realistic to ask what to change rather than whether or not to make changes. Change is essential for department survival and growth. In the face of internal and external pressures for change, department chairs need to preserve what is valuable and implement change that allows future viability. Effectively managing change is paramount to successful leadership. The department chair cannot assume that well-reasoned and needed changes will be automatically accepted and implemented.

For the department to change, its members must change—and faculty can tenaciously resist change. Change tends to be intensely personal in that members of the department respond to a proposed change based on how it affects them individually. Change invites resistance from individual participants who are focused on personal liability rather than on the department's welfare. Even a change that all recognize is important carries with it a sense of disruption. The challenge is to lead a department of individuals toward and through change that benefits the collective group.

The Objective

One goal of this chapter is to help department chairs understand that change is a dynamic process involving not only themselves but also others. Chairs need to identify the persons and pressures that influence the change process. Consequently, the management of change requires effective interpersonal communication skills. A second goal is to equip chairs with specific communication strategies for successfully implementing and managing change, including steps for making the department climate more receptive to change.

Defining the Task

Change is a dynamic process that is inherent in leadership. Consider the following definitions of leadership. Gmelch and Miskin (1995) define leadership as "an *influence relationship* between the academic leader and faculty members who intend real changes that reflect their mutual purposes (vision)." Tucker (1992, p. 56) defines leadership as "the ability to *influence* or *motivate* an individual or a group of individuals to work willingly toward a given goal or objective under a specific set of circumstances." Gardner (1990, p. 1) defines leadership as "the *process of persuasion* or example by which an individual (or leadership team) induces a group to pursue objectives held by the leader or shared by the leader and his or her followers." Finally, Bennis and Nanus (1985, p. 21) define leadership as *"influencing,* guiding in direction, course, action, opinion." All of these definitions of leadership describe the task of implementing change. Effective leaders are both successful change agents and change managers.

Change is inherent in the specific roles and responsibilities typically assigned to department chairs. Department chairs are change agents with faculty when conducting performance evaluation, supervising curricular revision, or soliciting faculty cooperation for administrative mandates. Similarly, department chairs are change agents with deans and central administration when seeking approval for curricular change, new faculty positions, more space, or greater department autonomy.

Change is a dynamic process. The act of implementing and managing change is never static because numerous individuals and conditions affect the change process and the outcome. The department chair is dependent upon the actions of other people for the successful implementation of change. Without skilled leadership and effective interpersonal communication, it is unlikely that all participants will move cooperatively in the desired direction. Finally, change is a process that does not occur in a vacuum. Environmental conditions influence and impact the process. Chairs must manage change, a process that is integral to their assigned duties but is also vulnerable to external and dynamic forces.

Relevant Communication Concepts and Strategies

The task of implementing change is not limited to those moments when external pressures or necessity mandate change. The department chair's role in implementing change includes prechange and postchange communication. A chair's daily communication with faculty, staff, and students can help to minimize resistance to change and set the stage for effective change implementation. The following communication strategies (Higgerson, 1992a) will help department chairs implement and manage the change process.

Establish preconditions essential for implementing change

Department chairs must recognize preconditions that influence the change process. Two critical preconditions over which the department chair has significant control are the department climate and the chair's credibility.

The department climate may not mirror the campus climate; a positive department climate may exist on a campus where morale is generally low and vice versa. A healthy department climate creates a supportive environment for change. Chairs who believe that they are helpless in establishing a productive department climate because of grim campus conditions do not realize the influence that chairs have over the department climate. Chapter 2 of this text addresses in more detail the chair's ability to influence the department climate.

A department climate is conducive to change if the following characteristics exist. First, the department mission must be understood and accepted. If members of the department understand and accept the direction pursued by the collective unit, they are more likely to see how the proposed change facilitates or impedes progress in that direction. A clear department mission must be supported by mutually accepted department goals. Some reward systems for faculty performance encourage individual achievement at the expense of recognized department goals; differential release time for research; counteroffers for faculty who may leave to accept another position: and new-hire salaries that create a salary compression problem between new faculty and longtime faculty whose salaries have not kept pace with inflation. The faculty must see department goals that are compatible with individual goals.

Second, there must be mutual respect among department members. Mutual respect implies open communication regarding department issues. Faculty air differences of opinion constructively and typically work through differences to identify the best alternatives for the collective unit. Faculty perceive the chair as treating all department members in a fair and consistent manner. When the department climate exhibits these characteristics, morale is typically good. In a positive environment, faculty are less defensive, less critical, and more receptive to change. Specific strategies for how a department chair can cultivate a healthy department climate are presented in Chapter 2.

The chair's credibility is another precondition that is essential to change. Credibility implies a trust that is essential to persuading individuals to change. Because change breeds anxiety and resistance, the chair's credibility is an important precondition to change. The more positive the chair's credibility, the more influence the chair has in the change process. Unfortunately, trust is hardest to establish during change when the chair needs it the most. Three specific components compose the department chair's credibility:

- perception of the chair's knowledge

- perception of the chair's motive or intentions

- perception of the chair's trustworthiness

Please note that all three components of the chair's credibility derive from perceptions held by others. A department chair may be knowledgeable, have good intentions, and be trustworthy. That chair, however, is credible only if others perceive him or her as knowledgeable, well-intentioned, and trustworthy. Credibility is an assigned attribute. Faculty, students, central administration, and other salient publics form assessments of the chair's credibility. It is helpful to understand how others assign credibility.

In assessing the chair's knowledge, faculty ask if the chair knows how to do the job. Does the chair understand the issues? Does the chair have the training and experience needed to do an effective job? Has the chair done the essential homework to do an effective job? The faculty may hold different assessments of their chair's knowledge to do the job. The differences result from diverse perceptions of the chair's role and varying notions as to what it takes to be an effective department chair. For example, some faculty weigh previous administrative experience as critical, while other faculty assess the chair's experience by published research. Those who assign a greater significance to administrative experience perceive the chair's role as one of managing administrative detail. Those faculty who value published research as an indication of one's readiness to assume a chair's position perceive the chair's role as "first among equals" in academic pursuits. They assign greater significance to the chair's reputation as a scholar when assessing the chair's experience to lead others in the discipline. It is also possible that the faculty and the administration hold different assessments of the chair's knowledge to do the job. A dean who perceives the chair's primary role as implementing the wishes of the central administration will assess the chair's knowledge and ability to do the job on very different criteria than faculty who perceive the chair's primary role as chief advocate for the department.

The assessment of the chair's motives or intentions is even more subjective. Faculty individually determine if the chair means well. Is the chair motivated by a personal agenda, or can the chair be counted on to pursue the department agenda? Here again, what some faculty perceive as evidence of a chair motivated only by a personal agenda, other faculty may view as essential to one's continued professional advancement. For example, some faculty take personal offense upon learning that the chair applied for a deanship at a different institution, whereas other faculty may view the action as the next logical step in the chair's career. Some faculty applaud a chair who manages to carve out time for research, and some faculty resent a chair who places the welfare of the department second to research even if only for one morning each week.

The assessment of the chair's trustworthiness considers whether the chair is honest and reliable. Are the chair's decisions predictable and consistent with the department's mission, goals, and objectives? Individual faculty tend to base this assessment on personal interactions with the department chair. Again, the faculty may not agree on how they view the same action. This component of credibility is central to the overall credibility rating. Aristotle pointed out that trustworthiness is essential to one's total credibility with others. If the faculty believe that their chair is untrustworthy, it doesn't matter that the chair knows the job or has good intentions. Chairs that "ride the fence," attempting to be everything to everyone, are likely to be perceived as untrustworthy. Faculty compare notes. Faculty listen to the chair's comments over time. Unexplained shifts in position lend themselves to assessments of untrustworthiness.

Unfortunately, it is easier to lose credibility than to acquire it. Consequently, the task of maintaining one's credibility as a department chair is never done. Virtually all of the communication strategies presented in this text work toward enhancing the department chair's credibility. For example, if the chair is clear and consistent in articulating the department mission (Chapter 1), and the chair's decision and actions are consistent with the articulated department goals and objectives, the chair will be perceived as more credible by the faculty. If the chair effectively conducts performance evaluations (Chapter 4), and the faculty realize that the chair is genuinely interested in their professional development, the chair will have higher credibility with the faculty. If the chair works effectively with the dean (Chapter 7) and other external publics (Chapter 8), the dean and other external publics will perceive the chair as credible.

Credibility is not the result of doing what others want you to do so much as the result of doing what others expect you to do in carrying out the duties and responsibilities assigned with the role of department chair. Department chairs can improve their credibility by clarifying for others the roles and responsibilities of the chair's job. This works internally with faculty and externally with the dean and other external publics. Only when others accurately understand the role of the department chair, the full range of assigned responsibilities, the parameters that facilitate or impede action, and other significant factors that define the chair's job can they accurately assess the chair's credibility.

The healthy department climate and the chair's credibility are critical preconditions to change because their presence facilitates change and their absence impedes change. If the existing climate is poor and the chair lacks credibility, it is virtually impossible to improve the department climate and the chair's credibility while undergoing change. If the preconditions are such that others remain critical and resist change, it is unlikely that the department climate and chair's credibility can be bolstered by the change process. If, however, preconditions are positive, a chair can further improve the department climate and enhance credibility by effectively managing change. Under positive conditions, the change process allows the department chair to demonstrate knowledge of the job, good intentions, and trustworthiness.

Determine the obstacles

The quickest way to determine the obstacles to planned or proposed change is to ask the following key questions:

1. Who will be affected by the change?

2. Is the change consistent with the department and institutional mission?

3. Is the change consistent with the department and institutional goals?

4. How will the change be perceived?

The answer to Question 1 identifies the potential resisters to change. Before department chairs can plan for the implementation of change, they need to know who will be affected by the proposed change. The answer may not be limited to department members. Change within the department can also affect persons outside the department. Take, for example, a decision to limit enrollment in a popular course to department majors. That change will affect other program advisors who recommend that majors take the course. By identifying those who will be affected by the proposed change, the department chair can anticipate reaction. That knowledge is useful in strategizing the presentation and implementation stages of change. Department chairs need to be cognizant of those expectations when identifying the obstacles to change.

It is important to know whether the proposed change is consistent with the department and institutional missions (Question 2). Ideally, the department mission is compatible with the institution's mission, but more specific in delineating the department's unique niche on campus and in the discipline. In advocating change upward or external to the department, it is particularly important to understand how the proposed change advances the institutional mission. For change within the department, the chair needs to recognize how the proposed change further advances the department mission. People within the department have expectations for what they believe should happen. The expectations may be unwritten and unspoken, but they influence each person's reaction to proposed change. Department chairs can help shape the expectations of members of the department by structuring and clarifying the department mission. As detailed in Chapter 1 of this text, the chair's efforts to establish a clear and acceptable mission for the department structures the way in which members of the department perceive and react to events. Once the initial understanding of the department's mission is established, it is easier to achieve change that moves the department in the agreed-upon direction.

Question 3 pushes the issue further by asking the relationship between the proposed change and the more specific goals and objectives of the institution and department. Ideally, the goals and objectives derive from the mission. They merely represent the more specific and immediate plans for achieving the general and long-term direction advanced in the mission statement. For each mission statement, there can be several specific goals and objectives. By analyzing how the proposed change achieves the immediate goals and objectives established for the department or the institution, the chair makes the proposed change more compelling.

Finally, chairs need to ask how the change will be perceived by those affected by the change. Will the change be seen as unnecessary, punitive, restrictive, or helpful? It is likely that the parties affected by the change will not have the same perception of it. Discerning the various reactions enables the department chair to determine the potential allies and resisters of the proposed change. Thinking through what the different reactions are likely to be enables the chair to prepare for and answer some of the objections in the initial presentation of information that describes the problem or need for change. Without preliminary analysis, good ideas for needed change can be derailed early in the process.

Define the problem or need for change

To accept change, faculty must understand the reason for it. When chairs fail to communicate the essential background information that demonstrates the need for change, they prevent people from understanding the conditions and principles that guide the proposed change. One way to demonstrate the need for change is to build on existing concerns. For example, a chair's initial communication may be directed toward the need to guard against further enrollment decline rather than advocating curricular revision. By starting with the conditions that call for change, the chair helps the faculty (or the administration) understand the potential risk of not changing. The chair also allows the faculty (or the administration) to realize the benefits of implementing change. The background information helps others in or outside the department understand the need for change.

It is often difficult to break from present routines to examine the status quo and discover the need for change. Yet, helping others perceive the need for change is an important step in implementing change. An effective chair gets the faculty to interrupt routine schedules and review relevant facts that enable them to recognize the need for change. The chair's role as change agent begins with getting faculty (or the administration) to perceive the problem and recognize that there are better ways of doing things.

It is also important that the faculty evaluate needed change in relation to the department mission and goals. For example, if the institution has a strong commitment to improving the quality of undergraduate education, a proposal for the addition of a new graduate concentration will be more readily accepted if the advantages to undergraduate students are identified in the proposal. Similarly, a department may have a specific goal of increasing enrollment. That goal can prompt faculty to support curricular revision that would otherwise be resisted if considered separately from the unit's need to maintain enrollment.

Repetition in communication that is clear and consistent can be helpful in focusing attention on the problem that requires change. The language may vary as the chair repeats the message. For example, the department chair must do more than send one memorandum articulating the department's need for additional space to the dean. The effective department chair will use every opportunity to reference the shortage of space in continued interactions and communication with the dean. This is particularly helpful if the need for space can be linked to college and university goals.

Solicit solutions to the problem
The act of soliciting solutions to the problem is an interactive process. Some chairs assert, "I explained what we had to do and asked for input." This is not an interactive process. It does not characterize a genuine dialogue or exchange of ideas. Nor is this statement likely to be perceived by faculty as sincere. Other chairs lament, "There was only one solution. Why take every-

one's time rehashing something that can't be changed?" Even if the outcome cannot be changed, there is tremendous benefit from having the participants analyze the problem and explore the full range of possible alternatives.

As an interactive process, the focus shifts from will we change to how should we change. The dialogue enables the department chair to encourage the faculty (or the administration) to take ownership of the problem and recommended solution. The chair's task is to assist others in conceptualizing and devising a strategy for successful innovation. During this part of the change process, the chair can help suggest specific strategies and encourage brainstorming of all possible alternatives. The outcome of the change process will be helped if the chair is able to structure a nonthreatening exploration of possible alternatives. It requires that the participants stay focused on the problem and the conditions pushing for change and not be allowed to view the department issue from the perspective of personal agenda. This participatory process for soliciting possible solutions enables the department chair to generate more support for change.

Provide reassurance

Any person's first reaction to proposed change will be to ask how it affects him or her in terms of job security, opportunity for professional advancement, promotion, salary increases, workload, and the like. Frequent communication with faculty before, during, and after the implementation of change can help to alleviate personal concerns. This requires clear and frequent communication at all steps of the change process. During any change effort, rumors tend to run rampant. To the extent that the department chair is able to defuse the destructive impact of rumors through consistent, clear, and frequent communication, the chair reduces anxiety and minimizes resistance to change.

The chair's communication can also help structure the task and build consensus. For example, the dean may make a request that faculty are likely to perceive as unnecessary busywork. The task may require some change in how the department assigns faculty time and measures productivity. Rather than merely announcing the dean's request at the next department meeting, the chair may find it advantageous to signal the forthcoming change through other communications with the faculty. The notice may appear in the announcement of the meeting or be discussed in informal conversations with faculty before it is put on the table in a more formal "get done" way. Often a specific request makes more sense (and is resisted less) if it is explained within a larger context. For example, the request to design and implement assessment measures of student learning outcomes is typically less objectionable if it is explained as consistent with the longtime faculty responsibility for evaluating student work.

Avoid rejection

Because change is a process, the chair can seldom implement change unilaterally. Successful integration of change requires that all faculty accept and facilitate its implementation. This makes it imperative that the department chair engage in communication with the faculty (or the administration) that will not result in outright rejection of the proposed or planned change. In addition to frequent and consistent communication about the need for change, the chair's communication must demonstrate that the chair acknowledges expressed concerns about the change. Without responding to the articulated concerns of the faculty, the chair appears to be unilaterally imposing change. This does little to build consensus about the need for change and does not allow the faculty to take ownership of the planned change.

It is possible to be a traditionalist in implementing change. Radicals tend to alienate prospective allies. There is a significant difference between demonstrating the need for change and attacking those who are responsible for the present practice. Even the best and most carefully conceived and executed process becomes obsolete in time. Chairs need to demonstrate their respect for past work while they make clear that changing conditions force a revision in current practice or policy. It's important for department chairs to remember that the process of implementing change does not mean that we have to discredit previous efforts or actions.

Endorsements from experts is another effective communication strategy for avoiding rejection. Chairs might explain how a similar change worked at a different institution or what leading experts in the discipline say regarding the issue. If faculty remain resistant to change, the chair can recommend that the department try the proposed action on an experimental basis. When doing this, chairs will be more credible if a timetable is set for the experiment complete with a date at which faculty will review the effect of the trial change.

Putting Theory Into Practice

The strategies suggested for implementing change involve precommunication, process, and postcommunication. Chairs can use these strategies to implement change within the department or to seek change with the central administration and other external publics. In Case 6.1, Another Mandate, the department chair must inform the faculty of yet another directive from the central administration. The chair knows that the faculty will perceive the initiative as busywork and as a negative comment on faculty effectiveness and worth. Place yourself in the position of Allyse Cartier, chair of the zoology department, as you read the following case.

Case 6.1, Another Mandate!

The Newest Directive from Central Administration

Allyse Cartier, chair of the zoology department, finds it hard to listen to the dean as she explains yet another directive from the central administration. Each department must implement an assessment program that will measure student learning outcomes. In short, the faculty are now being asked to document that students actually learn what academic programs claim to teach.

The assessment program must monitor the academic progress made by individual students. The assessment should use multiple measures given at regular intervals from matriculation to graduation. "Isn't that the purpose for assigning grades in each course?" thought Cartier. Clearly, this new mandate will monitor faculty effectiveness as much as assess student learning. The dean informed the college chairs that assessment data will be examined as part of the regular program review process.

Cartier could well imagine faculty reaction. She could hardly focus on the dean's presentation for thinking about how she might break the news to the faculty.

Background Information

In the past three years, the department responded to similar mandates designed to monitor faculty productivity, including workload studies and reports on plans to improve instructional quality. The faculty resented each new directive. In their view, the central administration does not trust them to do their work. The faculty believe that these policing tactics create unnecessary busywork that prevents them from using their time for teaching and research. Each new directive requires the faculty to spend considerable time defending their worth. Simultaneously, the faculty must contend with budget cuts that result in a loss of faculty positions and reduced support for professional travel, long-distance telephone privileges, and instructional equipment. Faculty morale continues to decline with each new mandate.

The central administration is aware of the adverse impact on faculty morale. The administration is also sensitive to the fact that the directives take time and resources away from teaching and research. The central administration, however, believes that the directives are essential in order to acquire data needed to respond to skeptical legislators and other external publics. It seems the only way to demonstrate that the institution is responsive to public pressure for increased accountability. How else can the central administration respond to charges of declining instructional quality and inefficient use of resources?

Breaking the News
Cartier can predict faculty reaction to this newest directive to assess student learning outcomes. The tenured faculty will be most outspoken. Many believe that the department should defy the central administration and not respond to these insulting directives. "After all, what can they do to us," is the typical retort of senior faculty. Untenured faculty are not comfortable with the direct defiance response, but grow weary of the time that each new request takes. Untenured faculty also fear that the department's response may in some way be used to grant or deny tenure. Cartier is certain that untenured faculty will perceive the assessment of individual student learning outcomes as a measure of teaching effectiveness. She knows that some untenured faculty will view the assessment mandate as a means by which the central administration might evaluate an application for tenure.

It is important for the department to respond to the assessment directive. Cartier believes that refusal to cooperate will be costly in terms of securing resources and support for the department. Yet, Cartier cannot continue to sell the central administration's point of view without jeopardizing her own credibility with the faculty. She understands their reaction to mandates that obviously question faculty worth.

Cartier knows that she needs to present this initiative in a way that makes it less offensive to faculty. But how?

Let's Analyze the Case

The chair of the zoology department feels the tension of the department chair's two roles: faculty and administrator. Frequently, the faculty perceive chairs as being more administrator than faculty, and central administrators perceive chairs as being more faculty than administrator. This places department chairs in a difficult position. Chairs typically understand the needs of both the faculty and the central administration and must interpret the needs of each party to the other.

Allyse Cartier knows that the faculty will perceive this newest mandate as bureaucratic wheel spinning. The faculty will suspect that the assessment initiative is an attempt to monitor the quality of teaching. Cartier realizes that they resent such policing tactics by the central administration. At the same time, Cartier recognizes the central administration's need to implement measures and collect data that will allow the institution to document instructional quality and faculty productivity. Cartier understands that the institution cannot ignore public distrust of higher education. Salient groups such as the state legislature demand more scrutiny over the expenditure of public funds in higher education.

Cartier's credibility with the central administration requires that she obtain faculty support for the new initiative. Cartier's credibility with the faculty, however, demands that she demonstrate her loyalty to the faculty. Should Cartier argue the value of an assessment program, she may appear to be joining those who question faculty worth. Many faculty hold the department chair responsible for protecting the department from unnecessary and time-consuming bureaucratic exercises.

To solicit faculty support for the new initiative, Cartier must present the mandate in a way that enables the faculty to see the initiative as a worthwhile activity. Should Cartier merely parrot the words of the dean, the faculty may perceive her as representing only the administration's interest. The chair's objective is to maintain her credibility with both the faculty and the central administration. The chair must secure faculty participation for the assessment initiative and lead the department in the development and implementation of an assessment program that has intrinsic value for the department.

It's Your Turn

Review Case 6.1 and think how you would present the assessment mandate to the faculty.

1. What are the potential benefits to the department from designing and implementing an assessment program? Will the assessment initiative, for example, improve program quality, help with student recruitment, or improve the department's opportunities for increased funding support? What benefits might individual faculty and students accrue from an assessment program? Would assessment scores serve other department purposes? Could assessment results, for example, be used to support an increased budget request or to reduce class sizes?

2. What objections do you expect the faculty to raise? How can the department safeguard against the major faculty concerns? What are the liabilities of refusing to design and implement an assessment program? How would you introduce the assessment mandate to the faculty? Would you present the request in a memorandum or call a department meeting?

Please Consider

It is important that the department chair consider the context when planning her approach to the faculty. This is not the first directive received from the central administration. The faculty complied with other mandates that took time and suggested a distrust of faculty. Past experience shapes our reactions to current events. If the chair wants a different reaction from faculty on the assessment mandate, then the presentation must allow faculty to understand how this directive is different from previous ones. The existing climate within the department has a direct bearing on how faculty react. If the faculty believe that they are abused by the central administration and morale is low, they will not have much enthusiasm for any mandate simply because central administration needs the data.

The chair must also read the context from the central administration's perspective. If the administration perceives the faculty as generally uncooperative or difficult, the chair needs to demonstrate that faculty response to the assessment mandate is constructive. This can be done in a number of ways. By articulating faculty concerns, the chair can illustrate that the department is working on the task. That makes it clear that faculty are not trying to avoid or sidestep the request. Some of the concerns mentioned should be indicative of the faculty's commitment to quality teaching. For example, one faculty concern that the chair may discuss with the dean is the time taken away from instruction to administer assessment measures.

Let's Recap

Review your strategy for presenting the assessment mandate to the faculty. If your approach does not incorporate the communication strategies for implementing change, you may want to review the material presented earlier in this chapter on how to effectively implement change. Does your approach

- assess the preconditions essential for implementing change?

- determine the obstacles to change?

- define the problem or need for change?

- solicit solutions to the problem?

- provide reassurance?

- avoid rejection?

Putting Theory Into Practice

Allyse Cartier elects to call a special meeting of the faculty. The mandate will be difficult to explain in a memorandum, and Cartier has no confidence that the faculty would read past the first paragraph. She elects to call a special meeting given the seriousness of the request from the central administration, rather than to add the issue to the agenda of the next regular meeting of the department faculty. Cartier sends the faculty a short memorandum calling a special meeting of the department to discuss "an important issue." After some thought, Cartier decides to keep the reason for calling the special meeting vague. She fears that the faculty might choose to skip the meeting if they know it is to discuss another directive from the central administration. Case 6.2, Spare the Messenger, offers an account of the special meeting. As you read Case 6.2, compare Cartier's method for presenting the assessment mandate with what you planned to do.

Case 6.2, Spare the Messenger

The Scene and the Players

Allyse Cartier enters the conference room about seven minutes before the scheduled special meeting. She notes that most of the faculty are already assembled. Dave Potter and Heresh Thakkar, two full professors, are engaged in a quiet, but serious, conversation. The other faculty are engaged in small talk and the room is filled with chatter.

Obviously, Cartier's brief memorandum announcing the need for a special meeting to discuss an important issue generated a lot of interest. Cartier is in the room less than two minutes before a dramatic quiet comes over the room. Small talk fades abruptly. Faculty stiffen in their seats. Cartier has their complete and undivided attention sooner than she expects.

The Tone

Dave Potter, the most senior member of the department, breaks the ice.

Potter: "What's this all about, Allyse?"

Chair: "Hold on, Dave. Let's make sure everyone's here before we begin the meeting."

Potter (turning to other faculty): "This must really be serious! She's afraid to give us a hint about the topic for the meeting."

Chair: "Take it easy, Dave. This is nothing we can't handle. It just wouldn't be fair to start the meeting ahead of time when everyone is not here." Just then Pamela Taub, an untenured assistant professor, enters the room. Before she can take a seat, Potter again breaks the silence: "Okay, Allyse, we're all here. Now what's all this about?"

Chair: "We have an important opportunity, but we're going to need to pull together and take control of the situation." Cartier notices that the faculty are leaning toward her as she speaks. She has the attention of absolutely everyone in the room. She continues cautiously.

Chair: "I'm certain that you share my view that the central administration is sometimes overbearing in documenting department work. First, we had to comply with the faculty workload study to demonstrate that faculty do work full-time and that this department is not overstaffed. Then we were asked to document faculty productivity in terms of credit hour generation. Each time we've complied with the request and presented information to justify faculty worth and effort. I want you to know that I appreciated your support in preparing department responses to those directives when I know that some of you would prefer to ignore them. We have seen some positive results of our labor."

Potter: "Sure, the dean doesn't come to our fall picnic anymore. That's one benefit."

Chair: "I believe there have been more tangible benefits. For instance, when the college had to surrender two faculty positions, the dean did not consider taking one from this department because our report on faculty workloads demonstrated that we are understaffed."

Thakkar: "We know all that. Now what's this great opportunity?"

Potter: "Maybe she's going to tell us we have an opportunity to free ourselves from senseless bureaucrats."

Chair: "Actually, you're close. We have an opportunity to shape a new initiative in such a way that could silence the central administration on the broader issue of instructional quality and teaching effectiveness."

Thakkar: "That would be some trick. I didn't know that it was possible to silence our dean!"

Everyone in the room started to laugh. The chair is pleased to have the levity because faculty are beginning to relax. They are certainly intrigued with the prospect of silencing the central administration.

Chair: "Let me explain. It seems that the central administration believes that it will be better able to represent the interests of the institution to external groups such as the governor and legislature if it is able to document that students enrolled at this institution learn what our programs claim to teach. Fortunately, it rejected the notion of purchasing and administering a standardized exam to all students regardless of academic major. Instead, the administration is willing to let faculty determine how to assess student learning."

Thakkar: "What? This doesn't make sense. We already evaluate what students learn. Each semester, every student receives a final grade in each class. That grade tells anyone how well the student has learned what we teach."

Chair: "There is some concern about grade inflation and whether or not grades in a course reflect accurately what students know and are able to do after graduation."

Potter: "Oh, come on. This sounds like one more effort to police faculty. Do they think we assign grades at random?"

Taub: "Let Allyse finish. She said this was an opportunity for us. At least we can listen to why she believes that."

Chair: "At first, I was skeptical. My initial reaction was similar to yours. After thinking about it, I concluded that it is an opportunity. Assessing student learning outcomes is not new in higher education. We've heard assessment horror stories from our colleagues at other institutions for several years. We all know that sometimes assessment is linked to the evaluation of faculty performance and used in making important personnel decisions such as granting tenure or promotion. Some institutions use assessment data to increase or reduce department budgets. At other institutions, students take a standardized exam regardless of their disciplines. This seems to be particularly unfair when the results are used to measure learning in the academic major."

Potter: "I wish you would get to the point. How does this affect us?"

Chair: "We are being asked to design and implement an assessment program that monitors student learning in this discipline. The good news is that we will have complete control as to what is measured and how. The only requirements are that we check students' progress at regular intervals throughout their program and that we measure student learning on a variety of assessment instruments."

Thakkar: "Tell me again how this is an opportunity."

Chair: "Look at it this way. It's obvious that the central administration is concerned with measures of accountability. They want to know and be able to document that faculty work hard and do an effective job. The mandate for an assessment program gives us license to design and implement a program that will collect the data by which we will be judged. How can we lose? We say what program objectives should be assessed. We determine how to assess student learning. It's like being asked to write your own comprehensive exam questions."

Thakkar: "I see your point, but it sounds like a lot of work."

Chair: "Not necessarily. We can divide the task by using a network of subcommittees. Remember, we don't have to assess every single course objective. We need only assess whether students have mastered the core program objectives. A review of the undergraduate catalog indicates that there are only four core program objectives that we should assess."

Potter: "I don't care how few objectives we have. We're not going to look good unless students take the exam seriously. I've heard enough about assessment programs to know that typically assessment scores cannot be used to determine the final course grades. So how can we make certain that students don't just write off the exam and make us look bad in the process?"

Chair: "You're right. We need to think that through carefully. We can brainstorm all the alternatives and decide which of those will make the exam most convenient for students to take.

Thakkar: "I have a colleague at an institution in the Midwest who went through an assessment mandate a few years ago. I recall that her department paid students to take the test and the result was still disastrous. Students came, accepted payment, and completed the test in 5 to 10 minutes by filling in answers without reading the questions."

Chair: "I've given this some thought. There is nothing that requires us to administer a separate exam. We could, for example, tuck a few assessment questions into the final exam of core courses. That way we could keep a running record of student progress as they completed each of the core courses designed to teach the core program objectives."

Taub: "Do you mean an assessment measure can be composed of a couple of questions?"

Chair: "Obviously, we're not prepared to make final decisions on such technical issues today. I'll want you to read the set of guidelines that I received. However, the guidelines do not specify the length or form of an assessment test. This is why I believe that we have an opportunity. Given the tone of the times, it is inevitable that we will need to do some type of assessment of student learning outcomes. Fortunately, the language of the assessment mandate gives us carte blanche to design and implement an assessment program. It seems to me that this is one test of faculty worth and teaching effectiveness that we cannot fail if we take positive and constructive action."

Potter: "What happens if we just refuse to comply with this directive?"

Chair: "I think it is likely that the central administration will find some way to measure our students. The question is, do we want to design our own assessment measures or have them designed by outsiders who are not familiar with our discipline?"

Let's Analyze the Case

Consider the decisions made by Allyse Cartier. First, she calls a special meeting of the faculty to present the mandate in person. This suggests that Cartier is more confident and comfortable with her ability to explain the new mandate in person than to write an informative, but persuasive, memorandum. The announcement of a special meeting piques faculty interest. Clearly, Cartier has the faculty's full attention. Second, Allyse Cartier presents the assessment mandate as an "important opportunity" for the department. She decides that the faculty will be more cooperative if they perceive that the mandate has some intrinsic benefit for the academic unit. Both decisions have an element of risk. For example, calling a special meeting without identifying the topic encourages faculty imagination. If there is a long delay between the announcement and the date of the meeting, idle speculation could develop into an obstacle to change. This is especially true if the department climate is such that faculty expect the worst and are defensive. Similarly, there is a risk in presenting the mandate as "an opportunity." Depending upon the chair's credibility with the faculty, they may perceive the chair as representing the administration's interest.

Cartier's decisions are consistent with her assessment of the climate and chair credibility preconditions. Cartier recognizes that the faculty are generally hostile toward the administration. The faculty do not trust the central administration to care about faculty welfare. Cartier takes every opportunity to distance herself from the administration during the meeting. Review Cartier's language in presenting the mandate. Early in the meeting she states: "I'm certain that you share my view that the central administration has been overbearing in documenting department work." This is a premise that Cartier knows faculty accept. When the faculty express uneasiness about the reason for the special meeting, Cartier is quick to say that it "is nothing *we* can't handle." She takes every opportunity to align herself with the faculty. When one faculty member makes a crack about "senseless bureaucrats," the chair encourages the faculty to view the assessment and mandate as a way to "silence" the bureaucrats on the broader issue of instructional quality and teaching effectiveness. Cartier admits candidly that she too was skeptical about the assessment mandate before she had time to think about it.

Cartier also demonstrates her understanding of the faculty perspective by listening to their concerns. When the faculty raise objections to various points of the assessment mandate, Cartier never dismisses their concerns as unreasonable or unimportant. Instead, she affirms the faculty view with a "you're right" or some similar acknowledgment of the concern before offering an alternate view. Cartier knows that she retains more credibility with the faculty if she does not appear to be an agent of the central administration. It is important, therefore, that she present the assessment mandate in a way that clearly demonstrates that she understands faculty concerns. Cartier must demonstrate that she values the faculty's perspective.

One obstacle to change in this case is the reaction of tenured full professors. Cartier predicts that at least some of the senior faculty may suggest that the department refuse to comply with the mandate. By presenting the mandate as an opportunity for the department rather than a request of the administration, Cartier prevents an argument to reject any request from the central administration. Instead, Cartier spends time helping the faculty discern the potential benefits of responding to the assessment mandate. Near the end of the meeting when Potter asks what would happen if the department refuses to comply with the directive, Cartier offers a very concrete example of the harm that could result. Specifically, the dreaded outcome of noncompliance is that the central administration will impose its own method of measuring student learning. That alters the discussion from *will* we design and implement an assessment program to *how* will we design an assessment program.

The faculty do not exhaust the discussion of possible solutions to managing the assessment mandate in this first meeting. Cartier makes it clear that it will be a collective effort. The fact that the faculty raise specific implementation concerns indicates that at least some of the faculty have accepted the mandate and are now thinking how best to design and implement an assessment program. Review Cartier's dialogue with the faculty. She never professes to know the answer. Nor does she argue for one best approach. She does, however, provide specific implementation suggestions when the concern is one that might derail the entire effort. For example, the faculty worry that students will not take the test seriously and that they will be judged by assessment results that do not indicate what students have learned. This single issue might be enough to cause the faculty to reject the assessment initiative. Particularly if the faculty perceive the administration's directive as excessive policing of the faculty, they are less likely to comply with any request that could bring harm to the department. By providing realistic and workable solutions to the more significant concerns, Cartier prevents the faculty from rejecting the initiative. She stops short, however, of presenting a plan of action. Her approach reassures faculty that their concerns will be addressed. It offers some assurance that collectively they can design and implement an assessment program that is free from serious drawbacks. By debunking the obvious reasons for refusing to comply with the assessment mandate, the chair avoids rejection of the proposed change.

It's Your Turn

1. How does Cartier's presentation of the assessment mandate compare with your strategy for explaining this initiative to the faculty? Did you identify the same obstacles? Were you prepared to present the potential benefits to the department from designing and implementing its own assessment program?

2. What are the ethical considerations involved when department chairs work to distance themselves from the central administration? What are the ethical considerations involved in balancing the chair's responsibility to the central administration with her responsibility to the department faculty?

Please Consider

The chair's management of change influences the department climate and the chair's credibility. Although climate and credibility are important preconditions to change, they are also affected by change. Cartier, for example, can enhance or damage her credibility with the faculty in her management of the assessment mandate. At the same time, Cartier can enhance or damage her credibility with the central administration through her management of the mandate.

To build credibility and improve the department climate, Cartier must manage the implementation of the assessment mandate in a way that allows others to perceive her as knowledgeable of her job, having good intentions, and trustworthy. Given that they are assigned attributes, it is not a simple task. In this instance the administration and faculty initially have different criteria for success. Cartier must convince the administration that the department is complying with the spirit and the requirement of the assessment mandate. Simultaneously, Cartier must demonstrate to the faculty that department concerns have her full attention. This does not mean that Cartier must be a hypocrite with one or both parties. It is possible to lead the faculty in compliance with a mandate issued by the central administration while safeguarding the interests of the academic department.

It's Your Turn

1. What is the chair's responsibility to the central administration in implementing the assessment mandate? Is the chair accountable for making faculty understand the central administration's point of view? What is the chair's responsibility to the faculty when implementing a request of the central administration? If the chair believes that a request from the central administration is unnecessary or somehow harmful to the department, is the chair ethically bound to implement the directive?

2. Review Case 6.2, Spare the Messenger, and strategize Cartier's next step. Would you, for example, appoint a subcommittee or work as a committee of the whole? How would you communicate progress being made within the department to the central administration?

Putting Theory Into Practice

The department chair's responsibility for implementing change is not limited to the academic department. Frequently, chairs must serve as change agents with the central administration and other external publics. Sometimes this takes the form of advocating specific proposals on behalf of the department. At other times it involves a long-term effort to alter external perceptions of the department. As the primary spokesperson for the department, the chair has the responsibility to recognize needed change and advocate the department's best interest.

In Case 6.3, A New Playing Field, the chair of the fine and performing arts department struggles to establish an effective rapport with the new dean of the college of arts and sciences. The relationship forged between the department and the new college dean is critical to the long-term welfare of the department. Place yourself in the position of the department chair as you read the following case.

Case 6.3, A New Playing Field

The Chair's Task

Anne Stein, chair of the department of fine and performing arts, is deep in thought when the night cleaning crew enters her office.

Custodian: "Working late again, Dr. Stein? My union may disapprove of your working my shift as well as yours."

Stein (smiling): "Don't worry, Joe, I've got my hands full managing this job."

Working late is routine since Vincent Das started as the new dean of the college of arts and sciences. Stein knows that it is important that she establish an effective working relationship with the new dean. She desperately wants to build a positive working relationship with him, but every effort seems to result in disaster. She is working late to prepare for a meeting with the dean the following day. The purpose of the meeting is to discuss ways in which the fine and performing arts department can be more cost-effective and productive.

Anne Stein has chaired the department for ten years, through two other deans. She is hardly a novice at establishing an effective working rapport with a new dean. She recognizes that chairs need to educate new deans about the importance of the discipline and the value of their departments. She realizes that every administrator will project a personal style that must be accommodated. Dean Das, however, is quick to judge the value of the fine and performing arts department without reviewing all of the relevant data. Dean Das believes that the fine and performing arts department is costly and contributes very little to the college. Worse yet, Stein senses that Das holds her responsible for the current situation. If the dean perceives Stein as ineffective, how can she credibly persuade the dean to perceive the department in a favorable way?

The New Dean

Vincent Das is in his sixth month as dean of the college of arts and sciences. A chemist of national renown, Das was hired from the outside. Before becoming dean of the college of arts and sciences, he served as dean of science at an institution focused on engineering and science. Das brings a lot of enthusiasm and energy to the position. He began working immediately with the campus office of institutional research to compile comprehensive data analyses of the units within the college. Sensing state and university concern for increasing productivity and greater accountability in spending public funds, the dean generated cost per credit hour data for each of the departments. He examined faculty workloads, which vary dramatically across the college. Finally, the dean studied enrollment patterns and projections for each program.

The dean uses this information to work with the department chairs collectively and individually. The dean's mission is to make every department within the unit cost-effective and productive.

The Department of Fine and Performing Arts

The department of fine and performing arts seems to be at the wrong end of every continuum used by the dean to evaluate program quality and program effectiveness. Enrollment in the department is modest when compared with the enrollments in other units. The faculty in the fine and performing arts carry the heaviest teaching loads within the college. While faculty in the sciences typically teach three courses each semester, faculty in the fine and performing arts teach four courses in addition to one-on-one instruction and indirect teaching through musical or theatrical productions. Because enrollment is low, the department is costly. The ratio of faculty to majors is small, making the cost per credit hour significantly higher than the college average.

The Conflict

The data report on the department of fine and performing arts does not surprise Anne Stein. She knows that the data are typical for most programs in the fine and performing arts. Actually, the department's total credit hour generation is slightly higher than that of comparable programs because the department offers a very ambitious production schedule. Each year, the department produces ten main stage productions. The productions include a combination of dramatic and comical theater, along with musicals and some light opera. The production schedule attracts nonmajors into the program who typically enroll in one or two classes for elective credit. This production schedule serves as a major link with the surrounding region. A highly visible and appreciated program, the production series draws season patrons from a radius of 150 miles.

Dean Das, however, finds the data generated for the department of fine and performing arts outrageous and unacceptable. Without seeking an explanation of the data, he informed Anne Stein that the department needs to be cost-efficient and more productive. Department chairs received the dean's analysis of their cost-effectiveness during the last college meeting. The dean instructed department chairs to examine the data and generate remedies. The dean announced that a meeting would be held with each department chair during which the dean would listen to the chair's plans for correcting existing inefficiency. Anne Stein and her chair colleagues found the dean's tone to be somewhat condescending. Clearly, the dean believes he has the answer.

Stein worked for weeks to prepare for tomorrow's meeting with the dean. She has, in her view, a logical explanation for each of the data points used by the dean. She recognizes that it will be difficult to get the dean's attention and to help the dean understand the special conditions that are typical of programs in the fine and performing arts. She needs to do this without alienating the dean. She cannot afford to have the dean conclude that the department of fine and performing arts is uncooperative or unsupportive of college goals.

Let's Analyze the Case

The department chair in Case 6.3 has a difficult task. Because the dean is new, the chair lacks an established rapport that might ease the conflict. The chair faces the prospect of building personal and departmental credibility with the new dean while refuting the dean's initially negative perception of the department. It is painfully obvious that the dean is unlikely to understand the department's perspective. Instead, the dean delineates criteria for judging departmental effectiveness that do not allow for discipline-specific variations. The dean's rhetoric suggests that, in his mind, all departments should be judged against the same criteria and standards. If the chair is to bridge the gap with the dean, she must present her information in a manner that is consistent with the dean's perspective. She cannot assume that the dean understands the peculiar nature of programs in the fine and performing arts. Nor can the chair assume that the dean will comprehend discipline-specific jargon or terminology. The chair needs to adapt her message, using language and a paradigm that will be familiar to the dean.

The analysis need not be limited to the immediate issue. For example, if the dean is impressed with productivity, are there other dimensions upon which the department can successfully demonstrate productivity? In completing this analysis, the chair is assessing the department's fit within the college mission as articulated by the new dean. The chair's success in establishing the program's credibility and value for the new dean hinges upon her ability to make the dean realize that the fine and performing arts department contributes significantly to the college mission and goals.

It's Your Turn

Review the facts presented in Case 6.3 and decide how you would approach the upcoming meeting with the new college dean.

1. How might the chair minimize the enrollment and cost-effectiveness data used by the dean to form an initially negative impression of the department? Is there other information that might persuade the dean to rethink the criteria used for evaluating program effectiveness? At what point would you brief the faculty on the brewing conflict with the new dean?

2. What other things might you do to encourage a more collegial relationship with the dean? What issues or department activities would help the dean form a more favorable perception of the department? How would you involve the faculty in the effort to improve the dean's perception of the department?

Please Consider

Climate and credibility are important preconditions to change. The chair of the fine and performing arts department is managing change that results from the hire of a new dean. This impacts the department in many ways. The chair must also work to change the dean's impression of the department. Because the dean is new, the chair has no initial credibility with the dean that facilitates these tasks. Since this one issue is a significant source of conflict between the dean and the chair, the chair needs to establish her credibility with the dean through communication and action on other issues. It is important that the chair not allow this single instance of disagreement to be the only dimension that defines her overall credibility with the dean.

Similarly, the climate improves if the chair does not allow this one area of conflict to affect the general rapport between the new college dean and the academic department. The chair must make every effort to find other opportunities for interaction that are positive and more conducive to building a healthy working relationship with the new dean. These efforts can help educate the new dean about the college. For example, a new dean that is sensitive to public reaction may be pleased to learn the regional popularity of the extensive production schedule conducted by the performing and fine arts department. Other more harmonious issues could provide a foundation for a more productive relationship with the new dean and, at the same time, educate the dean about the department.

Let's Recap

Review your strategy for the upcoming meeting with the new college dean. Consider your plans for this specific event in the larger context of managing change for the department as it responds to a new dean's administrative style and for cultivating a more positive impression with the dean. If your approach does not incorporate the strategies for managing change, you may want to review the material presented earlier in this chapter on how to effectively implement change. Does your approach

- assess the preconditions essential for implementing change?

- determine the obstacles to change?

- define the problem or need for change?

- solicit solutions to the problem from others?

- reassure the faculty and the dean?

- avoid rejection?

Putting Theory Into Practice

Anne Stein spent considerable time preparing for her meeting with the college dean. She collected information from the national organization. She can demonstrate how the department's credit hour production is higher than enrollment in comparable fine and performing arts programs. She can explain why one-on-one instruction skews the cost-effectiveness data. Finally, she can document program quality with comments from appreciative patrons who regularly attend productions.

Stein decides not to involve the faculty at this point. The faculty are very apprehensive about the appointment of a "science" dean. They are nervous that a dean trained in chemistry is likely to minimize the role and value of the fine and performing arts. She hopes to be able to improve the dean's impression of the fine and performing arts without confirming the faculty's worst fear. Case 6.4, Checkmate, describes the chair's meeting with the college dean. As you read Case 6.4, assess Stein's approach to the dean in terms of the strategies for implementing change.

Case 6.4, Checkmate

Anne Stein enters the office cautiously but cheerfully.

Stein: "It's a beautiful day. I enjoyed the walk over."

The dean does not respond but remains focused on reading data sheets. Anne Stein moves to a chair and starts taking the relevant file from her briefcase. She tries once again to break the ice.

Stein: "Are your wife and children enjoying their new home? There are numerous opportunities for families in this region."

Dean: "They keep busy. In fact, we all keep busy. Since we last met, I asked staff in the office of institutional research to generate a printout tracking each unit's cost-effectiveness and enrollment for the past ten years. This gives us a longer pattern from which to evaluate the current situation. Here is a copy of the data for your department."

The chair takes the printout. Before she has a chance to study it, the dean continues.

Dean: "As you can see, the fine and performing arts department has a long history of being very costly for this college. Obviously, we can't blame the current problem on any recent or specific condition. Your department has always been excessively expensive."

Stein: "It is true that the fine and performing arts department is more costly than many of the departments in this college, but–"

Dean (interrupting): "Actually, the fine and performing arts department is more costly than any of the other departments in this college. This has been the case for each of the past ten years. I suspect that we could go back further and find that the trend still persists."

Stein (sitting taller in her chair): "You have to understand that programs in the fine and performing arts are nontraditional and cannot be compared with more traditional programs in the sciences."

Dean: "I understand that the fine and performing arts programs are costly and a financial drain on the other programs in this college."

Stein: "Quality instruction in the fine and performing arts requires a lot of one-on-one instruction. We must maintain small course enrollments and individualized instruction if we are to retain a quality program."

Dean: "Of course, you have small enrollment in courses; you have very few majors for the number of faculty. You have the luxury of being able to offer one-on-one and small-group instruction. Other departments with healthy enrollments do not have that luxury."

Stein: "It's true that our enrollment is not large, but even if it were, we would need to offer individualized instruction. We cannot, for example, teach piano performance in a lecture hall. We are known for our performance focus, and performance courses require a tutorial method of instruction."

Dean: "Maybe this college cannot afford performance instruction."

Stein: "But performance is our strength. Without the performance courses we would not be able to staff the main stage productions that have been a tremendous source of pride for this institution. I brought a copy of the brochure for our current season. I thought you might like to see the range and depth of our production series. You'll notice that we do both classical and contemporary productions. It's a very popular series with our regular patrons and does a lot to enhance the total image of the institution within the community and region."

Dean (putting the brochures down without looking at them): "That's nice, but it doesn't do much for making the program more cost-effective."

Stein: "Well, the department's production series benefits the college as well."

Dean: "I understand that citizens in the community enjoy the productions. That's fine. I was hired, however, to make this college more productive and cost-effective. After months of analyzing the situation, I must tell you that the fine and performing arts department has the worst track record of any unit in the college. This statistic simply must change."

Stein: "But faculty in fine and performing arts work very hard. As you know, we have teaching loads among the heaviest in the college."

Dean: "I'm sure that the faculty do work hard. There is no reason for faculty to work this hard when we have such a low instructor-to-student ratio in the department. Now I want to hear your ideas for making the performing and fine arts program more cost-effective. I hope that you have given some thought to how you might reduce faculty workloads. I noted, for example, that you frequently offer multiple sections of the same course number without any of the sections enrolling large numbers of students."

Stein: "Those are the performance courses. It is important that the students receive small group or individualized instruction. For example, we cannot put all of the students studying piano in the same piano course. To separate the students' schedules, we've designated a different section number for each small group of students."

Dean: "Have you considered the possibility of enrolling all of those students in one class but allowing for individualized lab work for a portion of the course credit?"

Stein: "We can't do that. It would be too confusing."

Dean (looking more irritated): "Well, something must be done. We cannot continue the current practice simply because it's the way it's always been done. I'm very serious about this. It is time that you and your department quit stalling and face the facts. You must think of ways in which the department can improve its cost-effectiveness."

Let's Analyze the Case

Case 6.4 offers more insight into the personalities involved in this situation. The dean is highly structured and task oriented. In a somewhat abrupt manner, he moves right to the agenda without engaging in small talk. The chair, in contrast, has a difficult time getting to the issue. The chair is charged with the task of coming up with suggestions for how the cost-effectiveness of the department might be improved. The dean called this meeting in order to hear those suggestions. Hence, when the chair offers only explanations and no suggestions for remedy, she is perceived by the dean as making excuses and being uncooperative.

To be successful, the chair must first convince the dean that the department of fine and performing arts intends to cooperate. The chair must demonstrate a responsiveness to the concerns and issues raised by the dean. The chair must also demonstrate a willingness to evaluate current practice and to make revisions when necessary. To date, however, the chair has only succeeded in demonstrating her obstinate nature in defending current practice. It escalates the conflict in that the dean begins to draw a conclusion about the chair's management style that is likely to carry over into the dean's other interactions with the chair. The longer the chair appears to be difficult, the more likely the new dean will attribute the immediate conflict to the chair's (or the department's) pervasive attitude.

Stein's language is often unfortunate. There are moments when her choice of words makes it possible for the dean to take personal offense. Phrases such as "you need to understand," "we have always," or "that will never work" do not argue the point but demonstrate resistance to change. Similarly, the positive aspects presented about the department need to be linked to the dean's perspective and frame of reference. The dean is unlikely to be swayed by the value of a production series if the only benefit is community enjoyment and institutional visibility. To use the production series to improve the department's image within the college, the chair needs to establish its relationship to the college mission. The production series must have a value that will be recognized by the new dean. For example, what revenue is generated from box office receipts? If the production series is popular and well attended, it is likely that funds allocated to the fine and performing arts department are augmented by box office receipts. The chair makes little progress in describing the strengths of the fine and performing arts department because she failed to translate the information into a context that the dean can acknowledge and understand.

It's Your Turn

1. Review Case 6.4 and compare the chair's approach to the one you would use. How would you convince the dean that you are a team player? How would you sell the importance of the department to the college? Are there other groups on or off campus that might help improve the dean's assessment of the department?

2. Give careful consideration to the language you plan to use. Review Case 6.4 and substitute your language for the chair's comments. How will the dean respond to your presentation?

Please Consider

In Case 6.4, the dean states that his job is to increase college productivity. This is important information. When dealing with imposed change, it is helpful to view the change in the larger context. The chair needs to learn as much as possible about the external conditions prompting the change. Was the dean given a specific agenda by the provost when he was hired? What factors contribute to the dean's perception that cost-effectiveness is a critical issue? What are the trends (and pressures) at comparable programs within the state? Is the institution evolving a new mission? Are there external pressures that will result in increased accountability for each program on campus?

The answers to those and similar questions will help the chair identify the underlying motives behind the imposed change. If, for example, the dean's motive is to safeguard the college from future budget cuts, the dean's motivation for making departments more cost-effective is to build a more defensible case for maintaining the current budget level. It's possible the fine and performing arts department can help maintain current budget levels through other action. The department, for example, may be able to stretch the college budget by augmenting it with box office receipts. The department may be able to offer the college significant regional clout from performing and fine arts patrons. Those linkages, however, cannot be identified unless the chair considers the imposed change within the larger context. This requires that the chair read the suggestions being made from the dean's point of view.

Let's Recap

Effective department chairs are successful change agents. They recognize when the department must change and know how to ease in new policy and practice with minimal disruption. That is not easy because even desirable change can be uncomfortable for the very persons that the change benefits.

The department climate and chair's credibility are two important preconditions for change management. When the climate is healthy and the chair has high credibility, the faculty are less resistant to change. Similarly, department chairs are more able to effect change on behalf of their departments with the central administration if they have credibility with the administration. Change, however, can be difficult even in a healthy department and even when the chair enjoys high credibility with the faculty and the central administration. For that reason chairs need to carefully determine the obstacles to change. They must make clear the need for the change and the potential harm associated with preserving the status quo.

Finally, effective chairs know how to involve others in the change process. If faculty and staff (or the dean) participate in analyzing the need for change and identifying the best course of action, they will be more committed to making the change work. The process of reviewing possible alternatives helps to persuade those who would otherwise remain resistant to the change. Chairs must address and respond to individual concerns as the collective membership discusses the various and tentative solutions. Though time-consuming, this process is essential to effective change implementation. The ability to influence change is the essence of true and valuable leadership.

PART THREE

INTERFACING WITH EXTERNAL PUBLICS

This section of the text addresses the chair's responsibilities for ensuring effective communication with the administration and other external publics. The department chair is the primary spokesperson for the department and typically the sole interpreter of externally imposed conditions to the department faculty, staff, and students. Communication strategies for effectively interacting with external publics are presented for three of the more critical arenas: the dean, alliances on and off campus, and promoting the department.

Chapter 7: Working with the Dean
describes how the chair can improve the department's rapport within the college

Chapter 8: Building Alliances
includes strategies for cultivating important alliances with external publics on and off campus

Chapter 9: Promoting the Department
describes how the department chair can influence the perceptions held by the various external publics

7

WORKING WITH THE DEAN

Department chairs must maintain a productive working relationship with the dean if they are to successfully represent their academic departments. Effective communication characterizes a productive working relationship between dean and chair. In a productive relationship, the dean is receptive to information about the department and communicates essential information about campus issues to the chair. Both chair and dean share relevant information openly and in a timely way that, in turn, enables each to more effectively advocate the department's mission and resource needs. Deans need capable department chairs that they can count on to keep them informed about achievements and potential problems. In a productive working relationship, the dean and the department chair work together as a team to strengthen the department.

A department needs a dean who understands the department discipline, its strengths and resource needs, because it is the dean who communicates this information to the central administration. The dean cannot possibly represent the department's interests capably if there is a poor working relationship between the dean and chair. Without effective communication between dean and department chair, a dean is more likely to make uninformed decisions about the department, and the chair is likely to forward department requests that are ill-timed or ill-conceived in terms of the dean's perspective or campus politics. When there is a poor working relationship between the chair and dean, there is a greater tendency for each to respond to personalities rather than issues. Those reactions typically yield decisions that do little to enhance the department or college. Everyone loses when there is an ineffective working relationship between the dean and the department chair.

The Objective

One goal of this chapter is to help department chairs understand how their communication with the dean influences their professional credibility.

Communication is the primary vehicle for building one's credibility. Only if the dean perceives the chair as credible can the chair effectively carry out assigned duties. A second goal of this chapter is to equip department chairs with some specific communication strategies for improving their communication with the dean. Department chairs need to do more than respond to communication from the dean. They need to exercise leadership in initiating communication with the dean that contributes to an effective working relationship.

Defining the Task

A productive working relationship requires effective communication. Effective communication is more than sending memos and scheduling meetings, and exists only when there is a meaningful transfer of information between parties. Communication is a dynamic process that requires the sender to think about more than his or her purpose. The effective communicator considers his or her purpose in relation to the intended receiver's perspective, the context for the interaction, and the best possible channels for sending information. All of these constantly changing factors affect communication success. Perhaps the easiest way to illustrate what to do is to explain what can go wrong when a person fails to give communication careful thought. The following barriers to effective communication occur when a person fails to consider the full complexity of the communication process.

Unclear purpose

When department chairs communicate with unclear purpose, they pave the way for misunderstandings. The receiver attributes a purpose to communication whether or not it corresponds with the sender's intended purpose. By making the purpose for communication clear, chairs prevent the dean from guessing the agenda. When the purpose is clear, there is less opportunity for inferring a hidden agenda. Department chairs need to identify their purpose while considering the dean's need for the information. What is clear to the department chair may not be clear to the dean. To clearly state their communication purpose, chairs must use language that the dean understands.

A clearly stated purpose can be misunderstood if the chair presents it in a manner that makes it difficult for the dean to comprehend. The department chair may, for example, send a memorandum to the dean for the purpose of initiating a new student recruitment activity, an objective that most deans applaud. If the chair, however, constructs the communication so that the focus is on how the department cannot engage in student recruitment without more money, the dean may interpret the request as the department's resistance to recruiting students. If the chair focuses the request on the feasibility and potential gain from initiating a new student recruitment activity, the dean is likely to perceive the department as creatively engaging in an important college objective. In the second version of this request, the need for funds to support the activity takes a backseat to the merit of the idea.

Disregard for the receiver

Effective communication requires an other-centered perspective. The sender needs to analyze how the intended receiver will interpret the information. When department chairs fail to consider how the dean is likely to receive information, they increase the chance for faulty transmissions. Chairs need to consider the content, language, tone, and context of all communication with the dean. To evaluate the communication content from the dean's perspective, the department chair must consider what the dean needs to know and the relevance of the information for the dean. Chairs can analyze the effect of language by determining what words make sense to the dean. Provide data that are credible to the dean. If the dean has a bottom line approach to managing the college, statistical data may be more persuasive than other more subjective documentation. Avoid language that may evoke an emotional response. This can happen when the chair overuses certain language. If all department needs are "urgent" or "absolutely essential" to continued program quality, the chair may condition a standard response from the dean who may view this language as words from an alarmist who cannot separate major and minor issues. Department chairs must speak the dean's language when constructing a request or report. If the department chair advocates program expansion based on faculty interest when the dean is concerned about program quality and declining enrollments, the chair is not using language that is meaningful to the dean.

Communication tone affects the need to demonstrate support even when the chair disagrees with the dean. It is possible to disagree on an issue but retain strong mutual respect and an effective working relationship. As discussed in Chapter 5 of this text, it is possible to maintain a professional relationship during confrontation. Finally, chairs need to consider the context for communication from the dean's perspective. Department chairs must demonstrate that they understand the larger college issues while championing department-specific needs. Department chairs should demonstrate that they understand the constraints under which the dean must work. That can be done by referencing college priorities or needs in relation to the department request. Chairs can also accommodate the dean's perspective by carefully timing their communication. It is not a good idea, for example, to request anything when the dean is in a hurry, in between meetings, or distracted for any reason.

Noise in the channel

Channel noise refers to anything that distorts the clear transmission and reception of the communication. Sources of noise include distractions, information overload, choice of channel, inappropriate language, and distrust. Noise exists when a sender repeats a message without variation, causing the receiver to stop listening. A poor choice of words can create noise if the language used evokes a stereotypic response in the receiver that may have nothing to do with the actual content of the message. If, in attempting to achieve a different outcome, a chair labels the dean's action as discriminatory, the chair is more likely to evoke a defensive response from the dean than to persuade the dean to adopt a different view. In this instance, the language used becomes noise that adversely affects the purpose of the communication. A lack of trust between dean and chair contributes to noise that distorts virtually all communication. Without trust, each party is likely to infer a hidden agenda, discount the analysis, or misinterpret the purpose for communication.

To avoid unnecessary noise in the channel, department chairs must work to build trust with the dean. This requires performing the job in a manner that is consistent with the dean's expectations. Chairs must also use the appropriate channel to send their message. Is the message content best delivered through face-to-face communication or written memorandum? Would a written memorandum make a trivial issue more important? Would face-to-face communication minimize the effect of a significant problem? Chairs need to ask these and similar questions to select the appropriate channel for the message content. Noise attributable to distractions and overloads relates to the dean's style and position. Is the department chair's memorandum going to be one of 50 received on a given day? Will the telephone call placed after 5:00 p.m. become information overload? Effective communication requires that the chair transmit messages in a format and at a time when they are more likely to be interpreted accurately by the dean. Finally, the chair must construct the message so that its language and tone are appropriate from the dean's perspective.

No feedback loop

Feedback is the receiver's verbal or nonverbal response to the sender's message. Communication is a circular, not linear, process. The communication process is not complete until the receiver's response (feedback) allows the sender to confirm that the message was received. Feedback is the mechanism by which communicators learn whether or not they succeeded in communicating effectively. The receiver's response may signal that the message was misunderstood, and feedback tells the sender how to proceed. Is more detail needed? Should the language change to reduce defensiveness? Is this the wrong time to pursue the issue? The feedback loop in communication allows department chairs to adapt and improve their communication.

Department chairs need to continually assess their communication effectiveness in working with the dean. Did the dean interpret the message as intended? Does the dean understand the significance of the issue being raised? Does the dean accept the data presented in support of the department's proposal? Does the dean comprehend the issue sufficiently to present it to the central administration? The answer to these and similar questions will help department chairs judge the success of any particular communication and recognize the need for follow-up communication. It is also a good idea for chairs to tell the dean that they want feedback. Chairs can even tell the dean what type of feedback they want or would appreciate. A department chair, for example, might say, "I'd appreciate your reaction to this idea. I'm particularly concerned about the cost of the project." This practice can increase the chair's credibility with the dean because it provides an opportunity for the chair to demonstrate his or her understanding of college priorities and chair responsibilities. Chairs will undermine this effort, however, if they become defensive about the feedback that they requested. Chairs need to solicit and receive feedback from the dean, always treating it as information that enables them to improve their effectiveness.

Relevant Communication Concepts and Strategies

Department chairs can improve their working relationship with their deans through communication. This requires chairs to be continuously proactive in their communication with their deans. The following strategies illustrate how department chairs can use communication to demonstrate their administrative capability and to improve their working relationship with their deans.

Establish and maintain your credibility

As discussed in Chapter 6, the department chair's credibility is composed of three specific components: the perception of the chair's knowledge; the perception of the chair's motive or intentions; and the perception of the chair's trustworthiness. Department chairs remain credible to the dean if the dean perceives them as possessing those three attributes. A person's credibility determines his or her latitude for making mistakes. If a chair with high credibility makes a mistake, the dean is likely to dismiss the unfortunate instance as atypical behavior. If, however, a chair with low credibility makes even a small error, the instance reaffirms the dean's unfavorable perception of that chair. To determine what it takes for a dean to perceive a department chair as knowledgeable, having good intentions, and trustworthy, one must understand the dean's expectations for the department chair's performance. At a minimum, department chairs must demonstrate that they understand and can perform the duties assigned to them.

The way in which department chairs might evidence their commitment to the job can vary with the management style of the dean. Some deans place a high value on meeting deadlines and completing required paperwork. Some deans value most those chairs who can keep faculty working productively and who are supportive of the college. It is important for chairs to recognize and satisfy the dean's primary expectations for their job performance. Department chairs can evidence their knowledge of the job by learning campus policy instead of counting on the dean to answer trivial questions. The chair that relies on the dean to explain campus policy on such routine matters as how to handle a student grievance demonstrates an unwillingness to learn the job of department chair. Another important component that demonstrates the chair's knowledge of the job is a firm grasp of the academic discipline. Department chairs can evidence their understanding of the discipline by forwarding information about the discipline and the department's achievements. This has the second benefit of educating the dean about the discipline and the department's productivity.

Department chairs demonstrate their good intentions and trustworthiness by illustrating their knowledge of, and appreciation for, the college mission and goals. Department chairs build trust by evidencing the department's role in achieving college objectives. That includes forwarding information about the department that the dean may need. Don't whine when representing the department's interests, especially when the dean may view your bemoaning as inconsistent with college goals. Keep the dean informed about the department's achievements to help establish credibility for the chair and the department. News of department achievements serve as collateral against those instances when the department chair must disagree with the dean or when the department falls short in meeting a college standard. For example, the theater department with prominent alumni and a popular production series can use these achievements to offset a decline in undergraduate student enrollment.

Finally, chairs should not defer department decisions to the dean. Department chairs who ask the dean to order department priorities or seek the dean's help in "correcting" a department vote damage their credibility. Whenever the dean is asked to prescribe the department mission, rank-order department requests, or reverse department decisions, the chair is guilty of allowing the dean to make department decisions. Some department chairs may not realize that they are deferring department decisions to the dean. If, for example, the department does not take the initiative in championing the department mission to the dean, the dean will fill the void by defining the role that the department should fulfill, thereby prescribing the department mission. Neglecting responsibilities typically results in deferring authority to others.

Keep communication with the dean open and productive

The way in which department chairs communicate with the dean can build or destroy their credibility. Communication is open and productive when all parties exchange relevant information freely to serve mutually accepted purposes. Ideally, both the department chair and the dean want a strong department. If chairs accept that the dean is more friend than foe, it is easier to engage in open and productive communication. Chairs encourage open and productive communication when they treat every inquiry as legitimate and well-intentioned. If the dean is an ally of the department, there is no cause for chairs to sidestep issues or bluff responses. There is no need to personally attack the dean, making condescending statements such as: "If you understood this discipline, you would see the need to grant this request." Chairs gain more if, instead, they assume that the dean means well and they answer all inquiries directly. These instances should be opportunities to educate rather than to attack the dean.

Department chairs need to make full use of every available communication channel, including face-to-face conversation, telephone, informal note, typed memorandum, reports, and all other print and nonprint media. It is, however, essential that chairs recognize that each channel of communication provides a different context for the message. There is, for example, a difference between a request for funding that appears in a handwritten note on a half-sheet memo pad and a typed formal proposal. Which channel is most appropriate depends upon the message content, the dean's management style, and the working relationship between the dean and department chair. Some deans may only acknowledge formally prepared requests. Other deans may prefer to discuss an idea informally before receiving a written request for needed resources. Department chairs need to select the channel of communication for each item that will keep the communication with the dean open and productive.

Chairs can exercise considerable influence over the frequency and type of communication that they have with the dean. Department chairs do not need a formal issue to communicate with the dean. While some deans are more accessible than others, it is important that chairs communicate regularly with the dean. In virtually all instances, it is costly to avoid the dean. Instead, department chairs should initiate communication with the dean and not limit their communication to responding to their dean's requests for information. This allows the chair to maintain a continuous rapport with the dean. That rapport becomes the context in which difficult (as well as easy) issues can be discussed. If the department chair only approaches the dean when a problem erupts, there is little opportunity to build the type of rapport that supports an effective working relationship.

Department chairs need to follow up on their communication with the dean to learn the dean's reaction (feedback loop). It may be in face-to-face conversation or in writing. Meetings provide an opportunity to reinforce and clarify written communication. They also allow the chair to learn the dean's reaction to previous communication. Follow-up communication allows the chair to assess the overall effectiveness of previous communication. That assessment enables the department chair to alter the approach and gather additional information that responds to the dean's concerns. Using meetings in this way requires that the department chair listen in order to learn the dean's agenda.

Information obtained through active listening can be used to improve future communication with the dean. Active listening requires chairs to listen objectively. Chairs who listen with the intent to find fault in the message will not benefit from receiving the information. Active listening requires chairs to listen for the purpose of comprehending the dean's view. To do this, chairs must avoid unnecessary interruptions. It is one thing to interrupt to seek clarification on a particular point and quite another matter to interrupt for the purpose of quibbling with the point. Remember, the overriding objective is to encourage the dean to communicate more openly and productively with the department chair. That will not happen if the dean finds communication with the department chair punitive or counterproductive. Active listening implies an open mind on the issue, no distractions, and good eye contact between chair and dean. Done well, active listening is another practice that enables department chairs to increase their credibility with the dean.

Follow-up communication can also be written. Written communication is desirable when department chairs want a record of their dealings with the dean. This is more likely the case on technical matters, such as equipment requests or enrollment data. Issues with potential liability such as safety concerns or possible legal suits should probably be put in writing. Written communication documents that the department chair behaved responsibly in informing the dean. Because written follow-up communication becomes a matter of record for both dean and chair, chairs need to give as careful consideration to these messages as they did to the original correspondence. Specifically, chairs need to consider the reason for following up on earlier communication with the dean. What does the chair hope to accomplish, and is written communication the best vehicle for that purpose? Chairs need to consider the dean's reaction to written communication on that subject. Will the communication help or harm the chair's working relationship with the dean? Chairs need to consider whether the language and the tone of the communication are appropriate for the message and the intended receiver. Will the dean take offense at the chair's written communication?

Cultivate a team relationship with the dean

Seek the dean's counsel, but also become the dean's sounding board. Seek the dean's direction regarding college goals, but educate the dean on the department's integral role in meeting college goals. Seek the dean's interpretation of university policy and practice, but challenge the dean to implement policy with full appreciation of the department's needs. Respond to the dean's request for information, but also equip the dean with data for promoting the department. These and other mutually beneficial behaviors will forge a team relationship between dean and department chair. Fortunately, department chairs do not need to rely on deans to initiate these team behaviors. Communication is a vehicle for change. If a chair adopts the behaviors listed for engaging in open and productive communication, the dean must respond. Since deans have a vested interest in building effective working relationships with department chairs, they are likely to respond with positive behaviors that can further cultivate a team relationship. If, however, the department chair doesn't exercise leadership in communicating openly and productively with a dean who fails to encourage good communication, there is no motivation for the dean to alter the present practice.

Department chairs can also encourage a team relationship with the dean by engaging in those activities that the dean values. Department chairs should work to create a cordial rapport with the dean. It is important to be accessible and keep the dean informed of important issues and possible problems. This includes equipping the dean with data that the dean can use to promote or defend the department. Department chairs need to think of the dean as an advocate, not an adversary. It does not guarantee that the chair and the dean will agree on every issue, but department chairs must pick their battles judiciously. It is ill-advised to lose one's temper on the job. This does not mean that a chair should avoid varying the pitch or rate of speech to make a point. Reasoned discourse, even heated reasoned discourse, has its place. Temper is typically void of logic and can do much to damage the trust in any working relationship.

Finally, the department chair's performance should help the dean look good. This includes activities that enable the dean to be a stronger advocate for the department. Typically, deans do not appreciate surprise problems that are costly to the college. By keeping the dean apprised of potential problems, the chair does a lot to build trust and cultivate a team relationship with the dean. Whenever possible, make the department's achievements the dean's achievements. If the dean obtains funds from the provost to help support graduate student travel to a conference, have the students who benefit from the dean's generosity communicate their appreciation and the value of the conference experience. When a dean is able to feel a sense of pride in the accomplishments of the department faculty and students, the dean is more likely to value the department's role in the college. Chairs should keep the dean informed of the return on all college investments in the department. What did the dean's funding support yield to the department, college, and institution? This follow-up can pave the way for future requests.

Putting Theory Into Practice

In Case 7.1, Sharing the Liability, the department chair needs to get the dean's attention on an urgent matter. Previous communication from the chair did not yield the desired response. The chair must juggle the safety needs of department members and his rapport with the dean. Place yourself in the department chair's role as you read Case 7.1.

Case 7.1, Sharing the Liability

Background
For years faculty in the department have lived and worked among leaks. Physical plant workers have done their best to contain the leaks by using plastic tarps to direct the flow of leaking water into receptacles. Everyone

recognizes the need for significant roof repairs. The university is trying to secure capital funds from the state for this massive project. While the dean is sympathetic when the department chair complains about more leaks and water damage following virtually every rainstorm, Dr. Schmidhauser believes that the dean is too complacent about the problem. In his view, the situation is serious to the point of endangering faculty and students as well as damaging expensive department equipment. He is no longer content with the cajoling and shoulder shrugging that Dean Doherty uses to remind everyone that he is helpless in securing capital funds for the needed repairs.

Chair's Action

Jonathan Schmidhauser decides to escalate his complaint about the leaking roof by sending a memorandum to the dean. As he reads through the memorandum he plans to send, he can hear the dean's reaction. He knows that the dean will not appreciate receiving the correspondence, but Schmidhauser believes he must take some action. He doesn't know what else he can do.

Memorandum to Dean

To: Charles K. Doherty
        Dean

From: Jonathan Schmidhauser
        Chair

Subject: Strong Hall Roof

Our office experienced major leaks during yesterday's rains, as I mentioned. The physical plant crew who are trying to control the problem estimate that they removed more than 50 gallons of water from the attic area. Water drained through the light fixtures in Professor Sari's office for several hours and caused several ceiling tiles to fall.

This is not a new problem as the roof has leaked for years, but it is obviously getting worse. It is my understanding that the roof repair and replacement project for the building is scheduled for architect selection this fall and that the work is likely to be done some time next spring or early summer. It is important that the project move forward expeditiously so that the work can be completed as soon as possible.

In addition, I believe some interim measures are needed. First, I would ask that the situation be closely monitored on a regular basis until the project is completed. The problems from the recent rains cause a concern for personal safety of those working on the fourth floor, not to mention potential damage to equipment and furnishings. The problem has been controlled for years with buckets and plastic in the attic, but the amount of water now coming through has the potential to cause major damage and personal injury.

In addition, it is not clear to us what effect many years of leakage may have had on the condition of the wooden support structure for the heavy tile roof. A collapse of the roof itself, needless to say, could be disastrous. A thorough inspection and assurance that this does not present a safety hazard would help to ease our concerns in the coming months. If there is risk of such an occurrence, the offices affected should be temporarily relocated.

cc: University Risk Management

Let's Analyze the Case

Chair Schmidhauser believes that he must get the dean to recognize the serious need for roof repairs. Every time the chair raises the issue with the dean, he gets the same "shoulder shrugging" response. The dean is comfortable with admitting his helplessness in getting the needed roof repairs. There is noise in the communication channel on this issue in that the chair's repeated complaints evoke a patterned response from the dean. In desperation the chair writes a pointed memorandum to communicate the increasing severity of the leaky roof. The chair believes that he must write the memorandum to protect the safety of department members. If the chair only worries about the increasing danger from the leaky roof, the chair assumes greater responsibility should the roof collapse than if the chair alerts the dean to the pressing safety hazard.

Since we know little about the dean, we cannot predict how Charles Doherty might react to the chair's memorandum. The chair's credibility with the dean will shape the dean's reaction. If the dean perceives the chair as a conscientious individual, the dean is likely to take the memorandum seriously. If, however, the dean perceives the chair as an alarmist who whines until he gets his way, the memorandum is likely to anger the dean. Similarly, if the dean trusts the chair to speak from genuine concern for department members, the dean's reaction will be more positive than if the dean perceives the chair as grandstanding because the chair's motives are not trustworthy.

The dean will read the memorandum in the context of previous communication with the department chair. If the typical mode of doing business is through conversation, the dean will take greater notice (and perhaps offense) of a formal memorandum that documents the safety threat. The dean is likely to sense that the chair's purpose is to create a file document that places responsibility with the dean should the roof collapse. Since the dean believes that he is helpless in getting the roof repaired, he may take offense at being placed in this uncomfortable position. The chair's action may, however, prompt the dean to push central administration on an issue that he would otherwise ignore. The chair perceives the dean as content to shrug his shoulders about the problem. The chair needs to get the dean to take action on the department's behalf, which requires that the dean recognize what he might do to get the roof repaired. By changing the communication channel, the chair elevates the importance of the message. We are less certain whether the department chair jeopardizes his rapport with the dean by sending the memorandum. Notice also that the chair does not invite a reaction (feedback loop) from the dean. Rather, the memorandum only describes the action needed.

The chair's objective is to get the dean's support for securing an urgently needed roof repair without alienating his rapport with the dean. The chair needs to deliver unwelcome news in a manner that does not jeopardize the chair's working relationship with the dean. The chair needs to make clear that his purpose is to secure desperately needed roof repairs and not place blame upon the dean. The task is more challenging because word of a leaky roof is old news and the dean has a conditioned response to this routine message. The chair needs the dean to recognize it as a new issue that requires action instead of shoulder shrugging. Ideally, the chair needs to make the issue a top priority for the dean while cultivating a team relationship with the dean.

It's Your Turn

Think through how you would get Dean Doherty's attention on this issue.

1. Would you commit the matter to writing? If so, would you make any changes in the chair's memorandum in Case 7.1? How would you follow up on your memorandum to the dean to assess the effectiveness of your communication?

2. What precautions would you take to preserve your credibility with the dean? How might you safeguard your working relationship with the dean? How would you use this situation to cultivate a team relationship with the dean?

Please Consider

It may seem like an impossible task to raise an unpopular issue while preserving credibility and an effective working relationship. Yet, department chairs often find themselves in exactly this position. The chair, more than any other university administrator, is in a position to recognize pressing department needs. One factor that helps department chairs broach touchy issues is initial credibility. When deans perceive department chairs as responsible administrators, they expect to receive news of department needs as well as department achievements. Responsible deans will not take personal offense when department chairs do their job.

The manner in which chairs approach their dean about problems, however, can either strengthen or weaken their working relationship with the dean. Ideally, the department chair and dean can collaborate to remedy department problems. That is more effective in maintaining a productive working relationship than blaming the dean for the department's problems. Chairs can engage the dean in a collaborative effort even when the department chair must escalate an issue such as the situation described in Case 7.1. Chair Schmidhauser might, for example, phone the dean and inform him that the memorandum is coming. This tactic allows the chair to place a formal memorandum in context. In the situation described in Case 7.1, the chair might indicate that he intends the memorandum as ammunition for the dean who must secure the needed repairs from an uninformed central administration. It allows the chair to preface the harsh written communication, reinforce the team relationship between the chair and dean, and supply a rationale for committing the issue to writing that is not likely to cause the dean to take personal offense.

Let's Recap

Review your strategy for informing the dean in Case 7.1 of needed roof repairs. If your approach does not account for the possible communication obstacles, you may want to review the material presented earlier in this chapter. Does your approach

- make the purpose clear?

- show respect for the receiver?

- eliminate noise from the channel?

- include a feedback loop?

Consider whether your approach would strengthen the chair's working relationship with the dean. Does your approach

- establish and maintain the chair's credibility?

- keep communication open and productive?

- cultivate a team relationship?

Putting Theory Into Practice

The chair in Case 7.2, Passing the Buck, allows the college dean to prioritize department initiatives. The dean must evaluate the relative merit of individual department requests without guidance from the department chair. Consider the chair's responsibility for prioritizing department activities as you read the following case.

Case 7.2, Passing the Buck

Charley Madigan, dean of the college of science, muses over the latest memorandum from Barbara Bignet, chair of the mathematics department. As usual, the chair's memorandum is a brief note that covers a more thoughtful faculty proposal. The chair's memo reads: "I fully endorse the enclosed request from Professor Gobert. This activity is important to the department, and I hope that you can locate funds to support it."

Except for the name of the faculty member, the memorandum is identical to most received from Dr. Bignet. In fact, it is the third such request received from Chair Bignet this month. From reading the attached proposal, Dean Madigan learns that Professor Gobert has been invited to present a paper at a prestigious international conference in Australia. Professor Gobert is seeking funds to defray travel expenses. The dean believes that this is an important opportunity for Professor Gobert, and one that will accrue some visibility for the department and the institution. He is less certain whether the college should support this request over others received from the mathematics department.

A week ago, Dean Madigan received the same cover memorandum from Chair Bignet seeking support for a proposal prepared by Professor Milman-Posten. Professor Milman-Posten seeks funds to purchase computer equipment for instructional use in math courses that are taken by students majoring in engineering and several of the science programs. Before that, the dean received a proposal from Professors Arendsen and von Weber seeking support to develop a summer program for high school students to introduce them to possible careers in mathematics. This request also had the customary two-sentence cover memorandum from Chair Bignet.

The Responsibility

Dean Madigan is able to see merit in all three requests. He is also confident that he will recognize the merit of similar requests that Chair Bignet is likely to forward as the year progresses. Faculty in the department of mathematics are very creative and productive. The mathematics department boasts many strong faculty who engage in numerous important activities.

Unfortunately, the college budget is finite. Dean Madigan reserves a modest sum for sponsoring innovative requests. The funds are to help with special projects that may develop outside the normal department planning process. Dean Madigan recognizes that department chairs may not know about all faculty activities when preparing the department budget. Professor Gobert, for example, received his invitation to speak in Australia after the department budget was set for the current fiscal year.

Barbara Bignet, however, tends to forward all special requests to the dean for funding. Dean Madigan believes that many of these special requests could be (should be) incorporated in the department's planning. If, for example, the development of a summer program for high school students is a high priority, the chair should build this expenditure into the department budget. Similarly, the purchase of computer equipment to support instruction is an item that should be planned for within the department. At a minimum, the dean expects a thoughtful proposal that specifies what portion of the cost the department can bear in mounting larger initiatives.

The Decision

The department chair claims that every request is important to the department. Dean Madigan, therefore, must impose his own criteria for weighing the relative merit of each request. In deciding whether to support the three requests received this month, the dean weighs the affordability of each request against the potential gain for the college and the department. Given the state's emphasis on spending more time on undergraduate instruction and the campus pressure to preserve student enrollment, Dean Madigan opts to support the request from Professors Arendsen and von Weber to develop a summer program for high school students. This activity augments the college student recruitment program.

Let's Analyze the Case

The department chair in Case 7.2 delegates department decisions to the dean. For whatever reason, Barbara Bignet does not prioritize department requests for additional funds. This has one advantage in that no faculty member could accuse Dr. Bignet of playing favorites. Every faculty request gets the same support as she forwards it to the dean. The disadvantage is that requests receive funds in accordance with how they enhance college objectives, not necessarily department priorities. In this instance, the dean supports the request from Professors Arendsen and von Weber to develop a summer program for high school students because the activity supports the college effort to recruit students. Student recruitment may not be the top priority for the mathematics department.

The chair gives up more than her prerogative to prioritize department requests. By shirking this responsibility, Dr. Bignet allows the dean to establish an operational mission statement for the department. Student recruitment becomes a priority for the mathematics department whether or not it serves the department mission. It is possible that visibility at a prestigious international conference has greater value to the mathematics department than the college student recruitment program. By allowing the dean to make the decisions, the chair makes the task of promoting the department mission more difficult, especially if the dean's perception of the department's mission does not correspond with the department's self-image.

On a more personal level, the department chair sacrifices credibility with the dean. It is unlikely that Charley Madigan perceives Barbara Bignet as able to order priorities. That is a significant skill since there is seldom sufficient funding to support all requests. Department chairs must be able to order priorities. Worse yet, some of the special funding requests submitted by the chair impress the dean as initiatives that the department should integrate in the department's budget planning. It gives the dean reason to doubt the chair's ability to lead faculty through a planning process, another important administrative skill.

Barbara Bignet's practice of deferring decisions about department priorities to the dean will, in the long-term, jeopardize her credibility with the department faculty. The faculty will learn that the dean decides who gets funding. This practice conditions faculty to write for the dean instead of the chair. Consequently, the faculty begin to request college funds by demonstrating how the request supports college priorities. The faculty are likely to develop a greater allegiance to college priorities than department priorities. This undermines the sense of department community that helps department chairs manage more effectively.

It's Your Turn

Revisit Case 7.2, Passing the Buck, and develop a strategy for forwarding individual faculty requests to the college dean that does not surrender the chair's responsibility for ordering department priorities.

1. Assume that the department places a high priority on quality instruction and promoting the department's reputation. Which requests would you forward to the dean, and which requests would you plan to fund with department resources?

2. How would you introduce the requests to the dean? Can you place the individual requests in a context that enables the dean to understand the department mission and priorities?

Please Consider

The one short-term advantage to Barbara Bignet's practice of delegating decisions about individual requests to the dean is that faculty cannot accuse the chair of favoritism. However, the faculty can predict the relative merit of individual requests when they know and understand department priorities. If the mathematics faculty in Case 7.2 know that the department places a high value on quality instruction, they will not be surprised if Professor Milman-Posten's request to purchase computer equipment for instructional use gets funded before other requests that do not serve this department priority. As discussed in Chapter 1 of this text, a clear department mission provides both a blueprint for decision-making and a rationale for the department chair's decisions. Issues that might evoke a charge of discrimination or undue favoritism can be subdued, if not eliminated, when the chair's decisions are consistent with faculty expectations, given their knowledge of the department mission and priorities.

Putting Theory Into Practice

Case 7.3, Please Say No, involves the same mathematics department introduced in the previous case. This time we witness how Chair Bignet handles a difficult tenure application. Consider the relative responsibilities of department chairs and college deans in the tenure and promotion review process as you read Case 7.3.

Case 7.3, Please Say No

Charley Madigan, dean of the college of science, sits in his office ready for the next scheduled appointment, which is with Barbara Bignet, chair of the mathematics department. Dr. Bignet requested the meeting a few hours earlier but would not tell the secretary the purpose for meeting with the dean.

Dean Madigan isn't too worried. Dr. Bignet typically believes that she needs to talk with him "right away" about matters that could be communicated via memorandum.

The Meeting

Bignet: "Thank you for meeting with me on short notice."

Madigan: "You were in luck. I had blocked off a couple hours this afternoon to work on an enrollment report so my calendar could accommodate a last-minute meeting."

Bignet: "Well, it is important that we talk. I just heard that the college committee on promotion and tenure is meeting tomorrow to review the dossiers submitted this year."

Madigan: "Yes, and the application for Shih-Chung Chang in your department is in the stack of applications to be reviewed."

Bignet: "That's why we need to talk. I don't know if you have reviewed the dossiers, but Dr. Chang received the unanimous support of the math faculty."

Madigan (wondering what the problem could be): "That's great. I'm not surprised. Judging from Dr. Chang's annual performance evaluations, this is a person who has made steady progress toward promotion and tenure."

Bignet: "Not really. That's what I need to tell you."

Madigan (leaning forward as if to determine whether he's hearing Professor Bignet correctly): "What do you mean?"

Bignet: "The faculty believe that they had to vote in favor of tenure for Dr. Chang. Dr. Chang is, after all, a minority, and the faculty worried that a negative vote might be misinterpreted. Actually, the faculty believe that Dr. Chang should not receive tenure in our unit."

Madigan: "What? You can't be serious."

Bignet: "It's true. The faculty believe that Dr. Chang should not receive tenure, and I must say that I agree with them."

Madigan: "Why?"

Bignet: "For starters, Dr. Chang is not very proficient in English, and we believe this is a serious liability to effective teaching. You know the math faculty take great pride in offering quality instruction, and Dr. Chang's limited use of English jeopardizes the department's reputation for quality instruction."

Madigan: "This state requires that we certify new faculty members as being proficient in English at the time of their hire. As I recall, you certified that Dr. Chang is proficient in English when you hired him six years ago."

Bignet: "Yes, I remember signing some form, but we were desperate at that time. You'll remember that Dr. Wykoff retired on short notice a few weeks before the start of the fall term. Frankly, we did not have a very good applicant pool, and Dr. Chang was merely the best of a limited search."

Madigan: "But you recommended Dr. Chang for a continuing tenure-track appointment. You evaluated Dr. Chang every year throughout the six-year probationary period. Never before have you given any hint of a problem."

Bignet: "Surely, you understand that I couldn't do that without appearing prejudicial. Besides, I hoped that Dr. Chang's English would improve with time. It simply has not. If you deny Dr. Chang tenure, the department will have one full year to conduct a search for his replacement. I believe that we would be able to recruit a new faculty member with teaching abilities far superior to those of Dr. Chang. In the best interest of the department, I must urge you to recommend against Dr. Chang's application for tenure and promotion."

Let's Analyze the Case

The dialogue in Case 7.3, Please Say No, reveals more about the relationship between the mathematics chair and the college dean. Dr. Bignet shows disregard for the dean by scheduling meetings on short notice. We learn from the case that the dean has come to expect the mathematics chair to request meetings on short notice to discuss matters that are not terribly pressing. Barbara Bignet acts on her need even when it shows disregard for the dean, her intended receiver. To make matters worse, the chair refuses to alert the dean as to the purpose of the meeting. The dean has no opportunity to prepare for the meeting. It is more courteous to communicate the subject for discussion and allow others to prepare for a meeting. Meeting preparation may include reviewing a file, checking policy, or merely reflecting about the subject.

There is considerable noise in the channel of communication between the chair and dean. The chair's purpose is to tell the dean why he should recommend against tenure for Shih-Chung Chang. The dean tries to point out that the department chair gives him no basis for doing so. Shih-Chung Chang received favorable annual performance evaluations each year during the probationary period, and the department faculty voted to recommend Dr. Chang for tenure. The department chair does not understand that the dean has no basis to overturn the department's recommendation. The chair believes only that the dean should recommend against tenure for Dr. Chang for the reason that the chair explained. The chair is unable to consider the issue from the dean's perspective.

The department chair may have a legitimate concern about Shih-Chung Chang's qualifications if indeed Professor Chang is not proficient in English and this has an adverse affect on instructional quality. However, the chair raises the issue at the wrong time. As the dean points out, the department chair certified that Professor Chang is proficient in English at the time of hire. Furthermore, the department chair never raised this concern during annual performance evaluations of Dr. Chang. Unless some special circumstance caused Dr. Chang's proficiency in English to regress recently, the chair has no defensible reason to make it a basis to deny tenure. By not informing Dr. Chang of the deficiency and raising it now as the basis for denying tenure, the chair opens herself to charges of discrimination.

The department chair failed to fulfill her responsibility for performance evaluation. We have no indication that Dr. Chang knows there is any concern. If Dr. Chang's proficiency in English is less than desirable, the chair had an obligation to inform Dr. Chang of this early during the probationary period to allow time for Dr. Chang to remedy the perceived deficiency. This is problematic because Chang could claim that there was no deficiency since the chair certified that he was proficient in English at the time of appointment.

The interaction described in Case 7.3 does little to preserve the chair's credibility with the dean. The chair may believe that she can communicate openly with the dean. After all, the chair felt comfortable making this request in person and on short notice. This does not mean that the chair has an effective working relationship with the dean. The chair did not disclose her concern about Dr. Chang's qualifications for tenure throughout the six-year probationary period. Her behavior hardly suggests a team relationship between the department chair and dean.

It's Your Turn

Consider the problem described by the mathematics chair and think how you would manage the situation.

1. Would you certify Shih-Chung Chang as proficient in English at the time of hire because Chang was the best qualified candidate available following a last-minute search? How could you help Dr. Chang improve this deficiency? What is your ethical obligation to Dr. Chang and the other faculty? What is your ethical obligation to students?

2. How might the chair have worked with the dean earlier to address Dr. Chang's English proficiency? What is your ethical obligation to the dean in managing potential personnel problems?

Let's Recap

Review your strategy for informing the dean in Case 7.3 of Chang's deficiency in English. If your approach does not account for the possible communication obstacles, you may want to review the material presented earlier in this chapter. Does your approach

- make the purpose clear?
- show respect for the receiver?
- eliminate noise from the channel?
- include a feedback loop?

Consider whether your approach would strengthen the chair's working relationship with the dean. Does your approach

- establish and maintain the chair's credibility?
- keep communication open and productive?
- cultivate a team relationship?

Putting Theory Into Practice

In Case 7.4, Listen Carefully, the college dean and department chair talk past each other without ever communicating. Alan Kresky, chair of the geography department, finds the dean unsupportive of the department's desire to develop its program in land reclamation. The dean perceives the department chair as limited, if not stubborn, in his response to changing conditions within the state.

Case 7.4, Listen Carefully

The chair of the geography department, Alan Kresky, finds the dean of the science college, Andrea Rodriguez, unable to comprehend the resource needs and academic pursuits of the geography faculty. Repeatedly, Dr. Kresky advocates faculty interest to seemingly deaf ears. Dr. Kresky believes that Dean Rodriguez has a limited vision for the college and remains unwilling to support the geography department.

Dean's Message

Since hired from the outside three years ago, Dean Rodriguez has attempt-ed to make the college more cost-effective and responsive to state funding themes and university priorities. Rodriguez knows that the state will fund new programs and program expansions if they advance one of four state funding themes:

1. Making higher education more accessible to the state's population

2. Improving undergraduate instruction quality

3. Improving minority student recruitment, retention, and graduation rates

4. Bolstering the state's economic development

Rodriguez consistently reminds all department chairs of the four funding themes. The dean believes that the college can increase its resource base by responding to the funding themes. Unless the college increases its budget base by securing state approval for new or expanded initiatives, depart-ments must continually fight over the existing finite resources. To the dean, the possibility of securing new state dollars offers hope to an otherwise inad-equate budget.

The Geography Department

The geography department continues to advocate faculty interest in the area of land reclamation. The department boasts a number of faculty who have national reputations for their research. To remain competitive in this field, the department needs new technology and lab equipment. Chair Kresky pre-sents the department's resource needs at every opportunity. His proposals for new funding to support faculty research and teaching in the area of land reclamation include testimony from prominent researchers and other experts. He argues the need for graduate students to have course work in the area of land reclamation and the marketability of program graduates who have this training.

The department has a modest number of undergraduate students. The faculty have more pride and interest in the graduate program which attracts students nationwide. Currently, geography accepts 1 of every 10 graduate applications received. The department is relatively cost-effective because geography offers one core course titled "Environmental Issues" in the institu-tion's general education program. Enrollment in this course produces so many credit hours that the total instructional cost for the geography depart-ment is slightly below the campus average. The Environmental Issues course is taught through a combination of large lecture and small lab. Faculty present lecture material to large classes. Graduate assistants then supervise activities in labs with 25 students.

The Dilemma
Alan Kresky is unsure how to get the dean's attention. Department needs do not seem to correspond with the state funding themes. Somehow, Dr. Kresky needs to help Dean Rodriguez understand the department's need for additional resources regardless of the state funding themes.

Let's Analyze the Case

In Case 7.4, both the dean and the department chair have a specific message that each needs the other to hear. The department chair wants the dean to recognize and support faculty work in land reclamation. This area constitutes the primary thrust for faculty research and graduate instruction. The dean, however, wants the geography department to respond to the state funding themes. College funds are finite unless the college receives additional funding from the state to support new and expanded program initiatives. The state, however, will only fund program requests that are consistent with at least one of the four state funding themes. The dean wants to receive funding requests from departments that qualify for new dollars from the state.

There are a number of communication problems in Case 7.4. First, the message purpose is only clear to the individual senders. Both the department chair and the dean know what they want, but neither successfully clarifies that purpose for the other. If each would listen to learn the communication purpose of the other, the chair and the dean would know how to construct their messages for greater success. For example, if the chair were to link the department's resource needs to the improvement of undergraduate instruction or bolstering the state's economic development, the dean would be more receptive. If the dean explained that only proposals from departments that link funding requests to one or more of the state funding themes will be considered, the chair would know what has to happen to get the dean's attention. Instead, the chair perceives the dean as ignorant about the department's interests and resource needs, and the dean perceives the department chair as uncooperative and ignorant of the state's conditions.

Second, both the dean and the department chair show a general disrespect for the other. That is apparent in their communication, which is one-dimensional and does not take into account the receiver's perspective. Both focus only on what they need and want to say. Neither pays any attention to the concerns of the other. Third, the perception that each holds about the other contributes to noise in the channel. The dean doesn't respond to the resource needs of the department because she perceives the department chair as stubborn. The chair doesn't hear that the department can obtain new money only if the department's needs coincide with the state funding themes. Finally, there are no effective feedback loops to help either the department chair or the dean because both are stuck on merely repeating their initial message. For feedback to be effective, the sender must use the response to alter or elaborate upon the initial communication for the purpose of gaining a better understanding.

As a result of the ineffective communication between the department chair and the dean, both lose credibility with the other. The communication between chair and dean is not open and productive. Nor does their communication with one another help to cultivate a team relationship. Even though department chairs occupy line administrative positions that are below the dean in the university hierarchy, chairs can take action to remedy such ineffective communication as exists in Case 7.4. The department chair can exercise leadership by analyzing the present communication and determining how to alter the destructive pattern. Specifically, the chair needs to assess the dean's perspective and priorities to learn how best to champion the resource needs of the department. Only when the resource needs of the department fit with the dean's agenda will the dean recognize and be more likely to support them.

It's Your Turn

Place yourself in the role of department chair and decide how to break the negative communication pattern that exists in Case 7.4, Listen Carefully.

1. How might you present the department's resource needs so that the dean recognizes them as consistent with the state funding themes? Is such an adaptation of presentation harmful to the department mission?

2. What might you do to encourage the dean to perceive you and the department as cooperative team players within the college?

Let's Recap

Deans want and need department chairs to succeed because poor department leadership reflects negatively on the college dean. Deans cannot succeed unless department chairs are effective. Both chairs and deans have a vested interest in developing an effective working relationship. Effective communication is the cornerstone of any effective working relationship.

Department chairs can exercise leadership in cultivating an effective working relationship with the dean. The key is in communication. Department chairs need to communicate effectively with the dean. This includes making certain that the message purpose is clear, that communication exhibits a respect for the dean, and that potential "noise" is eliminated. It is also important to follow up on communication with the dean to learn how the dean received and interpreted the chair's communication. Building a feedback loop allows a sender to evaluate the message effectiveness with the express purpose of improving future communication.

Credibility is integral to effective communication. If the receiver trusts and respects the sender, there is a greater tendency to interpret messages accurately and constructively. Even in difficult situations, people are more likely to give the benefit of the doubt to those whom they trust and perceive as credible. Department chairs are never done working at maintaining their credibility. All communication to the dean says something about the chair and the department.

Through effective communication, department chairs can also cultivate a team relationship with the dean. This is particularly advantageous during times of adversity. In a team relationship, the chair and the dean work toward the same general goals. Both want the department, for example, to be of high quality, to receive adequate funding, to have healthy enrollments and other tangible evidence of success. Disagreements are easier to manage when both the chair and the dean want department success and both agree on how to measure success.

Open and productive communication is essential to a team relationship. Chair and dean need to exchange relevant information freely. Ideally, each pays attention to the perspective of the other through active listening and follow-up communication. If both practice active listening, they bring open minds to every communication exchange. Both answer questions directly without bluffing or becoming defensive. They listen to comprehend one another's message without becoming argumentative. When dean and chair disagree on an issue, they do so from full understanding of each other's view. Fortunately, chairs can exercise leadership to improve communication between dean and chair. By initiating the desired communication behaviors, chairs encourage deans to respond constructively with similar behaviors. Everyone wins when there is a productive relationship between the dean and chair.

8

BUILDING ALLIANCES

Academic departments do not exist in a vacuum but are dynamic units that must respond to external conditions and pressures. Durable departments build an intricate web of alliances with numerous constituencies. An alliance is a mutually beneficial relationship between two or more parties. Effective alliances with both campus and noncampus groups strengthen the department's posture within the institution. The campus is a political environment in that departments compete for finite resources. Unlike life in corporate America, competitors are not usually eliminated. To fare well from one year to the next, academic departments need effective alliances. Academic departments that provide important services to other units on campus are difficult to cut. Similarly, departments that enjoy a positive profile with important off-campus constituencies find it easier to demonstrate their value to the institution.

As the primary representative of the department, the chair must exercise leadership in establishing effective alliances. In describing the skills required today by leaders in higher education, Green (1988, p. 40) argues the need for coalition building. As Green points out, if one views the campus as a "political community with varied interest groups and diffused power," the leader's job will be to "build coalitions and consensus." An academic department that insulates itself from external groups becomes vulnerable to externally imposed change that may not be in the department's best interest. Department chairs can safeguard the future welfare of their departments by cultivating effective alliances.

The Objective

One goal of this chapter is to equip department chairs with specific strategies for building effective alliances so chairs can increase their departments' power in a political environment by cultivating important alliances. A second goal is to help chairs recognize when and how to use alliances. The benefit of having alliances is lost if the department chair does not know when and how to mobilize partners in support of the department.

Defining the Task

The term *alliance* refers to a mutually beneficial relationship between two or more parties. The department chair's purpose is to create a focused dialogue that allows for the establishment of common ground between the department and the various interest groups. Building alliances is the process of bringing together credible constituencies that have an interest in advancing a mutually beneficial agenda. An effective coalition creates movement. Sometimes this movement is in changing the direction of an issue. The department, for example, may use its alliance with alumni to persuade the central administration that a certain action is harmful to the department. At other times, a coalition creates movement by accelerating progress toward desired objectives. For example, an academic department may team up with area industry to promote the value of department research.

While the benefit of building alliances is obvious, the process of creating successful and effective coalitions is hard work. The task requires continuous effort. Even when the department enjoys successful alliances, the chair must nurture these relationships. A partner can only effectively advance a mutually beneficial agenda if that partner remains informed and motivated. For important alliances to remain supportive of an academic department, they must remain focused on both the needs and the achievements of the department. This requires continuous communication with the department. The department chair bears the major responsibility for engaging in dialogue with important constituencies.

Relevant Communication Concepts and Strategies

Not all alliances are successful or useful. Department chairs need to invest their energy wisely in order to cultivate alliances that carry the greatest benefit for their departments. The following strategies will help department chairs carry out this responsibility.

Select partners who are credible

Effective partners are those who have a vested interest in the department's mission and goals, but a department may have different alliances for the various components of its mission. A department may, for example, form an alliance with area industry in pursuit of the department's research goal and form a second alliance with alumni who support the instructional component of the department's mission. Not every partner needs to support with equal enthusiasm all the department goals. It is important that partners be perceived as credible by the central administration and others who have decision-making authority over the department. Little is gained, for example, from an alliance with an unaccredited program at another institution when trying to secure external grant funding for a cooperative research program. Department chairs need to give careful thought to the credibility of potential partners. There is little benefit in cultivating an alliance with a group that commands no respect from those who are in a position to affect the future of the department.

The same rule applies in selecting campus partners. An alliance with another unit on campus is only helpful if the central administration recognizes the partner as credible on the issue that forms the basis for the alliance. Mathematics and English departments may form alliances around support needs in the delivering of high-quality general education courses required for all university students. If the administration perceives these units as credible on this issue, the partnership can be an effective alliance in securing resources for general education courses taught in math and English. Chairs should look for potential partners among campus units that have similar conditions. Music departments, for example, may seek other departments that wrestle with the need to offer individualized instruction on a campus that accepts credit hour production as the most significant measure of department success. Chairs can help build department cases by forming alliances with credible partners on and off campus.

Identify and promote the mutual benefits

An effective alliance is a mutually beneficial relationship. The process of forming important alliances does not require the chair to plead for support. Rather, it requires the department chair to persuade potential partners of the mutual benefits derived from an alliance. Benefits are desired outcomes that partners lose should the alliance fail. For example, regional employers who rely on graduates of the department's program stand to lose an important benefit should the department fail to prepare the same number of qualified graduates. The English department's decision to decrease the enrollment in each section of technical writing may affect departments that require their majors to take the course. An effective alliance between departments enables units with similar conditions to remain united on such issues as course enrollment limits to preserve instructional quality.

Partners who perceive a benefit from an alliance have a greater commitment to the alliance and the common agenda, but even partners with a strong commitment to the alliance need information. If the regional employers that hire the department's graduates do not know the department's need for new equipment to train graduates who are proficient in using the current technology, they cannot help the department. Unless the English department knows that other programs on campus want to maintain a cap on course enrollment to preserve instructional quality, it may sense greater pressure to increase the English department's credit hour production. Credible partners are most effective advocates for the department when they recognize the benefits derived from strengthening the department and understand what the department needs.

In some instances, individual faculty may have a stronger rapport with a potential partner. The faculty who supervise student internships, for example, may be the first to develop a relationship with a potential partner. Chairs, however, must exercise leadership over the activity of forming department alliances, or individual faculty contacts may become productive alliances for faculty, not necessarily for the department. Faculty members can help with the process of keeping partners informed and motivated if they understand the department mission and objectives. It is important that the faculty consult with the chair when helping to cultivate department alliances.

Maintain continuous dialogue with partners

Effective alliances are not contractual agreements that individual partners must honor to avoid being in default. Rather, effective alliances are relationships that require continuous nurturing. Communication is the primary vehicle for maintaining an effective alliance. The most committed and motivated partners cannot fulfill their supportive role if they are uninformed about changing conditions that affect the department's progress. The department chair must communicate with partners about the department's achievements and resource needs.

Chairs should be careful to articulate program needs without giving the impression that the program is a lost cause. It is better to state resource needs as a condition of continued program strength or growth, not as evidence about how bad things are for the department. In some instances, department chairs may need to go one step further and help partners know how they can assist the department. Regional employers, for example, may be able to donate used equipment or allow for student training within industry offices. Chairs may need to help alumni learn that they can contribute more to the department than money and that the department welcomes alumni who serve as guest lecturers, employers of new graduates, or organizers on large fund drives. These pitches cannot be made in a single newsletter or piece of correspondence but must grow out of a continuous dialogue between the credible partners and the department.

Develop a strategy

When using an alliance to accomplish a specific purpose, it is important that department chairs not move ahead until they are certain that everyone is behind them. Alliances are only effective if partners agree on the same objective and engage in coordinated activity to accomplish the common goal. That takes time and careful preparation. The effective use of a particular alliance is the product of long-term planning and vision, not the result of spurious activity. Partners should work together to decide the collective plan of action so that individual partners understand their roles in the larger strategy. When department chairs merely dictate a specific role to each partner, they deny the partners an opportunity to strategize with the program leadership and thereby increase their commitment to the effort.

There are at least three times when alliances are particularly helpful to an academic department. The first instance is when there is a need for consensus on an issue and it is advantageous to work out a compromise rather than have a particular viewpoint imposed. Occasionally, two or more departments may engage in a turf battle over which department should teach a certain subject. To the extent that the departments are able to reach a consensus, they benefit more than if the central administration decides the issue. The first step in building such an alliance is to help potential partners perceive the benefit of reaching consensus without external interference. Most departments, for example, prefer to retain department control in defining the boundaries of the academic discipline. It is risky to let the dean or the provost whose training is in a different discipline resolve disputes over curriculum. It is usually preferable for the parties of the alliance to reach consensus among themselves.

A second situation when alliances are particularly helpful is when there is an advantage in aligning all interested parties on the same side of an issue. In this instance, the issue itself typically determines the interested parties. Departments of mathematics, English, and speech communication become an effective alliance on issues of delivering core requirements within a general education program. Most general education programs require all students to take a prescribed number of credit hours of English composition, math, and communication. These three disciplines form an appropriate alliance on issues related to staffing of the general education courses. Similarly, employers who have a vested interest in hiring graduates who are proficient in using the most current technology have a strong reason to help a related department secure new equipment. Working together, the employers and the department can decide their respective roles in pursuing possible sources for new equipment. The employers may have some influence with the central administration or an external funding source. With testimony from area employers, the department may have an increased opportunity for grant funding to purchase equipment. By working through the relative merits of each alternative together, the partners remain committed to the objective. This process also allows partners to know the efforts made by the department, which further enhances the alliance. A department that is willing to exhaust all options for new equipment in order to prepare graduates who satisfy the needs of regional employers will only endear itself to those employers.

Third, alliances are particularly helpful when a department needs to guard against changing conditions that threaten its welfare. Strong alliances with alumni, accrediting associations, industry, or area legislators can be an effective safeguard against the elimination of a particular program. These partners are important allies because they typically have some relationship with the central administration. Alumni, for example, are important to the university leadership as contributors of money, time, and good will. A vocal group of prominent alumni can influence the decisions of the central administration. Similarly, the state legislature can take action to alter the central administration's plans for a particular department. The legislature in a state with a large Spanish population, for example, may oppose a university's decision to eliminate the foreign language program. A department that can service the state's need to accommodate a multicultural population has value beyond the number of majors in the program.

Putting Theory Into Practice

In Case 8.1, Join the Winner's Circle, the department chair must secure external funding support for the debate team. Despite a long reputation for excellence, the debate team does not rate high as a campus priority during times of fiscal austerity. The chair must supplement the budget from outside sources. Place yourself in the role of department chair as you read the following case.

Case 8.1, Join the Winner's Circle

The debate team at Midwest University (MU) enjoys a long and prestigious tradition. For decades, debate teams from MU have excelled in forensic competition, bringing home countless trophies and plaques to the institution.

The forensics program is a source of pride for the speech department and the institution.

The budget for the debate team has not kept pace with increasing travel costs and other program needs. The budget does not permit the purchase of computer equipment that is essential for the team's research. The department chair failed to secure additional funds for the program from the institution. While the central administration acknowledges the instructional value of the forensics program, the academic dean does not wish to increase the debate budget because the program benefits only a few students. Debate competition requires a tremendous commitment from students. Traditionally, the size of the forensics program is lean, with the entire budget being spent on an average of eight to 12 students. In fact, the department chair hesitates to argue the point further for fear that the dean may decide that the college can no longer afford to spend the current budget on so few students.

Alternative Route

The department must seek sponsors for the forensics program off campus. The department chair requested that the debate coach submit a prioritized list of budget needs. At the top of the list is the acquisition of new computer equipment. Funds to defray travel expenses rank a close second. Debaters need the computer equipment to prepare evidence and debate cases for tournament competition. The team drives to tournaments whenever possible to reduce travel expenses, but travel costs still keep the team out of several tournaments each term.

With no hope of a budget increase for debate from the institution, the department chair decides to seek external funds for the forensics program. The chair lists the possible constituencies that might support the forensics program: alumni of the forensics program, area businesses, attorneys or legal organizations. The chair doubts that he can get much support from the alumni for two reasons. First, many of the debaters do not major in speech. Students in debate more often major in pre-law and political science. Second, all departments on campus recently completed their annual telephone fund drive in which faculty phone alumni to request a pledge. Most of the former debaters would have been called by faculty in other departments on campus. Besides, it would take a sizable sum of money to purchase computer equipment and increase the travel budget.

The department chair decides to approach area businesses. The chair is less certain whether to ask for cash or in-kind donations. The institution is located in a rural area of the state. Major industries include coal, farming, and one automobile manufacturing plant. It has been a bad year for farmers, and the coal mines have had to lay off more workers. There are a number of local merchants, but the chair doubts that any could contribute the sum of money that the forensics program needs so the chair elects to seek in-kind contributions.

The department chair hopes that an area business might be willing to donate used computers to the team when it upgrades its office system. The local computer store helps the department chair identify two businesses that are in the process of upgrading computer capability. The chair learns that the equipment being replaced in the area's largest law firm, Smythe and Wykoff, would suit the team's purposes perfectly. Acquiring the used computers proves easier than expected. The law firm is pleased to donate equipment for which it no longer has a use. In fact, the firm was not sure what to do with the old equipment. The old equipment has no trade-in value, and the firm does not relish the idea of trying to selling it. By donating the equipment to the university debate team, the law firm gains a tax deduction. In exchange for the gift of used computers, the department chair promises to make public the firm's generosity and keep the firm apprised of the debate team's achievements.

Each week when the debate team returns from a tournament, the debate coach takes the newest collection of trophies won by the team to the law office for display in the front lobby. Soon the firm's attorneys take a more personal interest in the team's success. Eventually, the firm requests a team picture to put on permanent display in the office. The debate coach takes a picture of the debaters with the firm's attorneys. The law firm enlarges and frames the picture. A few weeks later, the debate coach notices that the law firm has added a caption under the picture that reads: "Smythe and Wykoff join forces with Midwest University's winning team." The caption holds a lot of meaning because the Midwest University football and basketball teams have had losing seasons the past three years.

Area Networks

The department chair is not sure how to reduce the debate team's travel expenses. After reviewing the team's budget and expenditures for the last few years, the chair determines that the cost of renting university vehicles has increased significantly. Currently, the team pays to use cars from the campus auto pool. With budgets cut all across campus, cost recovery units like the transit motor pool have increased rental rates to balance their budgets. The department chair decides that it is worthwhile to try and get a cheaper rental rate from a local car dealer.

The chair approaches the largest car dealership to inquire about a rental agreement for the debate team. Given the chair's experience with the law firm, the chair hopes that the car dealership might be able to offer a special (lower) rate in return for a tax write-off. Perhaps the car dealership will see this as an opportunity to advertise business on the side of the van that carries the debate team.

The department chair soon discovers that the president of the car dealership, Charles Black, is in the same Rotary group as Jon Smythe, the law firm's senior partner. Mr. Black is familiar with the debate team's success because Jon Smythe boasts about the team's accolades at every Rotary meeting. Since Black and Smythe are long-time friends, Black frequently sees the newest batch of trophies on display at the law office. To the department chair's surprise, Mr. Black seems pleased to have an opportunity to associate his business with the winning forensics program. He volunteers to equip the debate team with a large van. The side of the van reads: "Charles Black's Ford Dealership Proudly Transports Midwest University's Champion Debate Team." The free use of the van is more than the department chair hoped to receive. The cost savings on travel to tournaments within driving range allows the team budget to cover airfare for the more distant competitions.

Let's Analyze the Case

The department chair in Case 8.1 faces the fact that increased funding for the department's forensics program will not come from campus sources. The chair has to build alliances with external constituencies that can support the program financially. The chair begins by a making list of possible partners. The chair then weighs the potential of each possible partner. The analysis causes the chair to reject alumni as a good source of funds. Notice how the chair's assessment of prospective partners enables the chair to invest his time more judiciously.

The department chair elects to approach local businesses. Again, the chair makes an informed decision to seek in-kind rather than cash contributions. The decision derives from the chair's assessment of the local economy. One might consider the computer store a potential source for computers. The department chair, however, uses the computer vendor to identify potential contributors. The computer store manager knows which area businesses are upgrading their computer capability. The computer vendor also knows the model and capability of the equipment being replaced. Approaching this local network is more efficient than trying to interest IBM or Apple computer in donating equipment to the Midwest University debate team.

The mutually beneficial relationship with the law firm of Smythe and Wykoff develops differently than the department chair anticipated. The chair's offer to keep the law firm informed of the team's success was a modest gesture of appreciation. The gesture escalated, however, when the debate coach took the team's trophies to the law firm. The trophy display attracted attention from clients, and the attorneys took more pride in their investment. The attorneys liked the trophy display and wanted to elevate the law firm's association with the successful debate team by hanging a team picture in the office lobby. The office lobby display preserves continuous communication between the department and the law firm. While the debate coach probably visits the law office more often than the department chair, the chair is aware of the coach's dealings with the attorneys and controls the nature of the alliance.

The law firm is a credible partner for the department's forensics program. The practice of law requires skills that are taught through the debate activity. Attorneys appreciate the training and skill required to be successful in debate competition. At the same time, the law firm has prestige within the community. That is apparent in the friendship between Jon Smythe, senior partner in the law firm, and Charles Black, the president of the car dealership. The chair's appeal to the car dealership was easier because of the impression that Mr. Black held of the debate team, an impression formed from conversations with Mr. Smythe.

Jon Smythe sets the stage for the department chair's appeal to Charles Black by illustrating the benefit of having an alliance with MU's debate program. Mr. Black is pleased to have an opportunity to associate with Smythe and Wykoff in their support of Midwest University's winning debate team. The department chair does not have to persuade Mr. Black that this alliance will be good for business because Mr. Black is already convinced.

It's Your Turn

Use the process followed by the department chair in Case 8.1 to identify potential partners for your department.

1. List the potential partners for your department. Are there specific activities within your department that would benefit from an effective alliance with external constituencies? Consider the mutual benefits accrued with each of the potential partners on your list.

2. For each possible partner, design a strategy for establishing an effective alliance. How would you maintain a continuous dialogue with each partner?

Putting Theory Into Practice

Jane O'Brien, chair of social work, has a problem that derives from the department's placement within a liberal arts college. In Case 8.2, Meeting Accreditation Standards, the department chair must pursue the department's accreditation despite the unit's low priority status within the liberal arts college. Place yourself in the role of department chair as you read the following case.

Case 8.2, Meeting Accreditation Standards

Jane O'Brien, chair of the department of social work, is not looking forward to the upcoming accreditation visit. She knows the department has several glaring problems that the visitation team will undoubtedly notice. The chair worries that the department may not receive accreditation. Unfortunately, Dr. O'Brien is the only one who realizes how slim the odds are that the program will be accredited. Before coming to Southern Research University (SRU), Dr. O'Brien served on many visitation teams for the national accrediting association. She knows the process well. In fact, it was her experience with the national association that helped O'Brien get the job of department chair at SRU.

The provost at SRU hopes to earn accreditation for the social work program. The social work program attracts a growing number of students from the region who then find work in the area after graduation. Since there is a high demand for persons trained in social work in this part of the state, the provost believes that earning accreditation for the program will improve the program's standing within the state, which should, in turn, help the program recruit more students from farther distances. Because the program graduates students who find employment within the state, the provost believes that the program will qualify for increased funding from the state once it is accredited.

The College
The social work department is one of 27 academic units in the college of liberal arts. With the exception of social work, the other departments fall into one of two general categories: humanities or the fine and performing arts. With an emphasis on training professionals, the social work department does not fit comfortably within the college mission and profile.

This uneasy fit produces numerous problems for the social work department. Specifically, social work tends to be a low priority on all issues reviewed by college committees. For example, the college committee on promotion and tenure does not understand the field research activities conducted by faculty in social work, and the social work faculty have a difficult time documenting how their work meets college standards for promotion and tenure. Similarly, college committees that deal with issues of long-term planning fail to recognize the merit of resource requests from the social work department. When the college must absorb a budget cut, the department of social work typically receives the biggest hit.

The Status Quo

The present situation in social work is both encouraging and dismal. Student enrollment is at its highest level ever and continues to grow. The department manages more than 300 undergraduate majors and roughly 50 graduate students working toward a master's degree. As enrollment grows, the number of faculty positions continues to decline. In the last five years, the department lost three tenure-track positions, reducing the total faculty size from 12 to nine. To manage the loss, the department streamlined its curriculum and lifted the cap on course enrollment. Some of the core courses in social work now have 60 to 75 students in them.

The social work department limps along teaching larger classes with fewer faculty. O'Brien tries to advocate the department's need for resources by documenting the unit's increasing productivity. O'Brien does not understand why the dean cuts social work's budget when there are numerous programs in the college with low enrollments. When she makes this argument to the dean, who holds tenure in the school of music, she receives lectures on the need for one-on-one instruction in the fine and performing arts. According to the dean, credit hour generation and other such data-driven measures of productivity cannot be used in the college of liberal arts because they do not take into account the conditions required for quality instruction.

Jane O'Brien believes that the department's location within a college of liberal arts is a serious liability. Many of her counterparts at different institutions enjoy a position on campus that is comparable to other professional units such as schools of law and medicine. At many institutions, the school of social work is led by a dean who holds a position that is equal to that of the liberal arts dean. It seems to Jane O'Brien that the social work department at Southern Research University is victimized by virtue of its location within the college of liberal arts. Given the college mission and priorities, O'Brien is not surprised when a college committee or the dean elects to make social work the last priority. The department cannot succeed as long as it is measured against criteria that do not fit the department mission and goals. At the same time, O'Brien is not certain how to raise the issue of moving the social work department out of liberal arts and elevating its status from department to school. Since this is only her third year as department chair, she worries that others would perceive such a request as motivated by self-interest.

Visit with the Accreditation Team

The accreditation team is impressed with the quality of instruction and individualized attention given to the large number of majors by a very understaffed faculty. The accreditation team notes the high level of professionalism and commitment to education exhibited by all faculty. The team is impressed by the department leadership. In just three short years, Jane O'Brien had the department ready for the accreditation review, which is a major undertaking. She obviously is well liked by the faculty and has cultivated a strong camaraderie within the department. Spirits are high and faculty investment in the program is great despite budget cuts and increasing workloads.

When the team raises the problem of lost faculty positions with the dean, they learn that these positions were needed elsewhere to meet the college's commitment to the institution's general education program. The dean explains that since more than 80% of the institution's general education requirement is taught within the college of liberal arts, teaching the general education sequence is a top priority for the college. In meeting with the provost, the accreditation team learns that the institution perceives social work as a "bread-and-butter" program. Teaching more than 300 undergraduate students with nine faculty makes the department very cost-effective. The provost explains that this statistic helps offset some of the other more costly units within the college that must teach small enrolled courses.

The accreditation team surprises Jane O'Brien when they meet with her for their exit interview. The purpose of the accreditation team's final meeting with the department chair is to review the recommendations that they plan to make in their report. Without any prompting from the chair, the accreditation team asks whether the department would be in favor of altering its reporting line. The team proceeds to explain that, in their opinion, the department of social work should report directly to the provost and be given school status. The social work enrollment and the provost's interest in the program support this action.

Let's Analyze the Case

The final meeting with the accreditation team should alert Jane O'Brien to the possibility of an effective alliance with the national accrediting association. Before the accrediting team's visit, O'Brien perceived the team as a neutral agent sent to review the program objectively. The team's suggestion that they recommend a different reporting line for the department elevates them to potential partner status. The national accrediting association for social work programs is a credible partner since the provost hopes to secure accreditation for the program.

Facts uncovered by the visitation team convince them that the social work program should not be housed in the liberal arts college. This does not imply that they are biased before the review or that they have a hidden agenda to elevate the status of all social work programs. Jane O'Brien probably has high initial credibility with the review team since she has significant experience as a reviewer for the national accrediting association. The team is also impressed with the faculty and students. In their objective and experienced view, the major obstacle to program quality (and accreditation) is the reporting line for the social work program. Specifically, the social work chair reports to a dean who obviously does not understand the program and its needs. Furthermore, there is no evidence that life will improve for the social work program as long as it must compete with the other liberal arts departments. The mission and priorities of the liberal arts college are not compatible with those of a professional unit such as social work.

Dr. O'Brien needs to respond to the visitation team's suggestion. They invite her comment on a recommendation that the institution change the reporting line for the social work department. The chair agrees with the review team's assessment but must consider the ramifications of placing this suggestion in the final report from the national accrediting association. The chair needs to anticipate the probable reaction of the dean and provost to the recommendation. She also needs to consider if other alliances might help encourage the central administration to act favorably on a recommendation to change the reporting line for the social work department.

It's Your Turn

Place yourself in the role of department chair and decide how you would react to the visitation team's assessment.

1. Would you encourage the review team to include in their report a recommendation that the social work department be removed from the

liberal arts college? What precautions, if any, would you give? Does this action risk accreditation?

2. Assume that the review team includes the recommendation for relocation in their report. What action can you take to support the review team's findings? How might you influence the campus decision?

Please Consider

The visitation team reaches the same conclusion as the department chair, namely, that the social work department suffers a disadvantage by being housed in the liberal arts college. Both believe that the social work program should move out of the college. Ideally, the department chair and the accrediting association believe that the social work department should be elevated to school status and report directly to the provost. This would make the social work chair comparable in rank to the dean of liberal arts.

The chair needs to give careful consideration to the visitation team's suggestion that their report include a recommendation regarding the inappropriateness of social work's placement in the liberal arts college. Even if the provost agrees that social work should not be housed in liberal arts, it does not automatically follow that the provost will want to elevate the social work department to school status. The provost will consider this request in the context of other issues and concerns. A provost, for example, may not be anxious to create a new school and dean position if there is pressure to reduce administration costs. The department chair needs to anticipate alternatives that the provost might suggest or accept. Are there other colleges that would be better locations for the social work department? Are there other structures that might work without requiring the creation of a new professional school?

The national accrediting association is a credible partner for the social work department because the provost wants the program accredited. We know from the facts in Case 8.2 that the provost perceives an institutional advantage to earning accreditation for the social work program. We do not know what the provost is willing to do to secure the accreditation. The department chair needs to anticipate whether the provost is likely to believe that the creation of a school of social work is worthwhile in terms of gaining an accredited program that will recruit more students. Unless the accreditation of social work is a high priority for the provost, the department chair takes a risk by encouraging the accrediting association to stipulate a condition that may make the price of program accreditation too expensive for the provost. An alliance with the accrediting association is helpful to the department if the provost places a high priority on receiving accreditation. If it is important to the provost that the social work department be accredited, then the accrediting association is in a powerful position to request changes on behalf of the social work program.

Putting Theory Into Practice

In Case 8.3, Marketable Collaborations, the department chair must devise a way to increase the marketability of graduates. The chair realizes that a poor job placement record can hurt student enrollment. The chair works to build a productive alliance with a unit that has no previous relationship with the department. To be effective, the chair must persuade the other unit of the benefits derived from the proposed collaboration. Think what you might do if confronted with the situation described in the following case.

Case 8.3, Marketable Collaborations

Abdul Mohjazi, chair of computer science, reflects on the increasing difficulty that graduates have in securing gainful employment with the BA degree in computer science. Employers prefer to hire individuals who are proficient in both computer science and management. Computer science majors who have a second bachelor's in management, or preferably an MBA degree, get the better jobs. Dr. Mohjazi believes that this employment trend discourages students from enrolling in computer science.

Students are more career oriented than they were 15 to 20 years ago. Students want to know what type of job they can get with a bachelor's in computer science before they decide to enter the program. The chair believes that the program loses students to the two-year associate degree program in information systems that is offered at the nearby community college. Prospective students want a "real" job as soon as possible. With an associate degree in information systems, students can get an entry-level position. For those students concerned about funding a college education, this route is attractive because they can take more courses in computer science after they have that first job. Some companies pay employees to take courses toward advanced degrees. However, students who have a bachelor's degree with training in computer science and management do start in higher-paid positions. Dr. Mohjazi needs to incorporate a management component into the computer science bachelor's degree in order to recruit students.

The institution offers an MBA degree, but most students graduating with a bachelor's in computer science find out that the MBA requires them to go back and take a lot of undergraduate prerequisites in business. Hence, the average student with a bachelor's in computer science needs at least two, and usually three, more years to complete the MBA The seven years required to complete both programs represents a major time and resource investment for students. Worse yet, students who remain to earn the MBA find that they lose touch with the current computer science literature, practice, and technology.

The computer science department advises undergraduate majors to use their elective credits taking management courses, but most of the management courses carry a "majors only" restriction. Consequently, computer science majors cannot take undergraduate management courses unless they declare a business major.

Possible Solution

Dr. Mohjazi hopes to convince faculty in the management department to collaborate on a special five-year baccalaureate in computer science. The five-year computer science program would encompass a core of management courses. This would increase the marketability of computer science graduates and make it feasible for graduates with a bachelor's in computer science to complete an MBA with just one additional year of course work. Clearly, this plan is ideal for students majoring in computer science. Dr. Mohjazi needs to think how best to present it to the chair of the management department.

Let's Analyze the Case

The management department is a credible partner for the computer science program because employers prefer to hire graduates with training in both subject areas. The job market suggests that an alliance between the computer science and the management programs would be mutually beneficial. A five-year program that allows students to earn both a bachelor's in computer science and a master's in business administration is likely to appeal to career-oriented students who seek gainful employment. Such a program will increase student enrollment in both computer science and management courses.

Dr. Mohjazi must persuade his counterpart in management of the benefits from collaborating on a joint degree program. To do this, he must first learn about the management program. Does the management department have a favorable reputation on campus? By reading the management program's promotional literature, the computer science chair can learn a lot about this potential partner. How large is the department? What is the undergraduate and graduate student enrollment? If the management department needs to increase student enrollment, the management chair may quickly perceive an advantage of a joint degree with computer science. The department chair would only need to demonstrate that there is a market for graduates with combined training in computer science and business and that the proposed joint degree program would increase student enrollment in both programs.

Dr. Mohjazi's persuasion must correspond to conditions in management. If the management program enjoys high student enrollment, then the advantage of recruiting more students will not appeal to the department chair. In this instance, the more persuasive argument might be the need to remain current with market demands for graduates. The department chair might present data regarding the success of similar joint degree programs at other institutions or demonstrate the attractiveness of the joint degree program to the institution. To build a persuasive appeal, the computer science chair must assess the current health of the management program in comparison to the relative attractiveness of a joint degree program for the management department. An effective alliance cannot exist when either of the partners has an "I owe you" status with the other member of the alliance. All partners must perceive the relationship as mutually beneficial. This requires that individual partners understand and sell the alliance from the partners' perspective. Dr. Mohjazi must determine why the management department might want to collaborate with computer science on a joint degree program to identify the more persuasive appeals.

It's Your Turn

Place yourself in Dr. Mohjazi's position as chair of computer science and develop your strategy for approaching the management department chair.

1. What data would you gather about the management program? How would you obtain this information? What sources would you use to assemble information about job market conditions to illustrate the need for a joint degree program?

2. How would you approach the management department chair? Would you introduce the idea in person or send a memorandum? How would you follow up on your initial communication? Would you enlist the faculty in this effort? If so, specify how you would have faculty help.

Please Consider

Information about the person whom the computer science chair plans to approach is important to deciding how to make the pitch. Whom Dr. Mohjazi needs to talk with will depend on where the MBA program is housed within the business college. If it is in one academic department, the computer science chair needs to talk with that department chair. Dr. Mohjazi believes that students majoring in computer science need management courses, so he is thinking of a joint degree program with management. If, however, a staff member at the dean's level coordinates the MBA program, Dr. Mohjazi will need to approach the person responsible for directing the program. Depending upon the institutional culture, it may be inappropriate for a computer science chair to approach a staff person in the dean's office of a different college. In that instance, Dr. Mohjazi will need to involve his college dean in approaching the business college dean's staff.

Once Dr. Mohjazi knows whom to approach, he must consider that person's management style. Has the computer science chair met the person who directs the MBA program? Does he know someone who knows that person? The connections need not be campus relationships. Often we learn more about people through our interaction with them at church or civic activities than on campus. Does this person prefer to iron out agreements through conversation? Is the person one who finds statistics more credible than qualitative reasoning?

These glimpses provide insights that help determine whether to approach the individual in person or through written communication. Often it is preferable to use a combination of oral and written communication. The computer science chair, for example, might introduce the subject in person but leave a document that details the need for, and the benefits from, the proposed joint degree program with the person during the initial meeting. Or the chair might broach the subject on the phone by saying: "I believe I have an idea that might help both our programs increase student enrollment. Would you be willing to spend 30 minutes talking with me about it?" Any clues about the person that the computer science chair hopes to persuade will help him know how to construct a more effective persuasive appeal.

Let's Recap

Review your strategy for persuading the management department to form an alliance with computer science. If your approach does not incorporate the strategies for forming productive alliances, you may want to review the material presented earlier in this chapter. Does your approach

- select partners who are credible?
- maintain continuous dialogue with partners?
- develop a strategy?

Putting Theory Into Practice

The department chair in Case 8.4, Campus Networks, learns the usefulness of campus networks. Even informal contacts can provide important information about campus practice. These data help chairs know how policy is practiced and when exceptions are possible. Campus precedent is seldom printed in the policy manual but can be important to handling the difficult situations that don't fit the routine cases addressed by policy.

Case 8.4, Campus Networks

Phil Worken, theater chair, is frustrated because the department must recruit a new technical director every five years. The technical director occupies a tenure-track faculty position, although everyone recognizes that the demands of supervising the scene shop and technical direction for stage productions make it virtually impossible for a technical director to satisfy the research standard for tenure. Technical directors don't have time to write articles for publication or engage in creative work that qualifies for tenure and promotion. Most tenure-track faculty in the department teach two 3-credit hour courses each semester and devote the remainder of their time to research and creative activities. The technical director works 12 months a year. For months surrounding each stage production, the technical director often works a 16-hour day supervising set construction.

Typically, technical directors stay through their probationary period and then leave the institution when they fail to receive tenure. While the department supports their applications for tenure, the dean and the provost typically point out the lack of scholarship or comparable creative endeavor. Consequently, the department must search for a new technical director every five years. Since Phil Worken became chair, he has hired three technical directors. Currently, the shop crew is doing exceptionally well under the leadership of Hamilton Maroney. Unless something changes, Dr. Worken is certain that Maroney will not receive tenure at the institution no matter how well he performs the duties of technical director. He wonders if there isn't another way to manage this situation.

The Lunch Bunch

As Hamilton Maroney reaches year four of his probationary period, this worry consumes more of Dr. Worken's time. He cannot think of a workable way around the current policy. He does not want the technical director hired on a term appointment because he fears that term appointees will act like second class citizens and invest less in the program. Yet, if the technical director holds a tenure-track position, the dean and provost will apply the promotion and tenure standards. One day, while having lunch with his tennis buddies, including the chair of speech communication, Dr. Worken laments out loud about this problem.

Worken: "You know how impressed I am with Hamilton Maroney. Well, I'm afraid we're going to lose him soon."

Others: "You're kidding. Why? He seems to be doing so well."

Worken: "He is doing a superb job. I especially appreciate his concern for shop safety. I can tell you that he makes my job a lot easier, but next year he comes up for mandatory tenure review."

Others: "Is that a problem?"

Worken: "It always is a problem for technical directors. In fact, the department has never had a technical director who qualified for tenure. They don't have the time to get the requisite number of peer-reviewed publications or creative products. This will be the third technical director that I've lost since becoming department chair."

McLeod: "Well, why don't you change the nature of the appointment?"

Worken: "I prefer to have a technical director on a tenure-track appointment. Term appointees tend to have less commitment to the program. Besides, we would still have to hire a different technical director every five years because university policy stipulates that a term appointment cannot be renewed for more than five consecutive years. The dean explained that the university has the policy to comply with AAUP guidelines for not abusing term faculty. It seems that the American Association of University Professors believes that an institution may keep faculty on term appointments to avoid granting tenure."

McLeod: "I'm not talking about making the technical director's position a term appointment. Why not hire the technical director as a continuing administrative professional? Administrative professionals typically have 12-month appointments, and they don't need to apply for tenure. Besides, an administrative professional on a continuing appointment has some job security in that he or she must get one full year's notice if the department decides to terminate the appointment."

Worken: "Oh, sure, I can see the administration going for that. Our technical director teaches. The administration isn't going to let us hire a faculty member as an administrative appointment."

McLeod: "Why not? Doesn't the technical director work seven days a week to supervise set construction with each main stage production? I know that the theater department puts on a lot of shows each year."

Worken: "Eleven; we produce 11 main stage productions each year. I can document that the technical director puts in a lot of hours, but so do faculty who direct or design shows."

McLeod: "How do the other faculty qualify for tenure?"

Worken: "Their work with the main stage productions results in creative products that satisfy the standard for promotion and tenure. The scenic designer, for example, has a set model that peers can review. The faculty who direct shows can use the press reviews of the production as evidence of the quality of their creative work. Technical directors supervise others. There is no creative product for peers to review."

McLeod: "That sounds like an administrative position to me."

Worken: "The department needs the technical director to teach at least two courses each term, and the administration is not going to let teaching faculty hold administrative appointments."

McLeod: "Well, they did in speech."

Worken: "What do you mean?"

McLeod: "I had the same problem with the debate coach. This is a person who works long hours 12 months a year and still had to meet university standards for promotion and tenure. It occurred to us that we needed the debate coach on a continuing appointment, but not necessarily tenured. As an administrative professional, the debate coach teaches courses in argumentation and persuasion but is not expected to meet standards for promotion and tenure. Our debate coach will never come up for tenure review."

Worken: "When did you make that switch?"

McLeod: "About seven years ago. We had a debate coach that I didn't want to lose. Like you, I was tired of beating the bushes for a replacement when the person on board was everything the department wanted."

Let's Analyze the Case

The theater chair has a recurring problem in that technical directors are not able to qualify for tenure. Specifically, the demands of the position prevent the technical director from completing the requisite amount of research or creative activity. The technical director position is so different from the typical faculty position that incumbents find it virtually impossible to meet university standards for tenure. The theater chair does not want to lose Hamilton Maroney, the current technical director. At the same time, he does not want to hire a technical director on a term appointment for fear that the person would have less commitment to the program. Until hearing the thoughts of his chair colleagues at lunch, Dr. Worken was resigned to an impossible situation.

The lunch conversation informs Dr. Worken of a campus precedent that he might use to argue a parallel exception in theater. Without this information, Dr. Worken believes that policy precludes teaching faculty from holding appointments as administrative professionals. This unfounded assumption prevents Dr. Worken from considering all possible alternatives to the department's dilemma. Department chairs sometimes think about university policy as unchanging or irreversible. Policies are meant to govern the norm, and most experienced administrators recognize that individual cases can warrant an exception to policy. To show the need for some variation in existing policy, the theater chair needs to demonstrate that the technical director does not hold the typical faculty assignment. This does not mean that the central administration is likely to waive tenure standards for the technical director. They may, however, acknowledge that the position is more administrative than faculty. If persons on administrative professional appointment can teach, it is a feasible alternative for the theater department.

It's Your Turn

Assume the role of the theater chair and decide how you would proceed to rescue the technical director from tenure review.

1. How can you use the information obtained informally at lunch from the speech department chair to propose a change in the technical director's position? What data would you assemble to demonstrate the need for an exception to policy?

2. How would you structure the request so the dean becomes a partner in forwarding the request to central administration? What benefits would you highlight for the dean that might encourage the dean to pursue the proposed change in appointment status?

Please Consider

There is another option for an alliance that might help Dr. Worken manage this problem of needing to replace technical directors. The department chair might enlist the college dean's help to secure a different set of criteria for tenuring the technical director. Perhaps certain tasks performed by the technical director could be added to the list of acceptable creative projects. A scenic designer uses set models as acceptable creative products for tenure review. Is there a way in which the process of supervising set construction can be reviewed by peers? This is the technical director's contribution to the creative activity of producing a main stage production. To engage the dean as a partner on this issue, the department chair must first help the dean understand the full scope of responsibilities performed by the technical director. Often, institutions use peer review to assess the quality of research and creative activity. The chair will have to help the dean know which of these duties require some artistic skill and might be subject to peer review.

The department chair also needs to help the dean realize the advantage of retaining the technical director. In the case of Hamilton Maroney, the dean should value the technical director's concern for safety. The department chair does not need to wait until the technical director's final year before tenure review to begin informing the dean about the advantages of having a technical director who pays close attention to safety issues. Also, the college dean is likely to understand the cost associated with conducting a search every five years for the same position. On a campus where salary increases do not keep pace with inflation and market value, it is particularly cost-effective to retain rather than replace good faculty. New hires command the market salary rate, which is usually more than the salary of the departing faculty member. This cost savings is in addition to the time and monetary expense of conducting a search.

Let's Recap

Academic departments function in a political environment in that all units compete for finite resources. Because departments do not exist in a vacuum, chairs need to develop alliances that advance the department mission and goals. A department may have numerous alliances, and some partners may hold an interest in only one component of the department mission. Patrons of the music department, for example, may be more interested in the concerts offered by the department than the curriculum. An alliance exists when two or more partners work together to achieve a common purpose. Effective alliances, therefore, are mutually beneficial to individual partners.

To form productive alliances, department chairs need to select credible partners. A department gains little from an alliance unless the administration and other agencies who have decision-making authority over the department perceive the department's partner(s) as credible. To remain credible advocates for the department, partners need information about the department mission and resource needs. The partners need to know about changing conditions that promise to affect the department.

Department chairs need to communicate regularly with partners to empower them to capably represent the department's interests. Chairs may enlist the help of individual faculty in keeping partners informed about the department, particularly when a faculty member may have a closer association with the partner. Chairs, however, must coordinate the total effort of building department alliances. This helps to ensure that partners work to strengthen the department, not individuals. It also prevents various partners from working at cross-purposes.

Finally, department chairs need to work with partners to develop a strategy for accomplishing mutually beneficial purposes. This takes time and careful planning but is essential to success. Ideally, partners work together to explore alternatives and devise strategies. The process, though time-consuming, increases the partner's commitment to the strategy and the desired outcome. Departments need credible partners who are committed to supporting the department mission if they are to flourish within the political campus environment.

9

PROMOTING THE DEPARTMENT

The dean, provost, and president form perceptions of each department. Similarly, other external publics develop favorable or unfavorable impressions of particular academic departments. Those perceptions represent the individual's or group's knowledge of the department but may or may not accurately reflect the department. The externally held perceptions of the academic department influence how the various external publics interact with the department. If, for example, the provost perceives the department as one of the institution's strongest programs, the provost is likely to safeguard that department's strength and reputation.

Department chairs must concern themselves with the department's external reputation. How is the department perceived by the various administrators on campus? What image does the department have with salient external publics in the community, state, and region? Department chairs have a vested interest in helping campus administrators and other external publics shape a favorable reputation of the department. By marketing a favorable image of the department, department chairs help to ensure the department's welfare. This activity serves as collateral against tough times.

The Objective

One goal of this chapter is to have department chairs recognize that the task of marketing the academic department requires careful planning and execution. A second goal is to equip chairs with some specific communication strategies for conducting an effective marketing campaign for the department. Even strong departments that enjoy a positive reputation on and off campus must continue to promote department achievements and activities.

Defining the Task

Marketing the academic department is the task of strategically advocating the mission and achievements of the department in order to enhance the overall reputation of the department (Higgerson, 1993). The task of marketing the academic department has two important defining characteristics (Higgerson, 1992c). First, marketing the department is an *attitude* as well as an activity. All communication (written and oral) from the department and about the department forms the department's public image on and off campus. Even informal comments made by the department chair or faculty can influence how others perceive the department. The candid comments can, in turn, affect how formal proposals are received. For example, the chair who comments casually that a proposed degree program may be too ambitious for faculty qualifications severely damages the chances that the proposal will be approved.

Second, marketing the department is a *campaign* and not a single activity. If the task of marketing the department is done effectively, the job is never finished. Marketing the department to the college dean does not start and stop with the submission of the annual goals and accomplishments report. Rather, the task of marketing the department is a dynamic communication process in which the sender, the receiver, and the message are constantly changing. An effective marketing campaign is responsive to changes in attitudes, perceptions, and environmental conditions. To be effective, the marketing campaign must be consistent. Department chairs cannot advocate images that appear inconsistent with the department and institutional goals. For example, the department that wishes to preserve a favorable reputation for delivering high-quality instruction cannot publicly bemoan that budget cuts have ruined the program. Marketing is advocacy, and effective communication is essential to advocacy. The marketing message must be understood by the intended receiver. Without effective communication, the very best idea can die. Without effective communication about department strengths, the strongest departments can lose favor with important external audiences.

Relevant Communication Concepts and Strategies

Departments that enjoy favorable reputations typically find it easier to withstand times of fiscal austerity and public concern about program quality. Department chairs can improve the department's status both on and off campus by promoting a favorable image of the department. Marketing the academic department is the task of strategically advocating the mission and achievements of the department in order to enhance the overall reputation of the department. Department chairs can use the following strategies to design and implement an effective marketing campaign.

Analyze the product

The product is every tangible outcome or benefit from department activity. It includes faculty and student achievements, service programs, retention and graduation rates, outreach activities, research programs, and public exhibits or performances. Department chairs must be able to clearly articulate the department mission and goals. Chairs should also know the scope of the department's influence. Does the radio and television department, for example, operate public broadcasting stations that serve a large population? Is the biology department's research on local crops important to area agriculture? Information about the department's influence on and off campus is important when requesting resources from the central administration.

The department chair needs to be familiar with the credentials of faculty, students, and alumni. It may be useful to keep a clipping file of activities and achievements. If computer technology is available, a database can be kept of faculty and student achievements that would allow the chair to recall activities that may be relevant to a particular audience. For example, when talking to prospective students at an area high school, it is helpful to reference former graduates of that high school who elected to enroll in the program. When soliciting funding support from area business, it is helpful to reference the ways in which faculty research enhances the local economy.

The department chair must be well informed about curricular and extracurricular programs offered by the department. Those activities contribute to the department's perceived value on and off campus. The department chair should assess the current and potential sphere of the department's influence. For example, does the department offer a general education course that is required for all students? What is the circulation of the newspaper published by the students majoring in journalism? Does the music department attract a large number of patrons from the surrounding region? Even service activities conducted by the department's student organization reflect on the department. Department chairs need to be aware of all department programs and the way in which they contribute to the department's reputation. An assessment of the department's influence on and off campus enables the chair to determine the department's niche in the university, the state, region, and the discipline.

Identify key audiences

The term *audience* refers to a specific individual or group that has a preconceived image (accurate or not) of the department and whose relationship to the department is important to its welfare. Academic departments must respond to several audiences, and the department chair needs to identify those audiences that are important to the department. On campus, the important audiences include key decision-makers. Chairs also need to identify informal decision-makers who are in a position to influence the final outcome even though they may not have line authority. That may include, for example, the dean's spouse who holds a degree in the department discipline and exercises significant influence over the dean's thinking about the department. Chairs also need to know what decisions are delegated to staff. For example, is it really the associate dean who controls how equipment dollars are allocated?

Off campus, department chairs must be aware of the key constituencies that are in a position to influence the future welfare of the department. These audiences include alumni, business groups, community organizations, granting agencies, accrediting agencies, area legislators, state boards of higher education, and prospective students. Is the president, for example, particularly responsive to prominent alumni?

An important step in identifying key audiences is to analyze the existing attitudes, biases, and predispositions held by each toward the department, the university, and higher education in general. For each of the salient audiences, department chairs should answer the following questions:

- What does the audience know about the department?

- Why is the audience significant to the department?

- What does the audience need to know in order to support the department?

If the department chair has no information regarding the audience's current predisposition toward the department, the chair might conduct some simple marketing research. For example, the theater department can survey patrons to find out such basic information as how frequently they attend, how far they travel to see a show, and their evaluation of production quality. That information is useful not only in learning how to improve the department's relationship with patrons but also to argue the department's need for resources.

Assess the political environment

Universities are political organizations in that all departments compete for finite resources. Department chairs must assess the political forces that influence decision-making on campus and become cognizant of campus issues that affect all departments. For example, hazardous waste is not a concern for only the college of science because the cost of hazardous waste disposal is typically shared by the entire campus community. It is particularly helpful to recognize when the department can make a unique contribution to resolving a campus problem. Faculty trained in public relations, for example, may play a key role in advising the central administration on how to disseminate information about the university's efforts to dispose of hazardous waste. Such contributions of expertise can increase the department's intrinsic value to the institution.

Department chairs must also assess the political environment off campus. Chairs need to be knowledgeable of salient state and national issues. It is easier to improve the department's image if the chair knows what questions exist in the minds of external constituencies, including accrediting agencies, state legislators, and governing boards. If, for example, accountability in spending tax dollars is a major state issue, then information that demonstrates the department's cost-effectiveness while preserving program quality does a lot to bolster the department's positive reputation. If there is a general belief that many departments neglect undergraduate education, budget requests that argue the need for resources in terms of the benefit accrued to undergraduate students will be received more positively than those that fail to show a benefit to undergraduate students. Department chairs must also pay attention to national issues that are likely to influence how groups of intended audiences perceive the department. A growing distrust for higher education culminated in the publication of several popular books including *ProfScam* (Sykes, 1988), *Impostors in the Temple* (Anderson, 1992), and *Illiberal Education* (D'Souza, 1991). Media coverage of these books influences the attitudes held by such important audiences as alumni, state legislators, and the parents of prospective students. Only when department chairs know what notions influence the public's attitude toward higher education can they construct proposals and other communication that create a favorable department image.

A critical aspect of assessing the political environment is knowing campus policy and precedent. There is no guarantee that campus practice treats all departments uniformly. For example, the cost of interviewing candidates for an open faculty position can be borne by the department, the dean, or the academic vice president. Knowledge of campus precedent helps the chair obtain the most favorable treatment for the department. The department is not likely to receive funds to cover interview expenses unless the chair knows to ask for them. Department chairs need to cultivate a campus network beyond the department in order to learn the boundaries set by campus precedent. This information is useful in securing resources for the department.

Plan a marketing strategy

Department chairs must use what they know about the product, the intended audiences, and the political environment to plan a marketing strategy for the department. To do that, chairs must first identify the department's unique niche. This is called strategic positioning. People typically remember things for their distinctiveness, not for their similarities. Any positive trait that distinguishes the department is typically worth promoting.

Department chairs need to construct the message in a way that makes it relevant to the intended audience. Chairs can use their knowledge of the intended audience's predisposition toward the department and the issue to craft a message that enables that audience to recognize department strengths and resource needs. Requests for increased funding, for example, are stronger if the chair links the basis for the request to institutional priorities. Too often, department chairs advocate a request based on the merits of the issue itself. Unfortunately, this is frequently less effective than linking the request to issues that are important to the administration. A chair seeking funds to support more graduate assistantships during times of fiscal austerity and declining enrollments increases the likelihood of success by linking the request to providing more sections of the general education course required for all incoming freshmen. The chair can further strengthen the argument by demonstrating that the current number of sections is insufficient to service all incoming freshmen and that there is a greater persistence rate among those students who are able to take the required course during their first year at the institution.

Message construction requires careful consideration of message channel. Effective message construction presents the information in a manner that will capture the attention of the intended audience. Are alumni, for example, more likely to respond to a request for financial support when the request is made in a letter from the vice president or through a telephone call from a former faculty member? Using the most appropriate message channel increases the effectiveness of the message. Faculty, for example, learn that information duplicated by a mimeograph or ditto machine is usually less important than information duplicated through photocopy. If this is the case, chairs can elevate the perceived importance of a particular message by using photocopy rather than ditto.

Timing is also important to communication effectiveness. Too often, the volume of work and the pressure of deadlines cause department chairs to sacrifice the advantage gained by strategic timing. Effective marketing requires the judicious timing of requests and other advocacy statements.

There is a need to connect some issues and disconnect other issues. For example, it is not prudent to submit a request to lower enrollment limits on all department courses immediately after the dean announces that a drop in college enrollment will have an adverse effect on next year's budget. However, if the dean asks the chair to assume responsibility for managing a major college initiative, it is an opportune time for that chair to remind the dean of the department's need for more computer equipment and additional secretarial support. Department chairs must take full advantage of every window of opportunity. If the central administration pronounces a renewed commitment to undergraduate education, a chair might provide the administration with an opportunity to demonstrate that commitment through support of a department activity that improves undergraduate instruction.

Share the responsibility for marketing the department

Since the task of marketing the department is an attitude and a campaign, more success can be realized if the chair shares the job with department members. Furthermore, it is hazardous to excuse department members from this important task. Well-intentioned faculty can undermine the best marketing strategies if they are uninformed. For example, faculty who articulate their belief that the department's weakest instructors teach the undergraduate courses undermine the chair's effort to promote the department as having a strong commitment to undergraduate education. Marketing messages are more credible if all members of the department participate in the marketing campaign. An effective marketing campaign enlists the help of both internal (on campus) and external (off campus) agents.

The potential internal agents include, but are not necessarily limited to, faculty, students, clerical staff, and friends. The internal agencies that fit the category of friends are any individuals or constituencies that have a vested interest in department activities and achievements. A friend might be another department on campus whose majors rely on courses taught by the department. A friend might be the spouse of a senior-level administrator who has a special interest in the department's discipline.

Potential external agents embrace, but are not necessarily limited to, alumni, community groups, private industry, other colleges and universities, funding agencies, regional groups, professional associations, state officials (elected or appointed), and accrediting agencies. Particularly in times of tight budgets, it is advantageous for a department to connect in significant ways with external audiences. External agents can be an important source of funds and support. The central administration is not as quick to cut a program that enjoys visible support from a vocal external constituency. For example, a costly theater program with low enrollment is better able to withstand campus budget cuts if the stage productions are popular with a sizable group of vocal patrons.

When chairs share the responsibility for marketing the academic department with internal and external agents, it serves two purposes. First, it helps to educate and update the external and internal agents as to the achievements of the academic department. Agents are more effective advocates for the department if they have a clear understanding of the department's strengths and mission. It is especially helpful if agents can identify with the department mission and goals. Second, by sharing the responsibility for marketing the academic department, the chair extends the scope and depth of the department's marketing campaign. The process of educating internal and external agents on the strengths and achievements of the department deepens their commitment to the department. Job descriptions for the position of department chair seldom list the task of marketing the academic department. That task, however, is imperative to the overall welfare of the department. Audiences on campus and off campus form perceptions of the department. An effective marketing campaign is essential to ensure that the perceptions held by these important audiences are positive.

Putting Theory Into Practice

In Case 9.1, Operating in the Dark, the chair of the theater department must convince the central administration to make a sizable financial investment in the department. The theater department's need for a new computerized light board becomes critical at a time when the university plans to reduce the institution's program inventory. The chair worries that the needed expenditure might prompt the administration to eliminate the theater program. Place yourself in the role of the department chair, Lucy Wieczorek, as you read Case 9.1.

Case 9.1, Operating in the Dark

Professor Wieczorek sits in the back row of the dark university theater contemplating what to do about the newest crisis facing the department. The theater department is to open a new production run in just four days, and the light board for the main stage is down. Worse yet, campus physical plant personnel report that the damage is beyond repair. For years, the physical plant workers have kept the light board in running order through a combination of handmade parts and ingenuity. Every time the repairmen have worked on the unit, they have reminded the department chair that the light board is more than 30 years old, a dinosaur in comparison with new technology.

Chair Wieczorek takes the warnings seriously. For years, the department has requested funds from the central administration to purchase a new computerized light panel to replace the old one. The department also has attempted to secure funds through external grants. The department chair has tried every argument imaginable, including linking the need for a computerized light panel to instructional quality. Students pursuing theater degrees with a specialization in technical theater would benefit from training on state-of-the-art equipment. All efforts, however, have proved unsuccessful, so the department has limped along making piecemeal repairs to the outdated equipment.

Timing

The chair senses that this may be the worst possible time for the light board to fail. This year the central administration announced that no longer will they amortize budget cuts across all departments. Instead, the central administration is evaluating all programs for the purpose of making vertical cuts in the institution's program inventory. The administration plans to target some departments and programs for elimination. Professor Wieczorek worried about the fate of the theater department before this latest catastrophe. Theater enrollment has remained steady over the last five-year period but is hardly robust. The department of nine faculty has an enrollment of 60 undergraduate majors and seven to ten students in the MFA program. The department's strength lies in its production series. The theater faculty mount ten main stage productions each year, including light opera and musicals. The production series is well received by the community, and the theater department attracts regular patrons within a radius of 150 miles. The production series has enabled the department to survive previous budget cuts. Currently, the department earns $.70 at the box office for every $1.00 spent on production from university funds.

Chair Wieczorek worries that the need for a new light board may prompt the central administration to eliminate the theater department. The chair recognizes that both the president and the provost do not have a great appreciation for the fine and performing arts. They attend productions infrequently and seem to be unmoved by appeals for needed resources. Chair Wieczorek recognizes that the long-term outlook for the department of theater is bleak. Without a new light board, it will be impossible to recruit and retain students who seek training and experience in technical theater. If the department cannot run main stage productions, it will be difficult to recruit and retain students interested in performance.

The Show Must Go On

The immediate crisis is how to handle the catastrophe that threatens the upcoming production. The department chair knows that she can count on the faculty to do whatever it takes to get the show up and running on time. Professor Wieczorek is continually impressed by the enthusiasm and professionalism exhibited by the theater faculty. They enjoy their work and take tremendous pride in mounting a very ambitious production schedule each year. The faculty enjoy doing high-quality main stage productions with student talent and effort. The training that students receive helps them secure work following graduation. The theater boasts a long list of successful alumni who have made a name in professional theater as actors, lighting designers, scenic designers, and directors. In addition, several alumni earned graduate degrees and moved into faculty positions in theater education.

It is the theater faculty who come up with the scheme for handling the current catastrophe. Located in the same building is the radio and television department which has a small studio equipped with a comparable light board. While the light board located in radio and television is also a dinosaur, it is at least in working order.

The theater faculty decide to run cable from the lights in the theater to the control panel in radio and television. This requires that a technician in the theater observation booth transmit the cues for light changes by radio headset to a second technician seated behind a remote control panel that is located more than 75 yards from the theater stage. The person operating the theater lights needs to make changes according to audio direction, not visual observation. This innovation gives the entire cast and crew a new challenge. The actors need to be more precise in their movements on stage that signal the lighting changes. One of the scenes in Act II begins with an actor flipping a light switch. The actor needs to regularize this action so it is more easily communicated to a technician who cannot observe the hand motion.

Chair Wieczorek marvels at the faculty and students as they go about executing this complex task. Enthusiasm within the department grows as everyone works hard to meet the challenge and open the production on time. The chair watches with genuine amazement as she muses how the central administration fails to see the immeasurable worth of the theater faculty and program.

Let's Analyze the Case

Lucy Wieczorek knows that the theater department is in a vulnerable position. The administration is evaluating all programs with the purpose of targeting some for elimination. The campus leadership believes that the institution's budget can no longer support the same number of degree programs, and they plan to make some vertical cuts in the institution's program inventory. The theater chair worries that the department is vulnerable because the program has a modest enrollment. The ratio of faculty to undergraduate majors is roughly one to six. At the graduate level, this ratio is one to one. The department is not a major producer for the institution in terms of enrollment, credit hour generation, or tuition revenue. To make matters worse, the theater department operates an ambitious production schedule each year. We know that the administrators are not regular patrons of theater productions. Although it is not stated in the case study, the chair may worry that the administration perceives the production series as frivolous during this time of fiscal austerity. In any event, the chair has not been able to persuade the administration to fund the purchase of a new computerized light board for the theater. This suggests that the administration does not rate the main stage production series run by the theater department as a priority for the institution.

Now the light board has failed and cannot be repaired. For the theater department to remain in business, the institution must purchase a new light board. Chair Wieczorek worries that this expense will help the administration decide to eliminate the theater program. For students majoring in theater, the stage is the laboratory. Without lights in the theater, it becomes impossible to teach theater courses or mount productions. Lucy Wieczorek fears that the timing of the light board failure will seal the department's fate.

The chair in Case 9.1 needs to think beyond the department's standing with the central administration. Specifically, the chair needs to identify the key external audiences that value the theater program and production series. We know that the production series is popular in the surrounding region and that devoted patrons travel as much as 150 miles one way to see a show. We also know that students benefit from the ambitious production series and that they typically secure work following graduation. Finally, we know that the theater department has prominent alumni who have made a name for themselves in professional theater as actors, lighting designers, scenic designers, and directors. The external audiences of patrons and alumni can be important sources of support for the department.

The theater chair is focused on the expense of a new light board and the declining institutional resources. She looks at the problem from the administration's perspective. Instead, the chair needs to influence how the administration perceives the theater department. The chair needs also to analyze the product. What does the theater program contribute to the campus and the surrounding region? Because the theater production series is popular with patrons, the theater program becomes a window for the institution in the surrounding region. In addition to being a public relations tool for the institution, the production series generates revenue. We know that the box office takes in 70 cents for every dollar spent on a production. The chair might argue that the theater program is a great investment for the university. After all, not many academic departments can recoup 70 percent of their support costs budget at the box office. Finally, theater offers a quality program. The faculty are resourceful and take great pride in the their work with students and the production series. Graduates get jobs in professional theater or go on to graduate school so they can teach theater. The department can boast the success of its graduates. Consequently, there is good reason to consider the theater program a showcase for the university.

In assessing the political environment, the chair in Case 9.1 limited her thinking to campus and, more specifically, the institution's budget situation. The relevant political environment is broader than that. The political environment includes such elements as the patrons' assessment of the theater program, the potential influence of prominent alumni, and the quality instruction that benefits majors. The chair's challenge is to present the department's strengths and resource needs in the larger context so the central administration can perceive the true worth of the theater department. The light board failure makes this need more immediate. Certainly, the chair did not need to wait to promote a more favorable image of the department with the central administration. Now the chair must manage a short-term crisis that will likely affect the long-term fate of the department.

It's Your Turn

Assume the role of department chair and think through how you would manage the situation described in Case 9.1.

1. How would you present the need for a new light board? How might you utilize patron and alumni support to strengthen your argument? Would you involve faculty and students?

2. When would you present your case? Would you wait until after the current production run? Would you dissociate the short-term crisis from the long-term need or link them?

Please Consider

Often departments treat academic quality as an internal goal, when it is also a marketable resource. It is important that departments with high-quality programs inform others about their success both on and off campus. By incorporating the concept of quality into the department's marketing campaign, the chair can help faculty identify those criteria that are appropriate for assessing department quality. This type of departmental review is important to maintaining quality programs and recognizing when curricular revisions are in order. The department, for example, may boast of a top-quality program on the basis of what students receive or where graduates are placed. In this instance, the type of training provided and the record of job placement success become two criteria for evaluating program quality.

Obviously, a clear department mission, a focused curriculum, and a healthy department climate help to promote a favorable image of the department. The most well-intentioned faculty member will be unable to promote the department in a positive way if the department mission and goals are ambiguous or unrealistic. Similarly, the most skilled department chair will be unable to advocate the program effectively if the curriculum lacks focus and relevance. For that reason, the information presented earlier in this text on structuring department mission and enhancing the department climate is relevant to the task of promoting the department.

Let's Recap

Take a moment and review your strategy for managing both the short-term crisis and the long-term department needs detailed in Case 9.1. If your approach does not incorporate the communication strategies for effectively marketing the department, you may want to review the material presented earlier in this chapter. Does your approach

- analyze the product?
- identify key audiences?
- assess the political environment?
- utilize a carefully planned marketing strategy?
- share responsibility for marketing the department?

Putting Theory Into Practice

In Case 9.2, Mobilizing the Fans, Chair Wieczorek takes a proactive approach to obtain a computerized light board for the theater department. Compare Lucy Wieczorek's marketing strategy with the one you designed for the situation described in Case 9.1.

Case 9.2, Mobilizing the Fans

As Chair Wieczorek marveled at the ability of theater faculty and their commitment to satisfy patrons, she had an idea. She knew that the devoted theater patrons would fully appreciate the extra effort expended by the theater faculty and students on their behalf. The chair contacted the local media and invited them to witness the preparation for opening night. The area paper ran a story picturing the massive amount of cable required to hook lights in the theater to the distant control panel. One picture in the paper showed a roped bulk of cables that measured more than three feet in diameter. Each cable in the roped bundle connected a stage light in the theater to the control panel located in the radio and television department. More than 120 different cables were needed to handle the lighting for the show. This massive tube of cable extended around several corners and down the hall for more than 75 yards where a technician would control the light changes for the production through audio headset.

When interviewed by the press about the activity, the department chair praised faculty ingenuity. She described in detail the creativity and supreme effort expended by both faculty and students to mount the production as promised. When asked when the theater might obtain a new light board, the department chair disclosed the department's unsuccessful attempts to secure grant funding to purchase a new computerized light panel. The chair candidly described the nature of the "dinosaur" equipment and the physical plant's claim that they could no longer find parts to keep it operational. The department chair added her concern that it was a difficult time for the university. She noted that the university administration would decide whether theater is a priority for the institution and the surrounding region. Wieczorek explained that the department would only receive funds to purchase a new computerized light panel if the administration believed the expenditure to be a priority for the university. The department chair made it clear that the decision to purchase a new light panel for the theater department rested with the central administration, not with the department. The department chair also made it clear that the central administration would consider the importance of the theater to area patrons as well as the quality of its instructional program.

Opening Night

The box office sold out for every scheduled production earlier than usual. The patrons and some newcomers were intrigued by the press coverage. The chair could hear patrons comparing notes on what they knew as they entered the theater. Large numbers bothered to walk past the cable that stretched down the long corridor to the radio and television department. A few brought cameras to take their own pictures of this extraordinary feat. The chair sensed that the house was impressed by the department's ingenuity. The chair's impression was confirmed in Act II when the audience applauded after the actor flipped the light switch on the stage wall and the lighting technicians responded accordingly. The audience was applauding the difficult lighting changes! The show received a standing ovation.

Seizing the Moment

The department added two matinee productions to the regular run. They were billed as bonus productions to accommodate audience demand. The department also announced publicly that the profit from the two performances would be applied to the cost of a new computerized light board should the central administration authorize the purchase. In addition, the department sold separate tickets for a backstage tour after the matinee performances. The tour included a walk through of the tricky light switch maneuver that occurred in Act II. Because of space limitations and safety concerns, the department announced that the tickets for the tour would be limited to 50 for each performance. The backstage tour sold out within two days of the announcement.

Channeling Queries

When concerned patrons asked about the purchase of a new light board, Professor Wieczorek reminded them that the decision to purchase a light board was in the hands of the administration. She also pointed out that the administration would weigh the importance of the theater program against other university priorities. She named everyone who would make the decision and what criteria they might use to decide the fate of the theater program.

The dean of the fine and performing arts college and the provost received dozens of calls and letters each day from concerned patrons who wanted to remind the administration of the importance of the theater program to the surrounding region. Based on those letters that the dean forwarded to

Lucy Wieczorek, the patrons did a great job of boasting about the quality of the theater productions. Several offered to pay more for their season tickets in order to keep the production season. It was painfully clear to the administration that the theater department had a vocal constituency of external supporters.

Let's Analyze the Case

Lucy Wieczorek links the immediate crisis to the long-term need. She hopes that publicity about the innovative way in which the faculty saved the show and honored their commitment to faithful patrons would help persuade the central administration of the department's worth. Most decisions involve some trade-off, and department chairs need to weigh the relative merits of each alternative. Professor Wieczorek runs a risk in pointing a finger at the central administration. She may alienate the administration and, by doing so, jeopardize campus support. Before this crisis, the administration did not approve the requests for a new light board so Professor Wieczorek has little to lose by trying to mobilize patron support on behalf of the theater program.

Professor Wieczorek is careful in how she points a finger at the central administration. She makes clear that they control the decision to purchase a new light board and lets the patrons know what criteria are relevant. The chair does not reveal that the administration denied previous requests. Her finger pointing is limited to factual information. She says nothing that would cause anyone to believe that the administration might eliminate the theater program or that they do not, for any reason, support theater. This frees the administration from defending past decisions that would be unpopular with patrons. It allows the administration to support the theater program without appearing to change their minds about campus priorities.

In Case 9.1 we learn that the theater program has some prominent alumni who have made a name for themselves in professional theater. The chair elects not to involve the alumni in any organized way. The alumni cannot voice their support because, unless they receive the local paper, they probably don't know about the situation. The chair decides to use the local constituency of patrons that she can mobilize quickly to help persuade the administration of the theater program's value and quality. This does not prevent the chair from seeking alumni support at a later time. Alumni are a potential source of support and resources. It is possible that some may be willing to contribute toward the price of a new computerized light board.

It's Your Turn

Consider the chair's response to the situation described in Cases 9.1 and 9.2 and decide if anything else might be done to improve the status of the theater program with the central administration.

1. Would you involve the alumni in the current situation? If so, what type of support (vocal, financial, professional expertise) would you want from alumni, and how would you obtain it?

2. Suppose this production run comes to a close and the administration has not approved the purchase of a new light board. What follow-up action would you take? How would you involve the patrons, alumni, faculty, and students? What other constituencies might be asked to help persuade the administration to purchase a new light board?

Please Consider

The theater chair does not use campus connections. As discussed in Chapter 8 of this text, departments can have effective alliances on campus that can lend support in situations like the one described in Cases 9.1 and 9.2. To determine the potential for support from campus alliances, the theater chair needs to determine if there are other programs on campus that depend on the theater department. Do students majoring in health education or recreation, for example, rely on theater courses in movement? Does the department offer a course on theater appreciation in the institution's general education program? Are there similar alliances that the chair might cultivate? Is there opportunity for the theater department to build an alliance with dance or other programs that have a need for a stage? The administration might be more willing to purchase a new light board if the theater stage can serve several academic programs. It takes time to form productive alliances, and ideally the theater chair would have campus alliances that could help with the crisis situation described in Cases 9.1 and 9.2.

Putting Theory Into Practice

The department chair in Case 9.3, Thawing the Hiring Freeze, must take action to minimize the likely impact of a college-wide hiring freeze on the English department. The chair recognizes that the department is vulnerable to a temporary, and perhaps permanent, loss of four tenure-track faculty positions. Place yourself in the role of the department chair as you read Case 9.3.

Case 9.3, Mounting an Offensive

Fiscal conditions at Central State University are especially acute this year. An enrollment decline coupled with a midyear rescission forced the provost to recall a portion of each academic college's budget. When the liberal arts and sciences dean learned the sum that had to be returned, he imposed an immediate hiring freeze. At a meeting of college chairs, the dean explained that a college committee would evaluate all open positions and rank them according to need. The hiring freeze would be lifted for only those few positions that the committee deems most essential to the college.

English Department

The English department is particularly vulnerable to the hiring freeze. Currently, the English department has four searches under way to hire new faculty. The English department is one of the largest units in the college with 29 faculty positions. The department services all undergraduate majors by staffing the six credit hour composition requirement in the institution's general education program. The department also services science and engineering majors who must take courses in technical writing. In addition, the English department boasts a strong emphasis in creative writing and 18th- and 19th-century literature.

The Decision

The dean establishes a college committee to evaluate department needs and rank-order the 19 open positions according to their importance. The dean estimates that the college will have a budget to fill seven positions. The college is composed of 28 academic departments, and 12 departments have one or more open positions. The department chairs with open positions may submit a written rationale for the proposed hires to the committee. To expedite the review process, the dean decides that the committee will work from written documents and not meet with individual department chairs. Everyone recognizes the need to lift the freeze as soon as possible so that the departments authorized to fill positions can act early enough to recruit the strongest possible candidates.

Perceptions

The chair of the English department worries that the department will lose at least two of its four open positions. The chair believes that the department has a strong rationale for filling all four open positions but recognizes that the college committee will perceive the positions in literature and creative writing as less significant than the positions in English composition. Most departments within the college view English as a service unit that must staff the general education requirement for composition. The chair is less certain that the dean and committee members recognize the excellence maintained by the English faculty in the areas of creative writing and literature.

The Strategy

The chair of the English department decides that the department cannot afford to allow the college committee's decision to be based exclusively on his report justifying the four open positions. Together with the faculty, the chair decides to become more proactive in advancing the positive reputation of the department's work in the areas of creative writing and literature. First, the department chair orchestrates a press release touting some of the recent awards earned by English faculty for works of poetry and fiction. The article runs in the area newspaper complete with a picture of the department chair surrounded by copies of the books and other works written by the English faculty during the last ten years.

Second, the department takes full advantage of its annual speakers' series. The chair usually releases an announcement featuring the speakers and invited scholars on literature later in the academic year. This year, the department releases the promotional materials on the annual speakers' series early. The announcement includes statements from recognized scholars in the field proclaiming the importance of the quality literature concentration at Central State University.

Third, the department chair incorporates in his report to the college committee some information that was not requested. The committee requested the usual data on enrollment, credit hour generation, faculty course loads, and graduation rates. The department chair complies with the college committee's request but adds information detailing what would be lost to the college in the event that the department lost any of the four positions. This information is more speculative but illustrates the department's track record. For example, the chair documents that faculty in the creative writing and literature areas submit on the average of 2.4 grant proposals each year. If the department were not able to fill the position in creative writing or the position in literature, the number of faculty in these areas would drop from nine to seven. The chair uses the reduced faculty size to project the decrease in grant applications and grant awards. Since the college receives overhead funds for each grant award, the cut of two positions translates into a significant loss of dollars for the college. The chair also demonstrates what courses would be unstaffed in the event the faculty were not hired. He shows how this weakens the degree offering for the specializations in creative writing and literature. Finally, the department chair produces evidence to illustrate that more than 70% of the English majors pursue one of these two specializations. Using this information he projects a corresponding decrease in college enrollment, which again translates into a loss of tuition revenue for the institution.

Let's Analyze the Case

The chair in Case 9.3 recognizes that the English department is vulnerable to the hiring freeze. English has four open positions at a time when the college can only afford to fill a fraction of its 19 open faculty lines. Worse yet, the chair realizes that those persons who will decide which positions to fill do not recognize the English department's mission. The dean and committee members recognize the English department's service role in staffing English composition and technical writing courses but do not acknowledge the department's work in creative writing and literature.

This case illustrates the value of an ongoing campaign to promote the department. If the chair knows that the campus does not recognize an important part of the department's program, the chair should take action to remedy the misperception before it poses a problem. The chair should not keep secret the department's strength and achievement in the areas of creative writing and literature. It is important to promote the department's full mission and corresponding accomplishments.

The chair knows that the college committee will recognize the need for faculty to teach English composition and technical writing courses, but the chair must make the college committee understand the department's need for faculty in the areas of creative writing and literature. To do this, the chair must determine what information would sway the college committee and how to present this information. Since the college committee expects department chairs to argue in favor of retaining their open positions in the written report, the English chair will need to consider other more objective channels for getting information to the college committee.

The chair takes three specific actions in order to convince the college committee and the dean that English cannot afford to lose the positions in creative writing and literature. At least two of the actions could have been done before the immediate fiscal threat to the department. The press release acknowledging some of the recent awards earned by English faculty is a good idea whether or not the department is vulnerable to a budget cut.

Similarly, the department could (and should) take full advantage of the annual speakers' series as an opportunity to promote the department each year. This activity helps to showcase the department's growing reputation within the discipline.

When department chairs market the department by making faculty activities more visible on a regular basis, they establish a reputation that helps to minimize liability. In Case 9.3, the faculty positions in creative writing and literature would not be as vulnerable if those making the decision on which positions to fill recognized the stature of the department's work in these areas. When done regularly and in advance of a crisis, the promotion is informative and, as a result, more credible. When done after the fact in response to a particular situation, the promotion appears defensive and less credible. While the English chair takes action to promote department strengths, it may not be sufficient to reverse existing perceptions at this point in the college committee's review.

The chair takes an offensive posture in preparing materials for the college committee. Instead of reporting the typical data, the chair takes the time to demonstrate specific and tangible consequences to the department and the college in the event the positions in creative writing and literature are not filled. This is helpful in that it translates the harm beyond the wishes of the English faculty.

Notice that the chair does not build a case for the positions in English composition and technical writing. The chair assumes that the dean will allow the department to fill those positions because they are integral to fulfilling the service mission of the department, a mission that is important to the college. The advisability of this action depends on the perceived value of the English department's service mission and on how others believe the mission might be satisfied. For example, the college committee may decide that fewer faculty can teach English composition to the same number of students if the college increases the enrollment caps from 25 to 35. Such a decision may jeopardize quality instruction and be unworkable for the English faculty.

It's Your Turn

Place yourself in the role of the department chair and consider how you would approach the situation described in Case 9.3.

1. What other strategies for marketing the English department would you use in advance of any immediate need to defend the department? How would you promote a favorable and accurate perception of the department's strengths and resource needs?

2. Would you build a case for the two positions in English composition? If so, what arguments would you make for retaining these positions while not undercutting the importance of the positions in creative writing and literature?

Let's Recap

Take a moment and review your strategy for minimizing the department's vulnerability to the hiring freeze detailed in Case 9.3. If your approach does not incorporate the communication strategies for effectively marketing the department, you may want to review the material presented earlier in this chapter. Does your approach

- analyze the product?
- identify key audiences?
- assess the political environment?
- utilize a carefully planned marketing strategy?
- share responsibility for marketing the department?

Putting Theory Into Practice

Case 9.4, Marketing the Department Mission, describes the challenge of marketing the department mission when the department goals differ from the expectations that others have for the department. Consider how you would handle the task described in Case 9.4 as chair of the zoology department.

Case 9.4, Marketing the Department Mission

The faculty in the zoology department at Eastern State University (ESU) are committed to building a concentration in fisheries. The department has offered course work in fisheries at the graduate level for some time. In recent years, the department conscientiously elected to build the concentration in fisheries. Under the leadership of Adolph Albrecht, department chair, the zoology faculty determined that their greatest strength resides in fisheries. This is one area in which ESU can outpace other institutions in the state and region. None of the other zoology departments have comparable faculty credentials or facilities in fisheries. ESU is a midsize institution located around many lakes and waterways.

Eastern's work in fisheries grew out of faculty interest. The zoology faculty perceive the surrounding lakes and waterways as a natural laboratory for fisheries research. Over time, the department filled every open position with new faculty trained in fisheries. Zoology faculty write grants to support their work, and funds received from granting agencies have enabled the department to purchase sophisticated state-of-the-art equipment for their research. This equipment also boosts the instructional quality for students enrolled in fisheries courses.

A few years ago, the department decided to escalate its offerings in fisheries for several reasons. First, fisheries remains an area that is of great interest to a large number of the faculty. Second, there are few fisheries programs at comparable institutions, so the department recruits graduate students who come specifically to study fisheries. Third, the faculty have ample opportunity to conduct research within the surrounding region. There is no shortage of natural laboratories in area lakes and waterways. Fourth, the zoology department's research links to the state's quest for economic development. Faculty use their expertise to benefit area industry. Agriculture and tourism are the two major industries in the area. Many farmers who have a difficult time making a living in crop farming can build fish farms with the help of zoology faculty. Fish farms raise fish as a food supply for restaurants and canneries. Health-conscious people consume more fish than beef. Fishing is also a recreational hobby that supports the area's tourism industry. People come to the region to fish. Faculty research on breeding fish helps stock area lakes for the tourism trade.

Supporters and Resisters
The zoology department knows that its work will continue to receive funding support as long as the research results have applicability for important state and national themes, including economic development, revitalizing rural America, and tourism. On campus, however, the department recognizes that the dean and the provost are less receptive. The dean must balance department needs for finite resources and space within the college of science. To build the program in fisheries, the department needs the institution's approval of matching equipment grants and the acquisition of land for a new outdoor laboratory that provides more control for experimentation than the area lakes and waterways. The department believes this is a good investment of state funds but recognizes that the dean and provost may be hesitant to commit the needed resources.

The Campaign
The zoology department has to communicate both the need for an expanded program in fisheries and a workable plan for meeting this need. Dr.

Albrecht believes that if he merely requests the outdoor laboratory and matching funds for equipment grants, the department is likely to find its plans aborted prematurely. Instead, the department decides to start working toward this direction while it promotes a department image that has a mission to build a larger fisheries program. The approach encompasses key audiences both on and off campus.

On campus, Dr. Albrecht sends "good news" on a regular basis to key administrators and the university press. In some instances, staff in the university relations office convert the news items into longer press releases, complete with pictures of the zoology faculty doing field research or consulting with an area farmer about starting a fish farm. The news communicated via these channels includes department achievements, the receipt of research grant awards, publications, presentations, seminars held for area farmers, and conversations with state leaders regarding economic development. All of the good news items demonstrate faculty credentials in fisheries, the state and regional need for fisheries research, and the unique service that zoology faculty at ESU can provide the state and region.

Off campus, the zoology faculty meet with farm cooperatives, farm bureaus, legislators, state economic development groups, area legislators, and other relevant agencies who have an interest in improving the state economy, shoring up the welfare of area farmers, or increasing the tourism industry within the state.

Dr. Albrecht is diligent in executing this marketing campaign on and off campus. He hopes that when the department submits its request for funding support from the institution, the administration will have a favorable impression of the department and recognize the value of making an investment in the fisheries program.

Let's Analyze the Case

The zoology department in Case 9.4 has a clear mission. The department believes that it can outpace other zoology programs in the area of fisheries. The department has redirected every available resource to increase the quality of its fisheries program. Now the department must convince the central administration to support the fisheries initiative. The department seeks funds from the institution for the construction of an outdoor laboratory and matching equipment grants.

Dr. Albrecht has analyzed the product and has identified key audiences. He knows the strength of the faculty credentials and their growing visibility off campus as researchers in fisheries. The chair recognizes that the fisheries program can support the state industries of tourism and agriculture. Sport fishing attracts many tourists, and fish farming offers an alternative to other crops for area farmers. The zoology department's program has an advantage over most other institutions because nearby lakes and other waterways provide natural laboratories for the faculty research.

In assessing the political environment on campus and within the state, Dr. Albrecht decides that the department needs a marketing strategy. The zoology chair fears that the administration will deny the department's requests unless they first adopt a favorable impression about the value of the fisheries program to the institution. The chair initiates a public relations campaign to promote the department. He informs the central administration about the program's success by disseminating "good news" updates of department achievements. The chair shares the responsibility for marketing the department with faculty who meet with area farmers, legislators, and state economic development groups.

Clearly, the zoology department has a mission that is consistent with the state priority of economic development. The faculty research in fisheries has direct application to the state's tourism and farming industries. It is less clear from the case study whether the department's objective to build its fisheries program is consistent with the institution's mission and priorities. The chair fears that the administration will not view the department's request for an outdoor laboratory and matching funds for equipment grants as a top priority. The chair must promote the fisheries program on campus so that the administration perceives it as consistent with the institution's priorities. The chair's marketing campaign includes off campus constituencies because he wants the region and state to recognize the true worth and long-term potential of the fisheries program. The marketing strategy described in Case 9.4 focuses on getting news of the department's strength and accomplishments to important constituencies. The plan does not enlist help from persons other than department members.

It's Your Turn

Assume the role of the department chair and think through how you would devise a marketing strategy for the zoology department in Case 9.4.

1. What other strategies for marketing the zoology department would you use to secure the central administration's support for the fisheries program? Would you share the marketing responsibility with off campus constituencies? If so, what support would you enlist from them?

2. How would you incorporate the perspective of the central administration in your pubic relations campaign? How might you align the department mission with the institution's priorities?

Let's Recap

Marketing the department is the task of strategically advocating the mission and achievements of the department in order to enhance the overall reputation of the department. It is a process of planting and fostering favorable and accurate perceptions of the department. As a process, the task of marketing the department is a campaign and not a single activity. The best strategy is a continuous one. Those in regular contact with the department form perceptions of the academic unit whether or not the perceptions are favorable or accurate. Consequently, the task of marketing the department is an attitude rather than an activity. Every communication from or about the department helps to shape the department's reputation and image. The chair needs to take a proactive role in promoting a positive perception of the department through all of his or her oral and written communication.

To effectively promote the department, the chair must first analyze the product. The chair must start with the department's mission, its strengths, and its resource needs. This requires the chair to be well informed on all aspects of the department. The chair must also know the department's ideal niche within the institution, the state, the region, and the discipline.

Once thoroughly familiar with the product, the chair can identify the key audiences. They include specific individuals or groups whose relationship to the department is important to the unit's welfare. Key audiences encompass both on campus and off campus groups. In working with each of the key audiences, the chair needs to assess what they need to know about the department and the value of the department to them. The chair must make certain that key audiences know the department needs. That requires closing the gap between their initial perceptions and the images that best convey the department's true worth.

All of this analysis must take into account the political environment. Departments compete for finite resources. They do not exist in a vacuum. What happens on campus can affect every department. What happens in one department can affect another whether or not their disciplines are related. If, for example, the physiology department develops an emergency need for renovation to prevent hazardous fumes from endangering the work environment, funds spent on that renovation are funds that no longer can support any other department. Knowing the political environment means understanding policy and practice. The chair needs to know how campus policy is practiced in other departments. When, and on what basis, are exceptions made? All advocacy documents originating from the department will be more effective if the chair takes into account the political environment when drafting them.

The chair needs to use the information about product, key audiences, and the political environment to plan a marketing strategy. This includes giving careful consideration to message construction, message channel, and timing. The chair will be most effective if the messages are prepared and sent in a manner that helps the intended audience recognize the relevance of the information. Marketing strategies are more credible if they continually communicate the same department themes. For this reason, it is imperative that the chair share the responsibility for marketing the department with faculty. This ensures that the faculty know what message the department needs to send and to whom. With an effective marketing campaign in place, the department is better able to withstand the immediate crisis.

REFERENCES

American Association of University Professors. (1990). Statement on professional ethics. In *AAUP Policy Documents & Reports* (pp. 73-85). Washington, DC: American Association of University Professors.

Anderson, M. (1992). *Impostors in the temple.* New York, NY: Simon & Schuster.

Bennis, W., & Nanus, B. (1985). *Leaders: The strategies for taking charge.* New York, NY: Harper & Row.

Cahn, S. (1986). *Saints and scamps: Ethics in academia.* Totowa, NJ: Rowman & Littlefield.

D'Souza, D. (1991). *Illiberal education: The politics of race and sex on campus.* New York, NY: The Free Press.

Gardner, J. W. (1990). *On leadership.* New York, NY: The Free Press.

Gmelch, Walter. (1991, Winter). The stresses of chairing a department. *The Department Chair, 1*(3), 1, 14-15.

Gmelch, W. H., & Miskin, V. D. (1993). *Leadership skills for department chairs.* Bolton, MA: Anker.

Gmelch, W. H., & Miskin, V. D. (1995). *Chairing an academic department.* Thousand Oaks, CA: Sage Publications.

Green, M. F. (1988). *Leaders for a new era: Strategies for higher education.* New York, NY: American Council on Education/Macmillan.

Higgerson, M. L. (1991, Spring). Strategies for managing conflict. *The Department Chair 1*(4), 1, 20.

Higgerson, M. L. (1992, Fall). Chair as change agent. *The Department Chair, 3* (2), 19-21.

Higgerson, M. L. (1992b). Communication strategies for managing conflict. *Proceedings of the ninth annual Academic Chairpersons Conference: Celebrating success* (pp. 266-272). Manhattan, KS: Kansas State University.

Higgerson, M. L. (1992c). Communication strategies for marketing the department. *Proceedings of the ninth annual Academic Chairpersons Conference: Celebrating success* (pp. 83-92). Manhattan, KS: Kansas State University.

Higgerson, M. L. (1993, Fall). Marketing the academic department. *The Department Chair, 4*(2), 5-9.

Higgerson, M. L. (1994, Fall). Strategies for conducting face to face faculty evaluations. *The Department Chair, 5*(2), 2-4.

Higgerson, M. L. (1995a). Facing faculty evaluation. *Proceedings of the twelfth annual Academic Chairpersons Conference: The many faces of evaluation* (pp. 74-81). Manhattan, KS: Kansas State University.

Higgerson, M. L. (1995, Winter). Tips for documenting performance evaluation. *The Department Chair, 5*(3), 3-4.

Higgerson, M. L., & Higgerson, R. G. (1994). A professional ethic for maintaining faculty morale. *Proceedings of the eleventh annual Academic Chairpersons Conference: Academic quality revisited* (pp. 126-134). Manhattan, KS: Kansas State University.

Higgerson, M. L., & Rehwaldt, S. (1993). *Complexities of higher education administration: Case studies and issues.* Bolton, MA: Anker.

Rest, J. R., & Narvaez, D. (1994). *Moral development in the professions.* Hillsdale, NJ: Erlbaum.

Rost, J. C. (1993). *Leadership for the twenty-first century.* Westport, CT: Praeger.

Sykes, C. J. (1988). *ProfScam: Professors and the demise of higher education.* Washington, DC: Regnery Gateway.

Tucker, A. (1992). *Chairing the academic department: Leadership among peers* (3rd ed.). New York, NY: American Council on Education/Macmillan.

INDEX

accreditation 11, 109, 238, 241

adversity 4, 31, 85, 227

alliances 22, 228-252

alumni 11, 49, 207, 233, 256-258, 264, 268

assessment (student outcomes) 114, 177, 181-183, 187-189

budget 23,25, 128, 199, 218, 233, 259-260, 263-264

campus (college and university)
   climate 42, 142, 171
   conditions 42
   culture 11, 246
   policy 81-82, 86, 96, 101, 106, 113-114,123, 130-131, 138, 143, 150-153, 207, 210, 247, 250, 257, 279
   priorities 10, 204, 206, 218, 226, 233, 258, 268

central administration 4-5, 10-11, 15, 16-18, 21-22, 30, 40, 42, 55, 128-129, 139, 145, 170,172, 178-179, 180-183, 187-188, 190, 200, 202, 206, 214-215, 229-230, 232-233, 241, 250, 255, 257, 259, 263-264, 268, 276, 277

change 38, 49, 68, 123, 128, 131, 135-136, 145, 147, 161, 166, 168, 228
   implementation 169-200, 210

communication
   channel 108, 203, 205, 208, 213-214, 221, 226, 258, 272, 279
   content 204, 208, 213-214
   context 10, 29-30, 34, 55, 70, 72-73, 109, 147-148, 161-162, 177, 182, 199, 204, 208-209, 213
   effective 38-39, 50, 57, 75, 142, 178, 227, 254, 258
   face-to-face 106-107, 110, 114, 132-134, 205, 208-209

feedback 111, 205-206, 209, 214, 226-227
   formal 55, 213
   informal 55, 208
   language 2-3, 71, 143-144, 152, 160, 162, 176, 187, 193, 203-206, 209
   listening 56-57, 61, 113, 129, 188, 209, 225
   noise 205,213, 221, 226-227
   nonverbal 155, 205
   open 171, 208-209, 226-227
   oral 246, 254, 278
   process 203, 205, 254
   productive 208, 210, 227
   purpose 203, 225-226
   receiver 203-206, 209, 221, 254
   sender 204-205, 225-226, 254
   tone, 4, 37-39, 68, 142, 156, 204, 209
   verbal 133, 144-145, 205
   written 205, 208-210, 215, 246, 254, 278

conflict management 38, 78-80, 139-168, 193-194, 198

consensus building 2-3, 5-13, 24, 29, 39, 57, 177-178, 232

credibility 24, 37, 40-41, 55, 79, 81-86, 97, 102, 106, 112, 138, 143-144, 152, 167, 171-174, 181, 187-189, 193-194, 200, 202-203, 206-209, 214-215, 222, 226, 230, 241

curriculum 23, 232
   committee 72
   core 21
   general education 41, 230, 232, 255, 258
   revision 39, 145

dean 53, 63, 72, 84-86, 111, 117-118, 129, 131, 146, 148, 153, 170, 172-173, 176-177, 181, 193-195, 198, 202-227, 241, 246, 251, 257, 272

decision-making 23-24, 43, 68, 75, 148, 168, 219, 230, 251, 256

department
    art and design 110
    biology 75-78, 87-89, 255
    chemistry 63-65
    climate 24-25, 36-68, 85, 111-112, 141-143, 162, 168, 169, 171, 174, 182, 187, 194, 200, 265
    communication disorders 14-15
    computer science 243-244
    culture 36, 69, 124-125, 163
    English 18-20, 230, 232, 270-272
    fine and performing arts 190-193,196-198
    foreign languages 31-33, 233
    geography 223-225
    information systems 243
    management 243-244
    marketing 149-150, 155
    mathematics 216-217, 219-221, 230, 232
    mission (see mission, department)
    morale 8, 42
    music 110, 115-117,119-122, 134-135, 230
    philosophy 157-160, 163-165, 163-165
    physics 57-61
    physiology 278
    policy 81-82
    political science 92-95,98-100
    priorities 4-5, 6,7-9, 10, 11, 16, 22-23, 28, 34, 160-161, 208, 218-219, 263
    radio and television 110, 124, 255
    social work 238-240
    speech communication 43-47, 232, 233-236, 248

theater 25-28, 207, 247-249, 260-262, 266-268

values 6, 16, 69

zoology 179-180, 183-187, 274-276

discrimination 89, 91, 143, 219, 222

diversity 6

ethics
    audit 81-86, 102-103
    department 69-103
    individual 70-71, 73

external publics 4,11-12, 22, 49, 71, 172-173, 178, 190, 201, 253-279

faculty
    complaint 151
    development 106, 109, 130
    grievance 91,100-101, 107, 132, 136
    minority 63, 124, 145
    morale 24-25, 35, 40-41, 112, 141-142, 148-149, 171, 182
    part-time 8
    perception 39-41, 48, 82-84,112, 143, 167
    tenured 28, 125, 130, 149, 188
    term 15, 125, 250
    untenured 28, 90, 148-149, 161, 166

instruction
    graduate 4, 10, 225
    individualized 13, 230
    objectives 136
    quality 12, 24, 33, 74, 112, 114, 181, 222, 230-231, 254, 264, 273
    undergraduate 4, 6, 10, 23, 225, 229

leadership 40-41, 43, 68, 71-75, 81-86, 97, 102, 125, 169-170, 200, 210, 226, 228, 231-233

legislature 233

liability 86, 210, 211, 273

merit pay review 38, 92, 95, 97,100-
101, 157
mission
    college 193, 198, 207
    department 2-35, 49, 86,160-161,
        173-176, 208, 218-219, 229,
        231, 231, 251-252, 253-255,
        260, 265, 272, 274, 276
    institution 4-5, 10-11, 174-175,
        277
    operational 5
    statement 3-5, 7, 9, 12-13, 22-24,
        34-35, 218
performance counseling 106-138
performance evaluation 23, 38, 78-80,
    84, 87, 90, 173, 221-222
physical facilities 41
planning 13, 218, 232, 253
president 16-17, 22, 253, 256
problem solving 39, 43, 85, 140
productivity 21, 36, 42, 70, 114, 128,
    142, 148-149, 181, 193, 207
program quality 195, 204, 241, 254,
    264
provost (vice president) 21, 198, 211,
    232, 241-242, 253, 257, 258

recommendation letter 154-156
roles and responsibilities 83-87, 96-97,
    100, 102, 106, 117, 130, 136-137,
    139, 141-143, 149, 150, 163, 170,
    173-174, 176, 180, 190, 206, 208,
    213, 216, 218-219, 229, 232-233,
    259-260, 277
salary increase 114, 131, 139, 151,
    160-162, 165-167, 177, 251
student
    complaint (grievance) 61, 136, 147,
        207
    enrollment 34, 128, 136, 145, 174,
        176, 195, 204-207, 226, 230,
        243, 244-245, 246, 258-260,
        263
    recruitment 33, 128, 203-204
tenure and promotion 78-79, 82, 84,
    91, 106-107, 111-112 , 115, 117,
    131, 135-136, 139, 142, 148-149,
    177, 199, 219, 221-222, 249-250
values
    campus 86
    department 6, 16, 86, 95
    shared 5-7, 29, 36, 50, 70